Celebrating African-American Achievements

WHO'S WHO
in BLACK
St. Louis®

THE THIRD EDITION

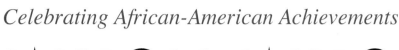

Photos taken at last year's *Who's Who In Black St. Louis* Unveiling Reception

Celebrating African-American Achievements

WHO'S WHO

IN BLACK

St. Louis®

THE THIRD EDITION

Who's Who In Black St. Louis®
is a registered trademark of
Briscoe Media Group, LLC

Purchase additional copies online @
www.whoswhopublishing.com

Corporate Headquarters
Who's Who Publishing Co., LLC
1650 Lake Shore Drive, Suite 250
Columbus, Ohio 43204

All Credit Cards Accepted
*Inquiries for bulk purchases for youth
groups, schools, churches, civic or
professional organizations, please call
our office for volume discounts.*

Corporate Headquarters
(614) 481-7300

**Copyright © 2006 by C. Sunny Martin,
Briscoe Media Group, LLC**

Library of Congress Control Number: 2006936026

Photo Credits
C. Sunny Martin

**ISBN # 1-933879-09-2 Hardback
$50.00 each-U.S. Hardback**

**ISBN # 1-933879-08-4 Paperback
$24.95 each-U.S. Paperback**

WHO'S *Who*

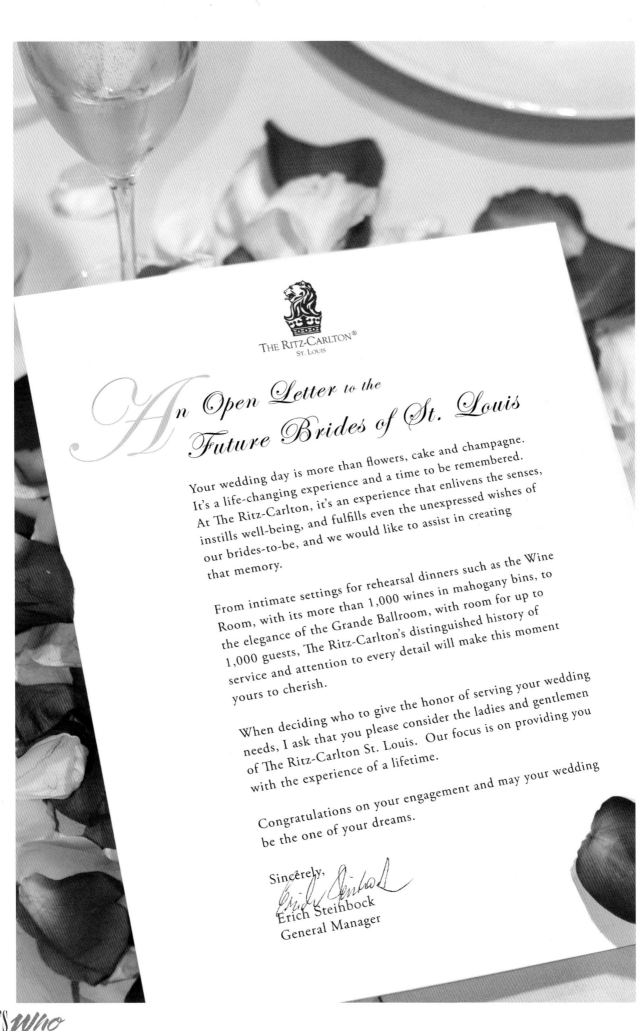

THE RITZ-CARLTON®
ST. LOUIS

An Open Letter to the Future Brides of St. Louis

Your wedding day is more than flowers, cake and champagne. It's a life-changing experience and a time to be remembered. At The Ritz-Carlton, it's an experience that enlivens the senses, instills well-being, and fulfills even the unexpressed wishes of our brides-to-be, and we would like to assist in creating that memory.

From intimate settings for rehearsal dinners such as the Wine Room, with its more than 1,000 wines in mahogany bins, to the elegance of the Grande Ballroom, with room for up to 1,000 guests, The Ritz-Carlton's distinguished history of service and attention to every detail will make this moment yours to cherish.

When deciding who to give the honor of serving your wedding needs, I ask that you please consider the ladies and gentlemen of The Ritz-Carlton St. Louis. Our focus is on providing you with the experience of a lifetime.

Congratulations on your engagement and may your wedding be the one of your dreams.

Sincerely,

Erich Steinbock
General Manager

WHO'S *Who*

CONTENTS

MEET THE TEAM

WHO'S *who*
PUBLISHING CO., LLC

C. Sunny Martin
Founder & CEO

Ernie Sullivan
Senior Partner

Keith Antone Willis, Sr.
St. Louis Publisher

Carter Womack
Regional VP

Paula Gray
Columbus Publisher

Melanie Diggs
Executive Editor

Aaron Leslie
Production Manager

Christina Llewellyn
Graphic Designer

Tamara Allen
Senior Editor

Jeanne Goshe
Copy Editor

Elizabeth Harris
Graphic Designer

Sarah Waite
Webmaster

Ann Coffman
Executive Assistant

Nathan Wylder
Senior Editor

Erica Bowshier
Comptroller

CORPORATE OFFICE
1650 Lake Shore Drive, Suite 250 • Columbus, Ohio 43204 • (614) 481-7300
Visit Our Web Site - www.whoswhopublishing.com

THIS BOOK WAS MADE POSSIBLE BY THE GENEROUS SUPPORT OF OUR

SPONSORS

PLATINUM SPONSORS

THE RITZ-CARLTON®
ST. LOUIS

DIAMOND SPONSORS

Allstate.
You're in good hands.

Anheuser-Busch, Inc.
ONE OF THE ANHEUSER-BUSCH COMPANIES

EMERALD SPONSORS

National City®

Behlmann
BUICK PONTIAC GMC
GMC

UNVEILING RECEPTION SPONSORS

Urban League
of Metropolitan St. Louis, Inc.

Ameren

WELLPOINT.

GMAC

AMERICAN FAMILY
INSURANCE®

United Way
of Greater St. Louis

Metro
www.metrostlouis.org

COLLIERS
INTERNATIONAL
TURLEY
MARTIN
TUCKER
Commercial Real Estate Services

Sparkman
Your Christian Classified Publication

Rams

community
Action
PARTNERSHIP
Helping People. Changing Lives.

sanofi pasteur
The vaccines business of sanofi-aventis Group

citigroup
SMITH BARNEY

TDG
THE DUKES GROUP
Construction Management

PRESIDENT CASINO
YOU'RE GONNA HAVE SOME FUN!

SSM
HEALTH · CARE

SIRVA
relocation redefined®

macy's

EXPRESS SCRIPTS®

MEDIA PARTNERS

The Saint Louis
Argus

BLACK
pages
THE INSTRUMENT OF
EMPOWERMENT

RCGA
ST. LOUIS REGIONAL CHAMBER
& GROWTH ASSOCIATION
Leading Businesses.
Leading Communities.℠

WESL-AM
Soul Classics
1490

RADIO
ONE
THE URBAN RADIO SPECIALIST

CLEARCHANNEL
RADIO

ST. LOUIS AMERICAN
NEWSPAPER

Diversity makes us better.

At National City, we know that diversity makes us a stronger, more competitive company. It improves our service. It opens our eyes to new possibilities. It helps create more effective solutions – for our customers and our communities.

Each day, we harness the power of diversity by:
• Attracting and retaining a diverse workforce
• Making our financial solutions available to diverse audiences
• Supporting and partnering with minority- and women-owned businesses
• Giving back to the community through volunteerism, charitable giving and sponsorships

Combined, these efforts are taking our company to new heights – proving the fact that building on our differences isn't just the right way to conduct business, it's a better way.

National City®

Rolls-Royce Motor Cars Atlanta
1-877-GA ROLLS (1-877-427-6557)
Serving: GA, TN, SC, AL, MS, LA & MO
www.rollsroycemotorcarsatlanta.com

Gregory Williams
Rolls-Royce: 404-237-6200
Mobile: 404-771-2799
gwilliams@hennessy-auto.com
3040 Piedmont Road, Atlanta, GA 30305

OFFICE OF THE MAYOR
CITY OF ST. LOUIS
MISSOURI

FRANCIS G. SLAY
MAYOR

September 23, 2006

It is my great pleasure and honor to congratulate you and the staff of *Who's Who in Black St. Louis* on the celebration of *Who's Who in Black St. Louis'* Third Annual Edition.

Since its founding, *Who's Who in Black St. Louis*, the largest African-American directory publisher in North America, has been highlighting the positive achievements of African-Americans in cities across the country. It is important that we recognize those outstanding citizens who represent the best in our communities. Doing so encourages us all and sets an example to which we can aspire.

This publication is not only an important civic contribution, but will no doubt serve as a tool to foster economic activity and opportunity for individuals and employers throughout the St. Louis Region.

I extend my best wishes to you and your staff for continued success as you continue to bring portraits of African-American achievement and excellence in the public eye.

Sincerely,

Francis G. Slay
Mayor, City of St. Louis

ST. LOUIS REGIONAL CHAMBER
& GROWTH ASSOCIATION

October 3, 2006

It is my pleasure to extend congratulations as you launch a new 2006 edition of **Who's Who In Black St. Louis**, acknowledging successful African-American leaders.

Highlighting African-American entrepreneurs, educators, business professionals and leaders in our community gives hope and inspiration to young African Americans throughout our community.

The RCGA is delighted to salute and congratulate those featured in this publication.

Sincerely,

Richard C.D. Fleming
President and Chief Executive Officer

ONE
METROPOLITAN
SQUARE

SUITE
1300

SAINT LOUIS
MISSOURI
63102

PHONE
314.231.5555
FAX
314.444.1122

http://www.stlrcga.org

BOARD OF ALDERMEN
CITY OF SAINT LOUIS
MISSOURI

September 20, 2006

To the Editors and Honorees of Who's Who in Black St. Louis:

I am pleased to congratulate Who's Who Publishing Company, LLC, the nation's largest African American directory publisher, on the third edition of Who's Who in Black St. Louis. For seventeen years, this organization has highlighted the positive achievements of African Americans in cities across the country and I am happy that St. Louis will continue the history of this successful publishing giant.

Who's Who in Black St. Louis will provide an opportunity to celebrate and recognize some of our city's finest leaders and it is my privilege to acknowledge them for the fine work they have done to build St. Louis into the cultural and economic force it is today. Each honoree serves as a living example of how hard work and strength of character leads to success.

It is no secret that St. Louis has a multitude of notable African Americans from politics to entertainment. However, I believe readers of this directory will be amazed at the diversity of career disciplines and experiences that have helped shape the character of our community and provided countless role models for our youth.

I would like to take this opportunity to thank the individuals on the following pages for serving as an inspiration to our city, our community and our youth – our city's future Who's Who in Black St. Louis.

Sincerely,

Michael McMillan

Michael McMillan
Alderman, 19th Ward

MM/als

OFFICE OF THE COMPTROLLER
CITY OF ST. LOUIS

GREETINGS,

As Comptroller for the City of St. Louis, I am pleased to offer congratulations to Who's Who in Black St. Louis on their third edition.

I commend Who's Who in Black St. Louis for its' providing an outlet to recognize the City of St. Louis's finest citizens and to acknowledge those individuals for the contributions they make to the cultural, economic, humanitarian, educational, political and social structures of the City of St. Louis.

May this 3rd edition of Who's Who in Black St. Louis be rewarding to all that are recognized in the publication and to those who will make use of the publication. Best wishes for continued success in your service to others.

Sincerely,

Darlene Green
COMPTROLLER

OFFICE OF THE LICENSE COLLECTOR
CITY OF ST. LOUIS
ROOM 102, CITY HALL
SAINT LOUIS, MISSOURI 63103

September 21, 2006

To the Editors and Honorees of Who's Who in Black St. Louis:

I am honored to be given the opportunity to publically congratulate Who's Who Publishing Company, LLC on it's third edition of Who's Who in Black St. Louis.

I personally know and have worked with many of the men and women whose names and personal histories of achievement are presented in your directory of African Americans in the St. Louis region. Their accomplishments and contributions to our community are deserving of recognition and will serve as a model for our youth.

I would like to extend to each individual so honored by your publication my sincerest congratulations.

Sincerely,

Gregory F.X. Daly

License Collector
City of St. Louis

GFXD/kg

September 14, 2006

Congratulations on another Edition of Who's Who in Black St. Louis.

With so much going on all around the world, it is important to both young and old to see the positive impact that African Americans can and do make in our society. With your publication, you focus on the dream coming true, as well as show others to work for goals and to set a positive example for our youth and community. Your publication is not only an inspiration but a source of encouragement to be read by all.

Publishing Concepts, LLC congratulates and salutes your hard work as the publisher, your staff, and all of those individuals highlighted in the publication. Thank you for allowing St. Louis to shine with diversity.

Sincerely,

Victoria R. Matthews
Senior Vice President of Business Development

Global Publishing Sales, LLC

PUBLISHING CONCEPTS, L.L.C.

MISSOURI
MEETINGS *&* EVENTS

6590 Scanlan Avenue • Saint Louis • Missouri • Phone: (314) 781-8880 • Fax: (314) 781-8848

SEEK...

Those businesses who

VALUE you

Be the market...Explode the market...

Value Self

Love Self

With DIGINITY

BLACK pages

333 N. Beaumont Street
St. Louis, MO 63103
314-531-7300

WHO'S Who

Diversity is a priority of the St. Louis Rams and we proudly salute Who's Who in Black St. Louis.

We are Always

THE DUKES GROUP
Construction Management

#2 Campbell Plaza
59th & Juniata
Building B
St. Louis, MO 63139
www.thedukesgroup.com

under **Construction**

The Dukes Group

Always The Best...Everytime...No Compromise!

WE ARE COMMITTED TO SERVICE.

WE SEEK TO EXCEED CLIENT EXPECTATIONS ON EACH PROJECT.

WE ARE COMMITTED TO BEING THE BEST AND THE SMARTEST AT WHAT WE DO. WE WORK HARD TO ACHIEVE THIS FOR OUR CLIENTS, AND FOR OUR FIRM.

WE ARE COMMITTED TO ETHICAL BEHAVIOR IN THE WAY WE CONDUCT BUSINESS.

WE ARE A TEAM.

WE ARE COMMITTED TO DEVELOPING PEAK PERFORMERS AND CREATING OPPORTUNITIES FOR PROFESSIONAL ACHIEVEMENT AND PERSONAL ENRICHMENT FOR ALL **TDG** EMPLOYEES.

WE ARE COMMITTED TO THE BETTERMENT OF THE COMMUNITIES IN WHICH WE LIVE AND DO WORK.

WE BELIEVE IN PEOPLE AND THE DIGNITY AND POWER OF THE HUMAN SPIRIT TO CREATE AND ACHIEVE EXCELLENCE.

WE PROVIDE OUR CLIENTS WITH SKILL, INTEGRITY, CONSTRUCTION KNOW-HOW, AND AN EXTRAORDINARY COMMITMENT TO EXCELLENCE.

Foreword

By Cheryl D. Polk

"Real leaders step up."

What an impressive group of men and women who are featured in the 2006-2007 edition of ***Who's Who In Black St. Louis***®!

As a native of Omaha, Nebraska and having lived in New York, New York for a few years, I moved to the St. Louis area 20 years ago to begin a new career. What I found upon arrival was a warm, caring community that was willing to embrace thought leaders and change agents who had energy and new ideas—even if they did not attend one of the local high schools.

Those individuals that you will find featured in this outstanding record of achievements by African Americans are some of the pioneers of this community, as well as the young professionals who are carving their own pathways to success and making an indelible mark upon this region. There is a rich history of medical professionals who were trained all over the world, but chose to practice at the renowned Homer G. Phillips Hospital and have outstanding medical careers. There are a bevy of entrepreneurs who have launched some of the most successful businesses this nation has ever seen, and there are the educators who bear the responsibility of educating our children and preparing them for their own successful journey. Being the daughter of a Baptist minister, I can certainly appreciate all of the religious offerings that exist within our community and provide much needed stability and outreach to our citizens.

There is no doubt that each one of the individuals you will find on the following pages had someone to influence their lives, besides their family. In my own life and career, I was fortunate to have a mother who challenged me to always be the best (and still does) and a father who shaped my moral being. I also had great teachers and real role models to support and nurture my every effort.

In my role as executive vice president and chief operating officer of the United Way of Greater St. Louis, I focus on our 16-county bi-state region to build a healthier community through the 200 agencies our United Way supports through our annual fundraising campaign. More than $65 million was invested in our community that served more than one million people in our area last year.

United Way's Charmaine Chapman Society, named after the first female and first African American to lead our United Way, has a stellar membership of leaders who pave the way toward improving the health and future strength of our African-American community. You will find many of our Society members listed in **Who's Who** because of their professional roles AND for what they do everyday to help people in our community. To date, they have invested more than $10 million through their generosity since 1995.

Yes, it is true. I am the first African-American female to author the foreword for **Who's Who In Black St. Louis**®—and only the second in the nation. While I am honored and proud to have served in this role, our region will only be better if I am not the last. For 2006, we still have too many "firsts" taking place, but I have no doubt that we will see fewer of them as we continue to support each other in all our endeavors.

Real leaders step up. As I look at the many accomplishments of those in this publication, I feel wonderful about all of the achievements and significant impact that African Americans are having on our communities throughout the region. These are the future thought leaders and opinion shapers, entrepreneurs, and medical and business professionals who will take our city to higher heights. Get to know them and embrace their caring and passion for our city.

If you are a pioneer, well established or up and coming— Congratulations! St. Louis, well done!

Sincerely,

Cheryl D. Polk

Executive Vice President & Chief Operating Officer
United Way of Greater St. Louis

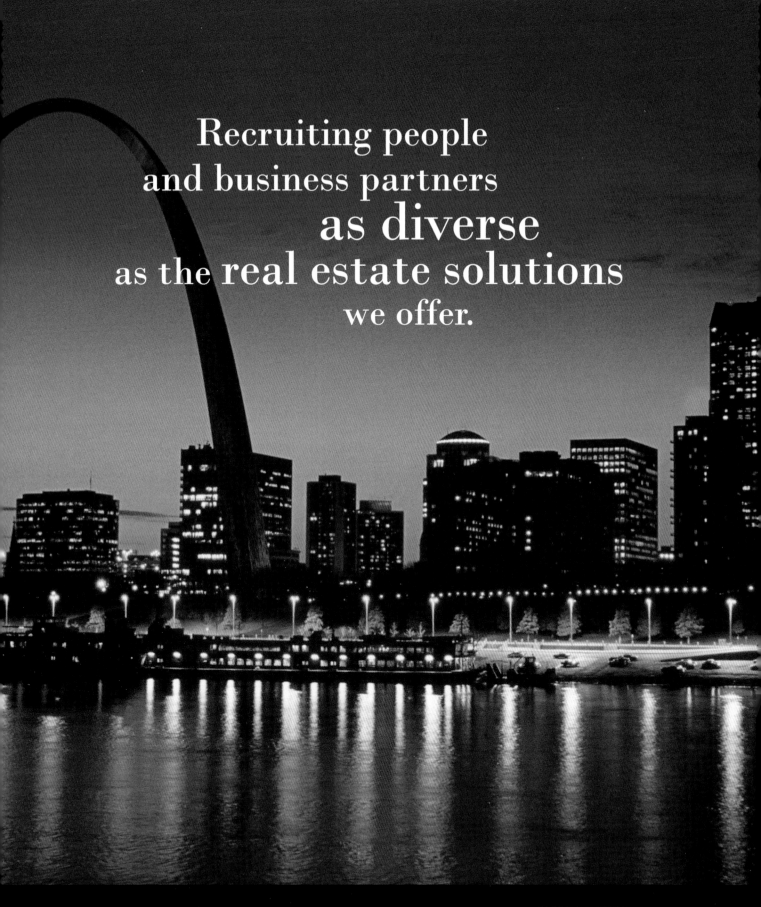

Recruiting people and business partners as diverse as the real estate solutions we offer.

ALL YOUR PROTECTION UNDER ONE ROOF

*Strong neighborhoods and communities provide opportunities for growth
and improved quality of life.*

*American Family Insurance applauds the accomplishments of African
Americans featured in Who's Who in Black St. Louis!*

*Thank you Who's Who for highlighting the accomplishments of African
Americans in our community.*

WHO'S *Who*

A MESSAGE FROM THE

Founder & CEO

C. Sunny Martin

"When you hear a man talking, then, always inquire as to what he has done for humanity." - Carter G. Woodson

Welcome to our third edition of **Who's Who In Black St. Louis**®. As I review this year's publication, one thing stands out – St. Louis is a city that places charitable giving and service as a high priority. This says a lot about the St. Louis African-American community and the spirit of giving that enables you to make a difference in the lives of current and future generations. In practically every profile and biographical sketch, I find people who are givers of time, service and resources. In reaching back, you have made giant strides forward and laid a humanitarian infrastructure upon which more can be accomplished.

To this end, I am honored to pay tribute in this edition to one of your most famous daughters, Katherine Dunham, a world renowned choreographer and great humanitarian in her own right. The impact she made on the world of dance lives on today. More importantly, she used her fame and talent as a voice for those who would not have been heard. This is community at the highest level.

Without the support of our sponsors and advertisers, this third edition would not be possible. You have not only supported our publication, but you have sown the stories and profiles of leadership and courage in the lives of young people by donating thousands of books to the youth in your region. Again, this is community.

I also want to acknowledge our St. Louis publisher, Keith Antone Willis Sr. Keith, your tireless efforts have benefited countless young people throughout the year and exhibit what makes St. Louis a great place to live and visit.

As we journey into 2007, I anticipate great things for St. Louis in the corporate, academic, arts, government and spiritual arenas. I look forward to your growth, influence and the dynamic outreach you will realize locally and nationally. St. Louis is great because its people give back. That is the essence of community.

Live life to the fullest,

C. Sunny Martin

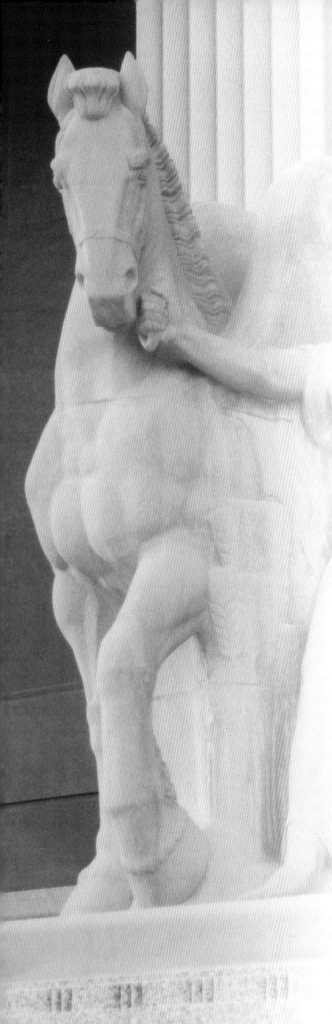

Criteria for Inclusion

Who's Who In Black St. Louis® is an opportunity for us to afford a measure of recognition to the men and women who have made their mark in their specific occupations, professions, or in service to others in the St. Louis community.

A sincere effort was made to include those whose positions or accomplishments in their chosen fields are significant and whose contributions to community affairs, whether citywide or on the neighborhood level, have improved the quality of life for all of us.

The names of those brief biographies included in this edition were compiled from customary sources of information. Lists of a wide variety were consulted and every effort was made to reach all whose stature or civic activities merited their inclusion.

In today's mobile society, no such publication could ever claim to be complete; some who should be included could not be reached or chose not to respond, and for that we offer our apologies. Constraints of time, space and awareness are thus responsible for other omissions, and not a lack of good intentions on the part of the publisher. Our goal was to document the accomplishments of many people from various occupational disciplines.

An invitation to participate in the publication was extended at the discretion of the publisher. Biographies were invited to contribute personal and professional data, with only the information freely submitted to be included. The editors have made a sincere effort to present an accurate distillation of the data, and to catch errors whenever possible. However, the publisher cannot assume any responsibility for the accuracy of the information submitted.

There was no charge for inclusion in this publication and inclusion was not guaranteed; an annual update is planned. Comments and other concerns should be addressed to:

C. Sunny Martin, CEO
Who's Who Publishing Co., LLC
1650 Lake Shore Drive, Suite 250
Columbus, Ohio 43204
Phone: (614) 481-7300

E-Mail: sunny@whoswhopublishing.com
www.whoswhopublishing.com

A MESSAGE FROM THE
St. Louis Publisher

Keith Antone Willis, Sr.

Welcome friends to our historic third edition of ***Who's Who In Black St. Louis***®! Historic in a number of ways, we have the first female to write our foreword, Cheryl Polk, executive vice president and chief operating officer of the United Way of Greater St. Louis. Another first is that we pay tribute to someone from East St. Louis, one of the city's most famous adopted daughters, Katherine Dunham. We lost her this year after nearly 97 years of life. She gave tremendously to this region and the world through dance, civil rights and humanitarian efforts.

It is an honor and a privilege for me publish ***Who's Who In Black St. Louis***®! As a resident since 1989, St. Louis is my adopted hometown. This city has given so much to me and my family personally and professionally: I live in the city of **St. Louis;** I work for **Mentor St. Louis;** my degree is from **Saint Louis University;** I met my wife in **St. Louis** and she works for the **City of St. Louis;** I love the **St. Louis Rams, St. Louis Cardinals, St. Louis Blues, and Nelly and the St. Lunatics.**

A wealth of extremely talented African Americans is highlighted in the following pages. However, I would like to point out that St. Louis is the home to the largest African-American-owned business in the country, World Wide Technology, according to *Black Enterprise* magazine. We have two institutions of higher learning, Harris-Stowe State University and St. Louis Community College, headed by African Americans.

It doesn't stop there. In a major way, African Americans in St. Louis support our United Way's Charmaine Chapman Society, a premiere national model for African-American giving initiatives. Since 1994, we have enjoyed two African-American mayors, two African-American police chiefs, two African-American comptrollers, and currently the first African-American fire chief and county executive.

In closing, we at Who's Who salute those featured for their contribution to our great city, a city where we are still writing our stories – stories full of passion, sacrifice, struggle and eventually, victory. Keep on winning St. Louis! To be continued...

Yours for a Greater St. Louis,

Keith Antone Willis, Sr.

Keith Antone Willis, Sr., aka Mr. St. Louis

Diversity Doesn't Just Happen...

We have 4 tools to help you succeed.

1 **DiversityInc Magazine** (12 issues)
The only business magazine focusing on diversity in the marketplace. Best practices and how-to from corporate diversity leaders.

2 **DiversityInc.com News Site**
Daily news and newsletters six days a week reported from an inclusive point of view. Hundreds of original online articles and resources to help you succeed with your diversity efforts.

3 **DiversityInc.com/Careers**
Visit the leading diversity career center on the Web that connects diverse candidates with companies committed to developing a diverse work force.

4 **DiversityInc Benchmarking**
A unique benchmarking solution that delivers the metrics needed for companies to make informed decisions around their diversity initiatives.
The DiversityInc Top 50 Companies for Diversity is also powered by this technology.

DiversityInc

Contact: Cecilia Fernandez • cfernandez@DiversityInc.com
DiversityInc • 570 Broad Street, 15th Fl. • Newark, New Jersey 07102 • 973-494-0506 • www.DiversityInc.com

In our hearts, we

DREAM.

In America, we turn dreams into

REALITY.

Honoring the remarkable achievements of
African Americans throughout history.

WWW.GMACFS.COM

© 2006 GMAC. All Rights Reserved. GMAC is a registered trademark.

KATHERINE
Dunham

BEHIND THE DANCE

Soul

By Renee Thomas Woods

Photos courtesy of the Missouri Historical Society

FEW PEOPLE CHANGE THE WORLD OVER THEIR LIFETIME.

As an anthropologist, humanitarian, political activist, writer, choreographer and dancer, Katherine Dunham was an exception to the rule. Her passing in May of 2006 signaled not an end to her work, but a continuation of her legacy. "We don't want her living to have been in vain. She didn't want to be eulogized," said Charlotte Ottley Dunham's executive liaison for legacy affairs. "She wanted to be modeled and be an example for the world." As a result, Dunham's legacy lives on in her adopted hometown of East St. Louis, Illinois and throughout the world.

On September 30, 2006 in New York, New York, hundreds gathered to pay tribute to Katherine Dunham. The show, "A Salute to the Extraordinary Life of Ms. Katherine Dunham," included performances by eight prestigious dance troupes from across the country. One by one ensembles such as the Alvin Ailey Dance Company, Dance Theatre of Harlem, PHILADANCO, Charles Moore Dance Company and the Louis Johnson Dance Company all performed in reverence to Dunham and her contributions to the world of dance and the arts. Amongst the ovations and accolades, the world-renowned professional dancers cleared the stage of the Symphony Space Theatre to make way for the headline act.

This wasn't the typical dance ensemble performing amongst their peers on a New York City stage. The company was made up of children and young adults between the ages of six and 18 from East St. Louis, Illinois. The Jackie Joyner-Kersee Performing Company filed onto the stage and danced their way into the audience's heart. The young dancers performed Dunham's original dance pieces like "The Rainforest" that captured the essence of Haitian and West African dance styles. Their celebration through dance symbolized the fruition of Dunham's vision to pass along culture and history to generations through dance. These young performers from the Jackie Joyner-Kersee Boys and Girls Club uphold the honor and uniqueness of African-American dance in the spirit of Dunham. At the conclusion of the evening's presentations, 97 white doves were released outside of the theatre to commemorate Dunham's 97 years of life. She died in May 2006 in New York City, a couple of weeks shy of her 97th birthday.

It may sound a little odd to associate three-time Olympic medalist in track and field Jackie Joyner-Kersee with dance and the performing arts. However, at nine years old, Joyner-Kersee was a dancer before she was an athlete. She was a student of the Dunham Technique at the Performing Arts Training Center in East St. Louis, Illinois where she grew up. After retiring from the competitive world of track and field, Joyner-Kersee opened her own Boys and Girls Club in 2000 to provide children and families in the community access to resources and programming to enrich their lives.

Ruby Streate remembers Joyner-Kersee from her days at the children's theatre. Streate started dancing with Dunham in 1969 and became an apprentice in Dunham's Teacher Training

Program at Southern Illinois University at Edwardsville (SIUE). Dunham's students not only learned how to dance, but also how to teach dance. They developed classroom management skills by working closely with Dunham as class monitors taking attendance and helping to correct students' movements as needed. Streate went on to oversee the Children's Theatre which opened in 1982 and was located behind the Katherine Dunham Museum near downtown East St. Louis.

Dunham came to East St. Louis in 1967 when she joined the faculty at SIUE. Once a booming town, the city fell victim to urban sprawl and an economic downturn that resulted from the closing of factories and meat-packing houses along with the decline of the railroad. The city's population became impoverished, mostly black and continues to struggle with high crime rates and a challenged political system. However, Dunham saw the beauty that laid within. She became rooted in the community just as she had in the West Indies decades prior. Dunham wanted to make an impact.

Katherine Dunham and brother Albert, Joliet, IL. 1917-21.

Today, Streate serves as cultural arts manager at Joyner-Kersee's center. Streate came to the center in 2004 after 20 years of working with SIUE. The cultural arts activities include Dunham Technique, ballet and visual arts. Voice and theater classes will be offered in the near future. Streate takes great pride in carrying on the traditions established by Dunham. "I had the utmost respect for Ms. Dunham because she had a hard time," Streate said. "But, she stood steadfast for what she believed. And as the kids say, she didn't let people 'punk her out.'"

Considered to be the "Matriarch of Black Dance," Dunham faced a number of difficulties throughout her life. At the tender age of four, Dunham's mother died leaving the young girl and her brother to be raised by their father in Joliet, Illinois. Because he traveled for work, Dunham's father left the two youngsters with relatives while he was gone. She took dance as a child and grew fond of the art form. Dunham had a creative soul even at a young age, putting on plays at home and church. She even played basketball in high school.

In 1928 when most women, white or black, weren't able to go to college, Dunham studied anthropology at the University of Chicago. In 1934 this young college student started her own dance company which she called simply, Negro Dance Group. During an anthropology lecture, Dunham learned of the remnants of African history and culture that had survived the slave trade. She delved into her studies to learn more about African history—her history.

Soul

Katherine Dunham. Inscribed on verso to Albert, 1934.

When Dunham came back to the states in 1937, she began to share with others what she had learned during her studies abroad. She began to meld the movement of West Indian dances with classical ballet and other dance styles that she had learned over the years. With a stroke of genius, Dunham created a new style that revolutionized the genre of dance. It became known as the Dunham Technique.

"Ms. Dunham is the first example of an American creating a modern-based dance technique," says Deborah Ahmed, dancer, choreographer and cultural and community activist. Ahmed also serves as the senior vice president of cultural programs for Better Family Life, a community-based nonprofit organization. Ahmed explained that Dunham effectively synthesized African, Caribbean and white western dances. "She was a pioneer. All that she did opened the door for dancers like Alvin Ailey, Arthur Mitchell and others," she continues.

Katherine Dunham infused the world with her vision of celebrating dance as culturally

Katherine Dunham playing a drum in the Paris production of "Afrique," ca. 1951.

She graduated with a bachelor's degree in social anthropology in 1936 and was awarded a grant from the Rosenwald Fund in Chicago to study dance in the West Indies. As an anthropology scholar, Dunham knew that to fully understand a people and a place you must become intimate with it. She understood that folklore—the customs, traditions and beliefs of a people—is passed on through oral traditions, crafts, music and most importantly, dance. Dunham did not merely stand on the outside as an observer, she immersed herself in the culture. She learned the history, customs and rituals of the people of Jamaica, Trinidad, Martinique and Haiti. Dunham even got involved in religious practices that were brought to the West Indies by slaves who had been taken from West Africa.

Katherine Dunham

and anthropologically significant. In 1947 she published what is considered to be the first scholarly study of ethnic dances, *Dances of Haiti*. Dunham brought dance to life like no one else before her had.

"Ballet is physical. You learn the movement but not the meaning behind it," said Streate. "In Dunham Technique you learn the soul behind the dance. If you immerse yourself in the culture, you have so much more to pull from creatively. That's why her dances were so authentic."

Audiences around the world began to appreciate it. The movements were powerful, energetic, and colorful. Dunham founded many dance schools and companies over the course of her career. She and her dancers would perform in plays and in films including the all-black productions of *Cabin in the Sky* and *Stormy Weather*. She was one of the first dancers to hire a manager to take a professional black dance company on tour. Furthermore, this was before the government provided subsidies for the arts.

In 1940 Dunham met John Pratt, a white costume designer. They began a relationship and despite their families' objections, the two

Katherine Dunham receives compliments of President Ronald Reagan on the occasion of the first Kennedy Center Honors Award at the White House, December 1983.

married and Pratt became the exclusive designer for Dunham's performances. The couple adopted a daughter, Marie Christine, in 1952, and the family continued to travel extensively with dance ensembles. Dunham's beloved husband passed away in 1986 after more than 40 years of marriage.

In one of her last interviews, Dunham reflected on her travels. "I would certainly say that travel has been one of the very important things. And if I had not traveled there are so many things I just wouldn't know," shared Dunham, the first black dancer to develop choreography for the New York Metropolitan Opera. "I think it's 57 countries of the world and that's a lot."

President Ronald Reagan recognized Dunham in 1983 with a Kennedy Center Honor for Lifetime Achievement for her contributions to the arts. She was the only female to be lauded among the likes of singer, Frank Sinatra; actor, Jimmy Stewart; composer, Virgil Thompson and filmmaker, Elia Kazan.

Katherine Dunham in conversation with the President of Senegal, Leopold Senghor, 1962.

Dunham used her knowledge and her celebrity to influence people to make a positive difference in situations of injustice at home in the United States or abroad. Even after she stopped dancing, she stayed active politically, staging hunger strikes and protests that brought international attention to issues such as apartheid in South Africa and the overthrow of Haitian President Jean-Paul Aristide in 1993.

As Dunham aged and her health deteriorated, she became confined to a wheel chair and had little money to support herself. Friends such as actor and singer Harry Belafonte took on the responsibility of caring for Dunham in New York City. She received continuous support from friends and supporters in her adopted city of East St. Louis and would make occasional trips back to visit.

Dunham made a permanent impression on the world with a special indentation in the St. Louis area. The SIUE theater and dance departments reside in Katherine Dunham Hall and soon the auditorium in East St. Louis Senior High School will be renovated and named the Katherine Dunham Performing Arts Center.

Katherine Dunham with Mor Thiam, master percussionist in residence from Senegal, and his wife Kine at the Dynamic Museum, East St. Louis, IL.

Katherine Dunham

Katherine Dunham in constume for "Death" from Rites De Passage, ca. 1943.

"I realize that she is a legacy and my responsibility as an artist, a dancer and a teacher is to keep lifting her name up," said Phylliss Newman, founder and artistic director of the St. Louis Dance Academy. "She gave hope to all dancers of color."

Dunham's last trip to the St. Louis area was in October 2005. A huge celebration was held in her honor at SIUE, and she was lauded with African drumming, dancing and poetry. During this visit she made a few poignant comments on the world of dance today.

"I think people have lost something. They have lost the idea of what dance is. Everybody seems to be in it just for matter of personal pleasure. And there's more to it than that... such as expressing your culture, expressing the meaning of life, the meaning of the people you came from, the meaning of your family and your roots," she said. "... Dance does this you know. It's in there. We just have to take it out and use it."

And on September 30, 2006 in New York City, the children of East St. Louis took center stage at the Symphony Space Theater at 95th and Broadway. They came to sing praises to Dunham through dance. Her voice speaks through the drums. Her spirit speaks through the dance. The children are her legacy and she is theirs. They understand and they won't forget.

Sources
"The Legendary Katherine Dunham" by Tracey Robinson-English, *Ebony Magazine*, February 2006.
"Miss Dunham Comes Home" by Gerald Pace, *St. Louis American*, June 29- July 5, 2006.
Black Dance in America: A History Through Its People, by James Haskins. Copyrighted 1990, published by Thomas Crowell New York.
"Living St. Louis: Katherine Dunham," produced by Anne Marie Berger, KETC-TV Channel 9, PBS.
"Transitions," *Dance Magazine*, August 2006.

Metro
C·E·L·E·B·R·A·T·E·S
Diversity

Metro. Connecting People with Places.

CLEARCHANNEL
RADIO

When you want to hear…

St. Louis' Hit Music Channel

Today's Best Country & All-Time Favorites

Your #1 Station for Hip-Hop and R&B

Today's Jams & The Best Old School

Oldies Radio and Rams Radio

Playing Songs of Faith and Joy

WHO'S *Who*

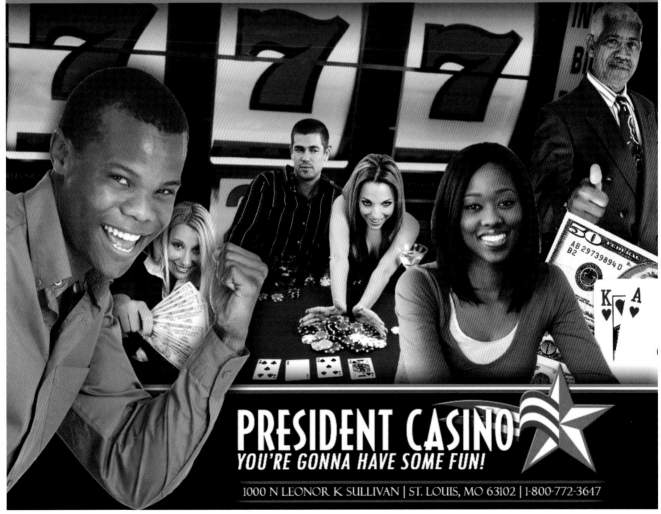
WHO'S *Who*

Ann Beverley Giustiniano
SSM DePaul Health Center

Homer Robinson
SSM DePaul Health Center

Gina L. Johnson
SSM DePaul Health Center

Phil Atkins
SSM DePaul Health Center

Mary Sanders
SSM DePaul Health Center

Wendell Reese
SSM Cardinal Glennon
Children's Medical Center

Deborah Henley
SSM Cardinal Glennon
Children's Medical Center

Cornelius Sanders
SSM Supply Chain Management

Denise Sykes-Collins
SSM - Information Center

Patricia Martin
SSM Health Care - St. Louis

Joe Conrad
SSM Health Care - Corporate

Janet Watley
SSM St. Joseph Health Center

Robert L. Smith
SSM St. Joseph Hospital
of Kirkwood

Diversity Development
Association

SSM Health Care (SSMHC) is committed to providing quality health care
as well as developing the leadership skills of its employees.
These highly motivated employees are all members
of SSM's Diversity Development Association (DDA).

www. ssmhc.com

WHO'S *Who*

Charmaine Chapman and the United Way
– a legacy of leadership and giving

Charmaine Chapman liked to say that she came from St. Paul to St. Louis on St. Valentine's Day; so saints must have meant for her to be here. She was president and chief executive officer of United Way of Greater St. Louis from February 1994 until her death in 2001. The first woman and first African American to head our United Way, Charmaine Chapman inspired the organization to achieve some of its greatest fund raising successes. Charmaine led United Way toward a new regional focus that identified critical issues and organized public and private collaborations to tackle those issues.

In 1994, Dr. Donald Suggs (right), president and publisher of *The St. Louis American*, founded the African American Leadership giving initiative to recognize African Americans who contribute $1,000 or more to the annual United Way campaign. To honor Charmaine's legacy of compassion and care, the African American Leadership Giving Initiative became the **Charmaine Chapman Society.**

Wayman F. Smith III 1994–95, 1997 Chair

David B. Price 1996 Chair

John E. and Barbara S. Jacob 1998–99 Co-Chairs

David L. and Thelma E. Steward 2000–01 Co-Chairs

Arnold W. and Hazel Donald 2002–03 Co-Chairs

Johnny and Minga Furr 2004–05 Co-Chairs

PledgeUnitedWay.org

United Way of Greater St. Louis

Celebrating African-American Achievements
ACROSS THE NATION

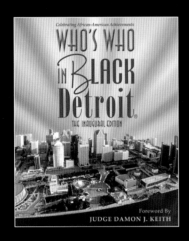

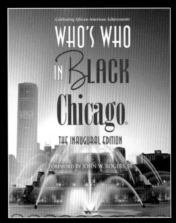

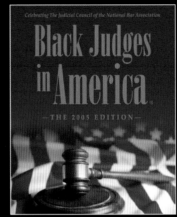

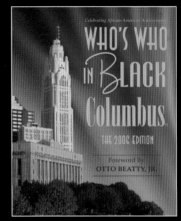

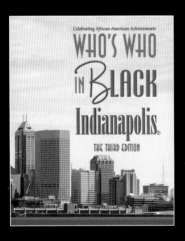

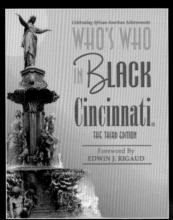

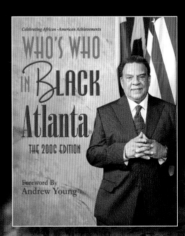

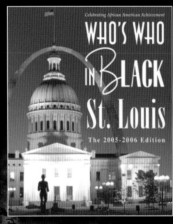

St. Louis'

INTERESTING
PERSONALITIES

 General Mills

WHEATIES

THE BREAKFAST
OF CHAMPIONS

100%
WHOLE GRAIN:

VITAMINS:

FIBER:

GOODNESS CO[...]

110 CALORIES PER SERV[...]

Jackie
Joyner-
Kersee

TED WHOLE WHEAT FLAKES

With Style and Grace

JACKIE JOYNER-KERSEE

By Pamela Bolden

The biggest difference between the Jackie Joyner-Kersee who soared to athletic wonderment in track and field throughout the '80s and '90s, and the woman she is today, happens to be a matter of style: "I wear better attire," she quips. "The same confidence, tenacity, aggressiveness that's needed on the athletic field is what I use to bring the best to my community."

She also brings endless enthusiasm, hope and determination to help her native East St. Louis, Illinois. In 2000 she opened the Jackie Joyner-Kersee Center, a 41,000-square-foot, state-of-the-art recreational center for the community. The center offers programs in education; character and leadership; culture arts; sports; fitness and recreation; and health and life skills to youth, ages 6 to 18. During the school year, the center serves about 200 people each day, and in the summer months, approximately 600 daily. Through its various initiatives and satellite programs, the center touches the lives of 10,000 families each year.

The Olympic medalist won silver, bronze and three gold medals and is often regarded as the best all-around female athlete in the world and the all-time greatest heptathlete. *Associated Press* named her Female Athlete of the Year in 1987, and in 1988 she became the first woman to win *The Sporting News* Man of the Year Award. *Sports Illustrated for Women* named her Female Athlete of the 20th Century and *ESPN* named her one of the 50 Greatest Athletes.

Joyner-Kersee, 44, uses her celebrity to encourage others to achieve their best. She is an ambassador for health and fitness, and a motivational speaker sought after across the country. "I enjoy it," she shares. With "having a voice," she says, "I'm able to achieve a goal I set out not only to benefit my dream and mission, but support so many people in the community." As someone who received lots of support and encouragement from coaches, family and friends, she delivers a message that, with preparation, anything is possible. "You can be whatever you want. Let your skills work for you, but go out to develop those skills," she implores.

"I believe there are lots of great people in East St. Louis. It's a gold mine. There's a lot going on here and I encourage people to visit both states (Missouri and Illinois)."

Joyner-Kersee believes the six-year-old center has been the catalyst for improved infrastructure and an economic boom recently seen in East St. Louis. She points to new housing in the Emerson Park community and new retail sprouting up around 25th and State Streets, as examples. Her future goals for the Center include building a theatre and an indoor track and field training area. "We want it to be a greater symbol of hope for the community at large," she says. "Whatever I have to do, I'm willing to do it. Failure is not an option."

Joyner-Kersee is married to her former coach and mentor, Bob Kersee, and is the author of two books, *A Woman's Place is Everywhere* and *A Kind of Grace*, an autobiography.

Photo by Maurice Meredith

A Journey of Success

JOHN JACOB

By Crystal Howard

John Jacob had already completed a 29-year career with the Urban League when he joined the senior management team of Anheuser-Busch and moved to St. Louis in 1994. With his initial thought to stay about five years—it is now twelve years later—he is still taking on new challenges for the "King of Beers."

Jacob's title is vice president of global communications and his responsibilities include counseling the company on external and internal communication, reputation management, and image-protection and shaping for the leading U.S. brewer. He serves as a member of Anheuser-Busch's board of directors and is one of 18 members of the company's strategy committee, which oversees all major policy and strategic issues of the corporation.

Prior to Jacob joining the company, Anheuser-Busch contracted most communication activities to an external company. However, Jacob focused on the goal of developing the right team to bring brand management communications strategy and leadership in-house. He convinced senior management it could be done. It took five years to achieve, but Jacob feels satisfied that Anheuser-Busch has a competent group of internal communications professionals to represent the company's products and image.

But don't think he was lucky to achieve his goals. Jacob doesn't really believe in luck. His philosophy is that success comes from being smart, having a vision, building relationships and being ready.

John Jacob earned his degrees in the late 50s and early 60s when opportunities for African Americans were still quite limited in corporate America. "I spent a lifetime in the civil rights movement and running a not-for-profit organization, which I loved," shares Jacob. "But I always wanted to be in an American corporation," he added. "While I may be 30 years later getting here—I'm not 30 years behind." African Americans arrived at corporate America's table a bit later, but they bring a wealth of experience and can demonstrate the ability to help companies thrive and achieve greater goals.

Jacob downplays his role in shaping the community. "There are so many African Americans in many organizations, including Anheuser-Busch, with significant contributions to the St. Louis area but they are flying just below the radar," Jacob notes. He wants that to change and strives to focus the spotlight on the great work of others. Jacob is proud to be a symbol of what this community is about and represent those people who typically go unnoticed.

He has served on several boards, both local and national, including Coca-Cola Enterprises, Inc., the Muny at Forest Park, Morgan Stanley, and Fair St. Louis, to name a few. Under the leadership of Jacob and his wife, Barbara, the Charmaine Chapman Society (the United Way of Greater St. Louis' African-American Leadership Giving Initiative), reached record numbers raising more than a million dollars.

Born in Louisiana and raised in Houston, Texas, Jacob received his bachelor's and master's degrees from Howard University. He also holds 19 honorary degrees from various educational institutions.

Jacob resides in St. Louis with his wife, Barbara. They have one daughter, Sheryl, who is manager of speech pathology at Howard University Hospital.

Photo by Maurice Meredith

Growing Deep Roots in St. Louis

DEBORAH J. PATTERSON

By Pamela Bolden

As the nation celebrated Independence Day on July 4, Deborah J. Patterson was once again dashing off on a month-long journey to Washington, D.C., Brazil, Hungary and Romania. As president of the Monsanto Fund and director of social responsibility for the Monsanto Company, Patterson works collaboratively across the company to ensure that Monsanto is a good corporate citizen. She also oversees the distribution of substantial resources through contributions and matching grants made in communities in which it operates.

Monsanto is an agricultural company that produces products and services to support animal feed, crop production and soil usage for farmers around the world. Under Patterson's leadership of nearly nine years, the Monsanto Fund has offered the kind of corporate giving that is hard to rival. In 2005, Monsanto contributed $12.6 million in grants worldwide.

The Monsanto Fund's commitment to the St. Louis region is just as generous. In 2005, the fund infused $4.4 million into the bi-state community to benefit local programs and services including the Donald Danforth Plant Science Center, the St. Louis Science Center, The Magic House, American Red Cross, COCA and Southwestern Illinois Resource Conservation and Development, Inc.

Social ethics and responsibility have been key ingredients at the heart of every major position the native St. Louisan has held. "My work in government provided me with the tools and skills I need for the work I do today," Patterson said in reference to her ten-year career in public service for the City of St. Louis, under former Mayor Vincent Schoemehl Jr. She was executive director of the St. Louis City Employment and Training Agency and later became the mayor's top advisor for housing and economic development.

"In the '80s, our team brought the first creative, innovative housing and community development program that the city had seen in 20 years," Patterson said. Mayor Schoemehl, one of her first professional mentors, provided Patterson with opportunities to grow and develop.

Her planning and leadership attributes led to a successful five-year reign as chief executive officer of the St. Louis Metropolitan Chapter of the American Red Cross. There, she credits another community leader, the late Gloria White, with mentoring her professionally and personally.

"St. Louisans are kind, compassionate and generous," Patterson said. "There are so many things we can do here for free—the Science Center, for instance—that differentiates St. Louis from other places. I like the size of St. Louis, you can get around, and you can get to work, with relative ease. We have access to theatre, culture, wonderful neighborhoods with great architecture."

Patterson's community involvements play an integral part of her life. She serves on the Sheldon Art Gallery advisory board, Girl Scouts of Greater St. Louis president's advisory board, Sisters of Mercy Ministries Foundation board, FOCUS St. Louis and the Vashon Compact executive committee.

The single parent of two adopted daughters, ages 8 and 10, says, "I feel very fortunate... through a lot of hard work, I've had lots of good breaks." The "good breaks" have been fortunate for St. Louis as well.

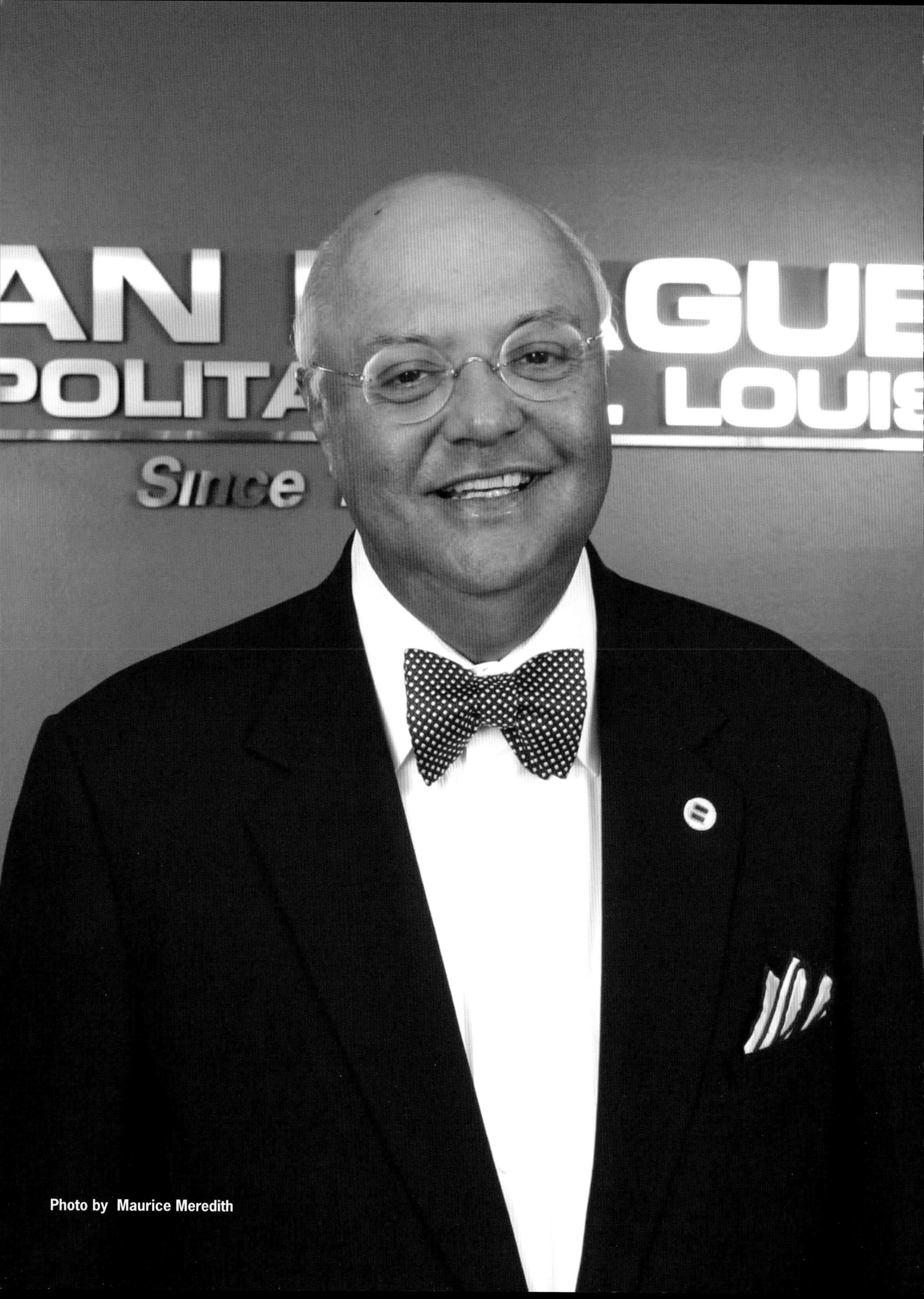

Photo by Maurice Meredith

Enfranchise the Disenfranchised

JAMES H. BUFORD

By Crystal Howard

The vision of the Urban League of Metropolitan St. Louis is that African Americans and others in the St. Louis region will have opportunities to create economically self-sufficient lives in communities that are flourishing with opportunity and growth. The Urban League serves as a catalyst for social and economic parity through its advocacy, coalition building, program services and promotion of communication and understanding among different races and cultures. The man at the helm of that vision is native St. Louisan James H. Buford.

President and chief executive officer Buford came to the organization with the diverse background needed to meet the challenges of managing the fifth-largest Urban League in the nation. Prior to his position with the League, Buford held positions with SmithKline Warner Laboratories, the State of Delaware, former Senate Majority Leader Howard Baker (R-Tenn.), and even studied for the priesthood when he was younger.

"As I got older, I saw what was happening to people and became more involved with the struggle for civil rights," stated Buford. At one point, he was an advance man for Rev. Ralph Abernathy. Eventually, the opportunity arose to head the Urban League in St. Louis. "I seized the opportunity to lead an organization that enfranchises the disenfranchised," he said.

Buford is only the sixth executive to serve the St. Louis affiliate since it was founded in 1918. He took the reigns in 1985 and his voice and leadership has helped guide the Urban League of Metropolitan St. Louis to rank number one in a national evaluation of more than 100 League affiliates.

St. Louis is one of only two affiliates nationally to serve a bi-state region: Missouri and Illinois. The Federation of Block Units, the advocacy wing of the League, began in St. Louis and was later adopted in the Chicago, Illinois and Gary, Indiana areas. Under Buford's leadership, the St. Louis office expanded its capacity to serve. Today, the agency has more than 50 programs promoting community organizations, education, fair housing and employment. Through its programs, the agency serves more than 66,000 people annually, including young adults, whose needs are addressed through the Urban League Young Professionals, which began under Buford's guidance.

Raised in a typical middle class environment, Buford holds a bachelor of arts degree in human services administration from Elizabethtown College and several honorary degrees from institutions including Harris-Stowe State College, the University of Missouri–St. Louis, Webster University, and Eden Theological Seminary.

He serves on numerous executive boards that include the St. Louis Council of the Boy Scouts of America, Chancellor's Council of the University of Missouri–St. Louis, Downtown St. Louis Partnership, Grand Arts Center, St. Louis ConnectCare, Heat Up and Cool Down St. Louis, and the St. Louis Muny Opera.

His awards are vast and include the 2006 Annie Malone Children & Family Service Center Making a Difference Award, Whitney M. Young Award from the Boy Scouts, St. Louis Gateway Classic Lifetime Achievement Award, and the Brotherhood-Sisterhood Award from the National Conference of Christians and Jews.

Buford and his wife, Susan, reside in St. Louis. He has two sons, James Jr. and Jason.

Photo by Maurice Meredith

"Good begets good."

GAIL HOLMES

By Jacquie Vick

When Gail Holmes relocated to St. Louis in the summer of 1998 from Westlake, Ohio, she looked for opportunities to positively impact the community. She did not have to look far. "St. Louis is a civic-minded area," she said. "There are so many helping organizations."

After graduating from Clemson University with both master of arts and bachelor of science degrees in industrial management, Holmes began her career with Energizer/Eveready Battery Company, Inc. in 1993. Today, Holmes is a brand marketing manager-retail merchandising with Energizer, responsible for building profit and market share while leading merchandising development in her division.

She spent the first five years focused on her career, honing her craft and improving her skills. With her career path on course, Holmes arrived in St. Louis with a desire to help others realize their full potential. She focused first on finding a place to call home in a safe and secure diverse environment. Next, she looked for a church home to feed her spiritual needs, and found fulfillment at Saint Alphonsus "Rock" in North St. Louis.

One of the first organizations Holmes joined was the National Black MBA Association, St. Louis Chapter. She continues to be an active member participating in fundraisers for college scholarships and mentoring opportunities for youth and young adults. As a past president and a charter member of POW (Professional Organization of Women), Holmes was instrumental in establishing the organization's 501(c) 3 status. In addition, she serves on numerous boards and committees including the Young Women's Christian Association, Blackburn College in Carlinville, Illinois; CORO Women in Leadership Program; Delta Sigma Theta Sorority, Inc.; Herbert Hoover Boys & Girls Club Young Professional volunteer; Regional Chamber & Growth Association (RCGA) Young Professionals Talent Group; and the United Way's Charmaine Chapman Giving Initiative - Women Giving Initiative.

Holmes' plate is always full, however, you will never see "inactive member" by her name. If she is on the roster, she is very much involved. A Charleston, South Carolina native, Holmes strongly believes in adding value to any organization to which she belongs. "Good begets good," she said. "Active participation propels you to other opportunities." A forward thinker, Holmes always looks to meet the next challenge, the next goal. The eldest of four children, she takes inspiration from her father whose encouragement helps her to keep pushing ahead and not accept less from herself. She hopes to inspire others the way her father inspires her to succeed with his unconditional love and support.

Holmes successfully balances work, community involvement and a personal life. In her spare time, when she is not busy with volunteer work, she focuses on personal growth and development, and is currently president of the Wall Street Walkers Investment Club. She enjoys playing golf, exercising and traveling.

Achieving Excellence in Community Service

BOB WALLACE

By Crystal Howard

Bob Wallace understands the magnitude of the position he holds with the St. Louis Rams. As executive vice president and general counsel, he is responsible for overseeing business operations and all revenue generating activities, broadcast and stadium negotiations, strategic planning, and departmental supervision and community outreach including the St. Louis Rams Foundation. Wallace is well prepared for the tasks at hand. One of the highest-ranking minority executives in professional sports, Wallace's NFL experience ranges from chief contract negotiator for the Philadelphia Eagles to a summer internship as a training camp assistant for the former St. Louis Cardinals. While earning his law degree, he was a legal intern for the late NFL Commissioner Pete Rozelle. This experience provides the perfect background for the challenges Wallace faces in his current position.

Named by the *St. Louis Business Journal* as one of the most influential minority business leaders, his leadership within the sports world has translated to the local region. Wallace has always remained focused on his goal to achieve excellence and serve the community. The Rams Foundation is designed to positively impact youth in the cornerstone areas of education, literacy, health, and youth football. "The Rams really make an impact through charitable endeavors," Wallace said. Through its community outreach programs, the Rams have contributed more than $5 million in cash, grants, merchandise and tickets to St. Louis area charities.

Wallace practices leadership by example both within the Rams organization and the various community and civic organizations he serves. "Limiting the number of boards I participate on allows me to devote meaningful quality time to each one," he added. Wallace serves in various capacities on boards locally and nationally, including president of the board of Giant Steps of St. Louis, a school for autistic children; Chancellors Advisory Committee for the University of Missouri-St. Louis; Sports Lawyers' Association; the sports entertainment division of the American Bar Association; secretary of the St. Louis Sports Commission; and chairman of the board for the Urban League of Metropolitan St. Louis, to name a few. Service to the Urban League is a family tradition for the Wallaces; his sister was president of the Urban League of Eastern Massachusetts for ten years.

Wallace earned his undergraduate degree from Yale University and a law degree from Georgetown University. As an instructor of sports law at Saint Louis University, Wallace shares his legal knowledge with the next generation. St. Louis Public Schools awarded him a certificate of recognition for his work on law and education projects for the district.

Although his St. Louis roots date back nearly 25 years, Wallace is a native New Yorker. He currently resides here with his with wife, Julie, and their two sons, Grant and Eric.

Photo by Maurice Meredith

Serving Where Her Passion Lies

MELBA MOORE

By Jason Bailey

Civil service is in Melba Moore's blood. Her father worked for Congressman William L. Clay for 24 years. She decided early in life that she would not follow in her fathers' footsteps. Moore swore she'd never get involved in politics. However, today she is the health commissioner for the City of St. Louis and she wouldn't change a thing.

Moore was hired to work as the sickle cell program coordinator during Mayor Freeman Bosley Jr.'s four-year term from 1993-1997. Bosley was the first African American to hold the position. She remembers a message in his inauguration speech that spoke directly to her. Bosley said that people who work for the city needed to live in the city.

"I was a contract employee and I lived in Chesterfield," Moore said. "Shortly thereafter I moved into the city and started my pursuit to become a civil service employee."

She went on to work at the American Lung Association where a coworker helped her find her purpose in life. Noting how busy Moore always seemed to be, her colleague asked what she really wanted to do with her life. After some thought, Moore realized where her passion lies. "I want to make sure that whatever I do improves the lives of women and children," said the native St. Louisan.

As health commissioner she and her team find solutions for St. Louis' health concerns and provide services to address St. Louisans' health care needs. She is focused on improvement, respect and accountability in her office and will work with whoever she can to get the job done.

There was a lot of house cleaning to be done when she first took the job. But if Moore knows anything she knows that nothing comes easy. She took responsibility and brought everything in line by identifying weak spots and forming alliances to help solve problems. One of the problem areas she saw was customer service in the department. Respecting the citizens that the health department serves is of the highest priority.

Her uncompromising stand made some enemies, but in the long run she changed the department's culture. And she did it with a smile. Her warm disposition and infectious personality is reflected in the smiles of the people she works with daily.

"You have to get rough sometimes," said Moore about keeping her department focused on safety. "You can't disregard the people in the community."

While Moore's ultimate focus is to keep the citizens of St. Louis healthy and safe through screenings, prevention programs and health services, she takes her duty to be accountable to St. Louisans just as seriously. She encourages her staff to remember that they are in their positions to serve city residents with respect and professionalism. When complaints and concerns come in from citizens Moore says that it is her department's duty to thoroughly investigate the allegations. She said, "They are the ones who put us here and it is our duty to serve them well."

Photo by Maurice Meredith

Harris-Stowe State University Yesterday, Now and Forever!

DR. HENRY GIVENS JR.

By Raegan C. Johnson

For the past 26 years, Dr. Henry Givens Jr. has been the powerhouse behind one of Missouri's oldest institutions of higher education. Since becoming president of Harris-Stowe State College in 1979, Dr. Givens has revamped the institution's image, propelled the school to university status and fulfilled his vision for its first residence hall.

When he first arrived at Harris-Stowe, the school faced relatively low enrollment and a paucity of funding. "I was determined to give this venerable institution a new life and a broader future in higher education—all to better serve residents in the St. Louis metropolitan area," Givens said. Harris-Stowe has evolved from a one-building teachers' college to a well-sought out university with six campus buildings including the Rev. Dr. William G. Gillespie Residence Hall and Student Center that opened in the fall of 2006. Additionally, Harris-Stowe boasts approximately 2,000 students, a dozen undergraduate degree offerings, several graduate collaboratives, and a reputation as one of the most affordable, accessible, diverse institutions in the Midwest.

In 1987 during a time when Harris-Stowe faced its own difficulties, Givens assumed the position of Lincoln University interim president at the request of then Missouri Governor John Ashcroft.

"Serving in both capacities presented a real challenge, but it allowed me to do something great for Lincoln University, my alma mater," he said. "I was able to perform fairly well because of the dedication and unwavering support of the faculty and staff at both institutions."

A St. Louis native, Givens, was educated in St. Louis public schools and graduated from Sumner High School. "I knew that black children were not allowed to attend public schools along with white children," Givens said. "However, I never accepted the implication that we black children were of lesser worth or intelligence than our white counterparts."

He went on to earn a bachelor's degree from Lincoln University, a master's from the University of Illinois at Urbana-Champaign, and a doctoral degree from Saint Louis University. In addition, he participated in post-doctoral studies in higher education administration at Harvard University. Givens attributes his passion for education to the conduct and professionalism black teachers displayed as he was growing up.

"I was extremely mindful as a youngster in a racially-segregated state and city that teaching was one of the few professions available to me," Givens says. He aspired to be like teachers who impacted his life such as educator Julia Davis, for whom a library in North St. Louis is named.

Givens began his career in the Webster School District, serving in several capacities including teacher, principal and assistant to the superintendent. Dr. Givens later went on to become principal of the first magnet school prototype in the nation, and the first African American to serve Missouri as the assistant commissioner of education.

Connections to the Motherland

SHEILA LITTLE-FORREST

By Lakeisha Clay

When Thelma and Russ Little Sr. founded Afro World in 1970, their daughter, Sheila Little-Forrest, never dreamed of one day running the family business. But after graduating in 1984 from Southwest Baptist University in Bolivar, Missouri, Little-Forrest returned to St. Louis to work with her siblings and ultimately begin her grooming process to one day take the reigns of the burgeoning hair products and supplies business.

She still finds her parents shoes hard to fill even though she has been president for three years. She prays for guidance and takes everything in stride. "Each day has enough challenges, so I don't get ahead of myself about tomorrow's worries," said Little-Forrest. A shrewd business woman, she always finds comfort in knowing that her father is never too far away in case a little help is needed. She keeps laughing and tries to find joy in something every day. Her approach is working.

Afro World International Hair Company Inc. is a force to be reckoned with in the hair care industry. Between retail, wholesale, in-store and e-commerce business, Afro World is a top provider of high quality hair products and hair pieces for both men and women. The business has carved out a specialty niche with the African-American market. Little-Forrest's quick thinking and business savvy have catapulted Afro World into the international business arena with business in seven continents thanks to the success of Internet sales.

Afro World's client list includes entertainers, celebrities and even stylists for the Ms. America Pageant. The business stands as a mecca of cultural enrichment in St. Louis with unique African and africentric fashions, accessories, fine art, jewelry and gift items.

Little-Forrest leads a pretty full life. In addition to running Afro World, this St. Louis native is married to Rev. Jeffrey P. Forrest, senior pastor of Blessed Hope Bible Church. The couple are the proud parents of three children: Justin, Joshua and Joye. Even with her busy life, Little-Forrest remains committed to giving back. "Taking an active role in the community to insure its continued growth both economically and spiritually has always been a part of Afro World's master plan," she said.

Many community events are held at the location such as health fairs, entrepreneurship programs, Kwanzaa celebrations, Soulful Santa, book signings, Forest Park Forever hat fundraiser, Charles Drew blood drive, Unity Theater, and a scholarship fund in her father's name for a high school senior. Sheila serves on numerous boards and committees including New City School board of directors and the Center of Creative Arts (COCA).

Afro World has received numerous awards and recognitions such as: the *St. Louis American* Salute to Excellence Business Award; 2004 Women Advocates for Children; Business of the Year by *St. Louis Sentinel*; Better Family Life Entrepreneur of the Year Award; Special Recognition Award: American Health and Beauty Institute; National Hair Association's Business of the Year; Carlson Craft Distinguished Dealer Award; Unity Theater Ensemble: Divine Channel for the Arts; Exhibitor of the Year by TSABCI; Normandy Community Forum Partnership Commercial Property Façade Improvement Award; and recognition by the Partnership for the New Work Force.

Photo by Maurice Meredith

Understanding the Value of a Dollar

HUBERT H. HOOSMAN JR.

By Marcus Ma'at Atkins

Investing money can be challenging. Today, as the cost of living continues to rise, it is imperative to have a nest egg for those rainy days as well as retirement. Hubert H. Hoosman Jr., president and CEO of Vantage Credit Union, understands the value of a dollar and is helping people invest their hard earned money wisely.

"We are a credit union, member-owned and operated," said the East St. Louis, Illinois native. "I can't find a better democratic model that works for the working class. I'm blessed to have a great board of directors and a great team to serve our members."

President and CEO since 1994, Hoosman manages Missouri's fourth largest credit union with assets in excess of $475 million. He began his career as a loan officer/teller/trainee in May of 1982. He moved up the corporate ladder as a loan department manager, branch manager, vice president of branch operations and senior vice president, before reaching his current position. Even though he lives in a world of numbers, Hoosman makes it a priority to focus on people rather than just making money.

"I enjoy coming to work every day," he said. "My job is to make someone else's life better and give them the tools they need to improve the quality of living for their family."

Hoosman is a graduate of East St. Louis Senior High School and earned a bachelor's degree in 1979 from the University of Missouri-St. Louis (UMSL) on a full basketball scholarship. Later, he became the first former athlete to receive the UMSL Distinguished Alumni Award.

He believes he has made a strong impact on St. Louis through Vantage's philanthropic efforts. "We try to support the educational community throughout the communities we serve," he said. Hoosman is proud to be a catalyst to an organization that is fair and represents the community.

Some of those support efforts include sponsoring University of Missouri-St. Louis basketball tickets for the Herbert Hoover Boys and Girls Club, donating toys to many youth programs during Christmas time, and assisting the World Council of Credit Unions with international credit union development. Through this organization, Hoosman has conducted training sessions for credit union management and volunteers in the African countries of Rwanda and Swaziland, as well as Brisbane, Australia.

Hoosman is also chair of the board of the Missouri Credit Union Association and vice president of the University of Missouri-St. Louis Alumni Association. He is a director of the African-American Credit Union Coalition, and the Consumer Federation of America, and a member of the World Leadership Development Committee of the Credit Union National Association.

Previously married, Hoosman is the father of Camille and Hubert III and attends Trinity United Methodist Church in East St. Louis, Illinois. His hobbies are traveling, listening and collecting jazz music and playing golf.

Photo by Maurice Meredith

Invested in St. Louis

DARLENE DAVIS

By Jason Bailey

Darlene Davis had a successful career keeping track of money for major corporations, but she wanted more. She realized that the 80-plus hours a week she spent tracking money for companies she didn't own was worth much more than what she was being paid.

Davis' husband, Tyrone, suggested that she start an accounting firm. She had never considered it. That was six years ago, and she hasn't looked back since. Awards and framed articles decorate the walls of Davis Associates as a testament that she made the right move. And as an added bonus, Davis' husband works as a partner in her firm.

In an industry dominated by white males, Davis doesn't look like the stereotypical accountant. You won't find her wearing a pocket protector or carrying a calculator. Her quick smile and dynamic personality make her warm and approachable.

"My clients come to me and they are just so happy to have a black, female CPA that they can go to," said the mother of three. "There was definitely a need and a market." Davis has clients that have been with her since the beginning of her full-service accounting firm, and she feels like a part of their business success. "The satisfaction of being able to help people is of the utmost importance," said the Saint Louis University alumnus.

Even as a child, Davis understood money. She would save her allowance and loan money to her brother and cousin who spent theirs on candy and snacks. When they repaid her, it was always with interest. She would even charge late fees.

"I gave them a dollar then they had until the next Friday to give me a dollar and a quarter," Davis said. As a University City High School student, Davis had her eyes set on the accounting field early.

She recalls looking for a summer job and noticing how many ads there were for accountants. She decided then that she would pursue accounting because there would always be a need. "I have fun every day," Davis said of running her own business. "It's not a job to me." She has carved a niche in the St. Louis market and can't see doing business or raising her family anywhere else.

Davis tells a story of congratulating her daughter, Olivia, after a successful school performance. When asked if she would take acting classes and become an actress when she grew up, Olivia's answer nearly brought Davis to tears. "I'm taking over Davis Associates when I get big," said the eight-year-old third grader.

Not only has Davis started a business, but she has also laid a foundation for the future right here in St. Louis. It doesn't get any better than that.

Photo by Maurice Meredith

Powering Communities with Energy and Commitment

RICHARD J. MARK

By Pamela Bolden

Richard J. Mark is not afraid to stand up for what he believes. And when it comes to giving young people the necessary tools to help them succeed in life, he will not relent. "You certainly won't win a popularity contest," he says of his penchant for making decisions that may not win popular votes.

The Collinsville, Illinois native has dedicated many years to community service. At age 25, he started a federally-funded, first-time juvenile offender's program in his hometown. In 1994 Mark was appointed by the State of Illinois to chair the State Financial Oversight Panel to improve School District 189 in East St. Louis, Illinois.

After ten years under Mark's direction, the panel was credited with leaving the district in sound financial standing with a $20 million fund balance and construction plans for eight new schools and an early childhood center. "The best way to help African-American youth is to educate them," he notes.

He lamented that no city can thrive without good schools. "The only way cities are going to revive themselves will be with strong educational systems. It should be the number one priority," he shares. "Without it, businesses move out; then people move out. It feeds upon itself."

His dedication and commitment to community service helps guide his decisions as senior vice president, Missouri Energy Delivery for AmerenUE. Mark is responsible for electric and natural gas distribution and customer service operations for AmerenUE in Missouri.

Before moving to this position in 2005, he was vice president of governmental policy and consumer affairs for Ameren Corporation. AmerenUE, Missouri's largest electric utility, provides energy services to approximately 1.2 million customers across central and eastern Missouri, including the greater St. Louis area. One-half of AmerenUE's electric customers are located in the St. Louis metropolitan area.

Prior to joining Ameren in 2002, Mark was president and chief executive officer of St. Mary's Hospital in East St. Louis, a position he held for six years. Mark initiated a plan that recruited more than 30 physicians to the East St. Louis community, greatly improving residents' access to healthcare.

Mark noted the importance of factoring community interests and concerns into corporate decisions. He says not-for-profits can benefit from the wealth of knowledge and resources business leaders possess. "A lot of times when people move up, they forget about the community. They can help bring resources to community organizations that they may believe in. We must balance the needs of the community with corporate interests. It's ultimately a win-win for everybody," he shares.

Currently, Mark serves on the board of directors for the St. Louis Black Repertory Theatre, the Major Case Squad, Forest Park Forever, Belleville Dioceses Catholic Community Foundation, Enterprise Bank and the St. Clair County Sheriff's Department Merit Commission. He and his wife have three children.

Your hospital
cares about you

If you do not have health insurance,
financial help may be available to you.

While you are here, please
let us know if you need help
to pay your bill.

Or, you may call us
at 618-463-7314.

All information will be kept
strictly confidential.

Photo by Maurice Meredith

Grounded in Faith, Family and Community

JUNE McALLISTER FOWLER

By Pamela Bolden

On Sunday mornings, June McAllister Fowler is a dedicated Sunday school teacher. Other times, she may be found roughing it with a group of impressionable youth at an area campsite or on other fun adventures as a Girl Scout leader. And as a Zeta Phi Beta sorority sister, she discovered the importance of being involved in a number of community outreach efforts. Fowler's community activism provides avenues for investing in the St. Louis community beyond her professional responsibilities as vice president of corporate and public communications for BJC HealthCare.

BJC HealthCare is one of the largest nonprofit healthcare organizations in the United States and the largest provider of charity care in the state of Missouri. It delivers services through 13 hospitals and multiple community health centers in urban, suburban and rural communities throughout the greater St. Louis, southern Illinois and mid-Missouri regions.

Fowler is responsible for articulating the organization's commitment to improving the health and well-being of the people and communities BJC serves. She is responsible for media relations, executive communications, community affairs, corporate marketing, creative services, Web development, media services and the "BJC Today" employee newsletter. She is also heavily involved in public policy.

Fowler earned a bachelor's degree from the University of Missouri-Columbia and a master's degree in urban affairs from Washington University in St. Louis. However, her business practices are grounded in her belief system. "My faith is a huge part of my life," says Fowler. "It orders my steps and directs my path and is the foundation for how I think." Her belief system influences the many aspects of her life—her career, family and community. Fowler is a native St. Louisan who was nurtured and protected by a community rich in values. There were parents who instilled work ethics, dynamic teachers who taught handling conflict and emotions, a school principal who taught integrity, and a neighborhood that taught the meaning of community.

Fowler puts into practice lessons learned. She serves as vice president of the St. Louis County Economic Council; on the boards of the St. Louis Science Center, Forest Park Forever, Associated Industries of Missouri, UMB Bank St. Louis advisory board; and as past chair of the Girl Scout Council of Greater St. Louis and the Metropolitan Association of Philanthropy.

Some of the recognition she has received include the 2001 Coro Community Leadership Award, the 2002 National Eagle Leadership Institute Award and induction into the YWCA of Metro St. Louis Academy of Leaders in 2004. Additionally, Fowler was named one of the Most Influential Minority Business Leaders by the *St. Louis Business Journal* in 2005.

Fowler has been married to her husband, Flint, for 25 years and they have three children. Jessica, 22, a recent graduate of the University of Virginia, has been accepted into the Duke University School of Medicine; Evan, 18, is a freshman at Morehouse College; and Stacey, 15, is a sophomore at John Burroughs School in St. Louis.

EXPRESS
Charting the Future

Building People and Their Careers

MICHAEL HOLMES

By Marcus Ma'at Atkins

"To whom much is given, much is required." This is the philosophy that Michael Holmes of Express Scripts lives by. "I've been blessed in my life and I'm trying to give back and make a positive contribution to St. Louis." These words provide a window into the character of this highly-respected executive. Holmes, new senior vice president and chief human resources officer of Express Scripts, grew up in Berkley, Missouri and is heavily vested in this community.

He views his role as the leader of the organization's human resources operation to build infrastructure that will support the company's explosive growth. With 14,000-plus employees across North America, Holmes guides the strategic direction of human capital within the firm, including the culture; recruitment and selection; training and development; compensation and benefits; talent planning; and employer relations.

"My overall plan is to ensure our human resource strategies are focused on driving the business forward and helping to make Express Scripts the number one pharmacy benefit management company," Holmes says.

Express Scripts ranks 134th on the 2006 Fortune 500 list with more than $16 billion in revenue. The company is currently headquartered in Maryland Heights, but will relocate in the spring of 2007 to a newly-built corporate headquarters on the University of Missouri-St. Louis campus. Express Scripts' mission is to "make the use of prescription drugs safer and more affordable" for its plan sponsors and 50 million members.

Holmes, who graduated in 1979 from Washington University in St. Louis with three degrees, emphasizes the importance of assisting others within the organization. "I get to work with people across the organization and mentor individuals," Holmes says. "As a leader in human resources, I'm able to help people in the beginning stages of their careers."

A 25-year veteran of the human resources field, Holmes returned to university life in 1993 and received his master of arts degree in business from Webster University. "I wanted to round out my knowledge of the financial side of business," he explains. "It's imperative to understand how the score is kept and to have basic business acumen such as the ability to read financial statements."

One of his favorite past times is his philanthropic efforts, which are currently focused on the United Way of Greater St. Louis, Harris-Stowe State University, and 100 Black Men of America-St. Louis Chapter.

Holmes served as chairman of Mary Institute and Saint Louis Country Day School (MICDS) and the national board of directors of the Sickle Cell Disease Association of America. He is also the past co-chair of the St. Louis Inner City Competitive Alliance. "As a community that has given so much to me, St. Louis has influenced my value system and my understanding of philanthropy," notes Holmes.

The Berkeley High School graduate has been married to his wife, Gail, for 25 years and has two children, Brooke and Michael II. "St. Louis is home and is a great place to live and raise a family," he said. "It's where most of my family and friends are located. People have good values here."

Photo by Maurice Meredith

Helping Girls Grow Strong

THERESA E. LOVELESS

By Crystal Howard

Theresa Loveless is no stranger to the St. Louis area. She was born in the Metro East, raised in Arkansas and returned to the St. Louis area in 1971 to work with the Girl Scout Council of Greater St. Louis. Loveless has more than 35 years with the Girl Scouts helping young ladies become leaders in the community, and it all began for her in Fort Worth, Texas. Today, Loveless leads the Council of Greater St. Louis as chief executive officer and has renewed focus on supporting girls and expanding volunteer opportunities.

A number of things motivate Loveless, "…helping girls grow strong, understanding their potential and how to move forward. There's more than one way to serve a girl," she said. At the helm since 1996, Loveless has taught area girls that there is more to Girl Scouts than just cookies. They offer a variety of programs to appeal to girls on many levels.

Unique to the St. Louis area, during April Showers Girl Scouts collect more than one million personal care items for local families in need. These crucial items cannot be purchased with food stamps.

Making Cents in the City is a new three-year progressive program focusing on building awareness, knowledge, and confidence with money management. Experts in various fields cover different financial programs throughout the year.

Girl Scouts Beyond Bars offers girls with incarcerated mothers the opportunity to maintain the mother/daughter bond and break the cycle of crime. Loveless is particularly proud of Project Anti-Violence Education (PAVE), which serves girls primarily in school settings and helps them prevent violence in their lives.

Her support of diverse programs has helped the Girl Scout Council of Greater St. Louis continue to become the largest Girl Scout Council in the United States for the past seven years, currently serving more than 62,000 girls and 17,000 adults. New challenges await Loveless in the near future when the council expands and mergers with the Becky Thatcher Council. This move will extend the organization's reach to the Iowa border and add roughly 1,500 more girls.

A widow and mother of a grown daughter living in Florida, Loveless knows what is important in life. She keeps the organization's focus on the girls they serve and not the administrative struggles that may arise.

In addition to the Girl Scouts, Loveless is active in the St. Louis community. She is involved with numerous boards and committees including Women of Achievement (past president); Parents As Teachers (board member); Missouri Botanical Gardens sub-district committee (past president); St. Louis Alumnae Chapter of Delta Sigma Theta Sorority, Inc. (past president); Leadership St. Louis/Focus St. Louis (past vice president); and a charter member and past chair of the Charmaine Chapman Society, the African-American Leadership Giving Initiative for the United Way of Greater St. Louis, to name a few.

Loveless' awards include the President's Advocacy Award from the NBA Echo Emergency Children's Home, Trailblazer Award from the St. Louis Forum, Faith in Action Award from Lutheran Family & Children's Services, Unsung Hero Award from Top Ladies of Distinction, and Soror of the Year from the Central Region of Delta Sigma Theta.

"I believe we can make a difference."

MARTIN L. MATHEWS

By Crystal Howard

In 1958 Martin Mathews coached a baseball team of 30 neighborhood boys for what he thought would be a one-year commitment. The young men played teams that seemed to have everything...nice fields, and new uniforms and equipment. Martin's team appeared to have nothing. But appearances are deceiving...those boys had Martin Mathews, a man who would make a difference in their lives. Martin gave them $25 to join the league and coached the boys when no one else would. With two years of hard work and proper coaching, they were successful—sometimes playing five teams in one day—but they won the league!

By 1960 Mathews and his friend, the late Hubert "Dickey" Ballentine, met under a shade tree in St. Louis' Handy Park to discuss how to form leagues and keep the neighborhood boys having fun and out of trouble. Mathews could not have dreamed that day was the beginning of an organization that to date has served more than a million girls and boys.

As president, chief executive officer and co-founder of the Mathews-Dickey Boys' & Girls' Club, Mathews has a passion for helping children succeed. He mortgaged his home to help pay for the club's first building. "I believe we can make a difference," Mathews said.

"Given the opportunity, a strong support system, and preparation—any kid can succeed," he added. "If you buy into that 'bad background' excuse, people like Oprah Winfrey should not be where she is today." Mathews' philosophy is that all our children deserve a chance. By bringing together parents, schools, churches, and the business community, the children at Mathews-Dickey can have the opportunity to achieve.

With a board of directors list that reads like "Who's Who in St. Louis," Mathews assembled a support team of local business and charitable organizations, including the United Way. "St. Louisans are the greatest givers, but you have to be proven," he continued. His enthusiasm and love for the children managed to garner the support needed to expand from their humble beginnings. Literacy programs and activities for girls were eventually added to the club.

In 1982 President Ronald Reagan declared the club a model for the country. NBC's *Today Show* recognized the club in 1994. A Hall of Fame was created to capture a pictorial history, secure memorabilia from the club's earlier days, and to honor distinguished alumni, community supporters and board members who have made significant contributions to their community and the Boys' & Girls' Club. Mathews even had a hand in helping to establish the Jackie Joyner-Kersee Center located in East St. Louis, Illinois.

Although his plate was full, Mathews still served as an advisor to many local boards and organizations including St. Louis Job Corp, CORE Leadership Fund, Fair St. Louis, the Missouri Athletic Club and several others. He received numerous local and national awards, including the Amateur Baseball Hall of Fame; President's Council on Youth Opportunity; St. Louis Board of Education's Outstanding Community Service; the Missouri Athletic Club's prestigious Jack Buck Award and an honorary doctorate from Webster University. President Ronald Reagan honored Mathews with the United States Presidential Citizens Award in 1982.

Staying on Task, Raising Academic Performance

THERESA SAUNDERS, ED.D.

By Pamela Bolden

Lending her vocal skills at a school program may be a bit unorthodox, but that shows a glimmer of the complexities of Theresa Saunders, Ed.D., the new leader of School District 189 in East St. Louis, Illinois. Saunders, originally from Jackson, Michigan, has been shaped by many influences in her life.

"The first was my mother and aunts who were teachers and helped shape both my thinking and work in education," Saunders said. She became superintendent of the public school system in October 2005. The district serves about 10,000 students who live in East St. Louis, Centreville, Alorton, Washington Park, Fairmont City and Brooklyn, Illinois. The district is primarily comprised of African Americans, with the second-largest population consisting of a growing number of Hispanic students.

She is no stranger to urban education settings, having studied in urban schools abroad in England, the Netherlands, South Korea, and in several western African countries. Saunders earned a doctorate in urban education and school finance from the University of Southern California in Los Angeles. She was most recently superintendent of the Highland Park Schools in Highland Park, Michigan.

Saunders has lofty goals for the East St. Louis school district. "I have three primary goals," she said. "First, is to have all schools make their AYP (Adequate Yearly Progress) requirements; secondarily, to have all programs in the district compliant with state and federal mandates; and third, to grow the district in student/families and the development of appropriate programs and services."

So far, her greatest challenges have been to decentralize staff and programs to the site level for direction and implementation. However, Saunders says she has been encouraged by the enthusiasm of staff, students and community members for new ideas and processes for improving the education of children and families.

One of the superintendent's first acts, the reinstatement of monthly parent forums, has been an overwhelming success. The forums open dialogue between the district, parents, guardians and others interested in public education. The one-hour sessions are used to discuss such topics as classroom instruction, parental concerns, and avenues for enhancing student achievement.

In other encouraging developments, the school district is closing six schools in preparation of welcoming three new, larger elementary school buildings in the fall of 2006 — Paul Laurence Dunbar Elementary School, Gordon Bush Elementary School and the Dr. Katie Harper Wright Elementary School. Additional schools scheduled to open in 2007 are Clark-Mason Middle School in East St. Louis and the Leroy Ducksworth Elementary School in Washington Park.

Saunders, a member of Alpha Kappa Alpha Sorority, Inc., is a newly licensed minister in the Anglican Church. In addition, she is writing a book entitled, "Leadership as Mastered Disciplines" and a children's music book, "The Wisdom of Children's Worship." She serves on the board of the Center for Health, Education and Advocacy in Detroit, Michigan and the education committee for the Anglican Church Worldwide.

Photo by Maurice Meredith

Answering Life's Calling

DR. HENRY SHANNON

By Jason Bailey

Dr. Henry Shannon's record of distinctions, awards and service in education stretches across three decades. From junior high school history teacher to his current position as chancellor of the St. Louis Community College system, Shannon has been in the forefront of molding minds.

As the seventh chancellor for the system, Shannon is fulfilling his purpose. The system is the largest community college system in Missouri, serving more than 130,000 students at three campuses and four education centers throughout the St. Louis metropolitan area. The college also serves the business community through counseling, consulting and training services.

"Our mantra is to be accessible, affordable and very responsive," he said. Shannon sees the community college system as a servant of the common man. Founded in 1962, the institution's mission is to expand minds and change lives everyday, especially those without access to other education options.

With more than 30 years in education, Shannon wants the college's students to have every advantage and opportunity regardless of their backgrounds or academic plans. In his view, education is the only road to an internationally-level playing field. Looking to the future, Shannon says the time for totally non-skilled labor is coming to an end. "The jobs of the future will require some type of post-secondary education," said the Mississippi native.

Shannon was born in a small town and moved to what he calls "up South" to St. Louis when he was eight years old, shortly after the historic Emmett Till murder. Like many others, Shannon's family feared for the safety of their children in the face of the racist violence that claimed Till's life.

When Shannon graduated from Soldan High School in 1965, St. Louis was a segregated town. He wanted to be a professional basketball player but eventually realized there was only one choice that made sense. He went to Harris Teacher's College and earned his bachelor's degree. He continued on to obtain both his master's and doctoral degrees from Washington University.

Despite his degrees and credentials, there are no pretenses about Shannon. He has always had an open-door policy to students and employees. He doesn't get as many office visits these days, but he keeps in touch via email and frequent visits to SLCC campuses.

He passed his attitude about education on to his four children and shares a special bond with his high school sweetheart and wife of 36 years, Gwendolyn. As an educational trailblazer in her own right, Mrs. Shannon served as the first African-American junior high school principal in Jennings.

"I like helping people. I like seeing students succeed. And over the years I've come across many young people I've been able to help in some way," said Shannon.

Some of Dr. Shannon's students have become professors, judges and one, Freeman Bosley Jr., became the first African-American mayor of the City of St. Louis. He enjoys hearing from old students and is proud and humbled as they pay homage to him and credit him as being a mentor and role model. He smiles when he thinks of it because he knows he has answered his life's calling.

Our *Mission*

Through our exceptional health care services, we reveal the healing presence of God.

Committed to Affecting Change

YVONNE TISDEL

By Jacquie Vick

Yvonne Tisdel's passion to help, serve and protect began with a 20-year stint in the United States Navy and continues in her professional and personal work in St. Louis. She settled in St. Louis after retiring as a lieutenant commander from the Navy in 1995. Tisdel joined General Electric Capital Mortgage Services as an operations leader—one of only three minority managers. "I immersed myself in the community and became very passionate about the history and culture of the city," she says.

In 1998, she joined SSM Health Care and has been working to increase diversity awareness and promote diversity not only throughout the organization but in the community. In her role as corporate vice president, human resources and system diversity for SSM Health Care, Tisdel provides system-wide strategic leadership in human resources and workplace diversity to SSM Health Care's 20-plus hospitals, nursing homes and health businesses. She is committed to affecting change and creating diverse professional environments to help attract a diverse talent pool to St. Louis. "Place yourself in an area where a need has not been met," she advises.

Tisdel is a community activist. She sits on the board of three organizations (Guardian Angels Association, St. Louis Workforce Development and the YWCA); serves as chair of the United Way/SSM Health Care African-American Giving Initiative; co-chairs the Walk as One National Conference for Community and Justice (NCCJ); and serves as a supplier diversity committee member for National Premier, Inc., and a mission and ethics committee member for CHRISTUS Health Care.

She has been instrumental in organizing diversity forums in St. Louis to support diverse employees in management. Additionally, Tisdel has been recognized for her efforts by the St. Louis American Foundation as a Stellar Performer in the Salute to Excellence in Health Care, and a Woman of Distinction by the Professional Organization of Women. She has also received awards from the Young Women's Christian Association (YWCA) and the Navy.

Growing up in Memphis, Tennessee during the civil rights era, Yvonne is all too familiar with the hardship, struggle, devastation and disappointment of workers fighting for equal pay for equal work. She witnessed it at 12 years old with the onset of the garbage strike and knows what it was like to be one of the few rising through the military ranks. She knows the adversities minorities face in corporate America also.

During her free time Yvonne enjoys interior decorating, traveling, the performing arts and the rich history of the city. And she wants tourists to take pleasure in the city as much as she does.

Yvonne obtained a master of science degree in administration from Central Michigan University in Mt. Pleasant, Michigan; a bachelor of science degree in business administration from Lemoyne Owen College in Memphis, Tennessee; and a Society for Human Resource Management (SHRM) professional certification. She is a member of Delta Sigma Theta Sorority, Inc. and has numerous professional human resource affiliations.

SPARKMAN
YOUR CHRISTIAN CLASSIFIED PUBLICATION

Celebrating Six Glorious Years!

Our Invitation To You!

*We greet you in the Mighty name of Jesus our Lord and Savior!
It is with great joy that we embrace our faithful readers and we
invite those who have not read our publication to experience a
powerful Media Ministry!*

About Our Publication

Sparkman Your Christian Classified Publication is the leading Christian
Publication in the metropolitan and surrounding areas. Founded in 1999
and named in honor of "Mother Ida M. Sparkman," Sparkman Publication
is an exciting and diverse publication dedicated to serving the Christian
Community. We are distributed in over 700 area Churches, Christian centers,
Christian bookstores, libraries, restaurants, colleges, universities, area
hospitals, beauty and barber salons, and many private business locations.
We strive to provide our readers with employment and real estate opportunities,
soul-stirring spiritual and educational articles, up-coming Christian events, a
comprehensive Church Directory, information about our Sparkman Lecture
Series 2005 and more!   *   *   *   *   *

We Do Our Best To Inspire And Empower The Hearts & Minds Of
Our Readers!

*Marilyn Parker
Founder / Editor*

*Dr. Bessie L. Reece
Executive Director
Co-Owner*

How To Find Us

For more information about us, how to receive our free Christian
Publication for your Church or establishment, or information on
advertising with us please call us or visit our web-site!

*   *   *   *   *

"And I thank Christ Jesus our Lord, who hath enabled me, for he counted me faithful, putting
me into ministry". I Timothy 1:12

We Thank You For Your Support Over The Years...May God Bless You! ....Evangelist Marilyn Parker & Dr. Bessie Reece

www.sparkmanpublication.com   Ph: (314) 535-7210 or Fax: 535-7310

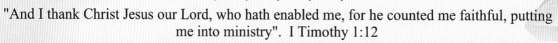

The City of St. Louis Department of Health

Stay in tune with the "Rhythm of Health" by using Public Health!

Programs and Services:

- Health Promotion Education
- School Health Services
- Show Me Healthy Women
- Childhood Lead Poisoning
- Prevention Program (CLPPP)
- Refugee and Immigrant Health

- Community Health Program
- Communicable Disease
- Metro AIDS
- Maternal/Child Health Services
- Investigation Services
- Environmental Health Services
- Bioterrorism Response Planning

"Working with you to improve the health of the citizens of St. Louis"

*Pertussis*Protection™
Around the Whole Family

Two steps to protect babies from whooping cough

A serious illness: Whooping cough (pertussis) is a serious illness in infants that can result in hospitalization and death. Children younger than 6 months old are at highest risk. In the United States (US), almost 80% of babies 6 months old or younger with whooping cough are admitted to the hospital.[1]

A continuing upsurge in whooping cough: In 2004, the number of reported cases of whooping cough reached a 45-year high.[2-4] Reported cases of whooping cough are highest among these groups: infants too young to be vaccinated, adolescents, and adults. A study has shown that babies often get whooping cough from their mothers or other family members.[5] The protection provided by childhood pertussis vaccines "wears off" in adolescents and adults, who may then spread the infection to infants. But there is a way to protect your baby.

Take 2 steps to protect your baby

Vaccination for children: Today, children in the US are routinely vaccinated with a combination vaccine for diphtheria, tetanus, and acellular pertussis (DTaP). The Centers for Disease Control and Prevention (CDC) recommends vaccination at 2, 4, 6, 15-18 months, and 4-6 years of age.[6]

Vaccination for adolescents and adults: Protection from pertussis "wears off" so predictably that, in 2005, the CDC Advisory Committee on Immunization Practices voted to recommend a single booster of tetanus, diphtheria, and acellular pertussis (Tdap) vaccine for adolescents and adults (11-64 years of age) who have close contact with infants less than 12 months of age.[6,7]

Please talk to your family doctor about immunizations to protect your baby from pertussis.

References: 1. Centers for Disease Control and Prevention (CDC). Rate of hospitalizations for pertussis among infants aged <6 months—United States, 1994-1998 and 1999-2003. *MMWR*. 2005;54:1027. **2.** CDC. Summary of notifiable diseases, United States 1994. *MMWR*. 1995;43:68-77. **3.** CDC. Summary of notifiable diseases—United States, 2003. *MMWR*. 2005;52:69-77. **4.** CDC. Final 2004 reports of notifiable diseases. *MMWR*. 2005;54:770-780. **5.** Bisgard KM, Pascual FB, Ehresmann KR, et al. Infant pertussis: who was the source? *Pediatr Infect Dis J*. 2004;23:985-989. **6.** CDC. Recommended childhood and adolescent immunization schedule—United States, 2006. *MMWR*. 2006;54:Q1-Q4. **7.** Advisory Committee on Immunization Practice recommends adult vaccination with new tetanus, diphtheria and pertussis vaccine (Tdap) [press release]. CDC; November 9, 2005.

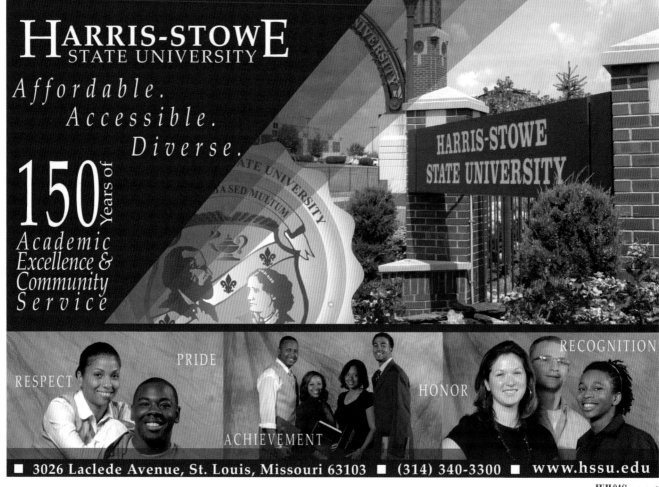

FRUSTRATED *TRYING TO STRETCH YOUR DOLLARS????*

Let **HDC** Help!!!!
We offer
"FREE SERVICES"
To income eligible residents in St. Louis City and Wellston

Services provided

- ✔ Food and Clothing
- ✔ Employment Assistance
- ✔ Energy Assistance
- ✔ Health/Nutrition
- ✔ Wellston Youth Coalition

- ✔ Homeless Prevention
- ✔ Emergency Food
- ✔ GED
- ✔ Computer Learning Center
- ✔ Christmas Assistance

- ✔ WIC
- ✔ Life Skills
- ✔ Job Fair
- ✔ School Supplies
- ✔ Family Support

The Human Development Corporation of Metropolitan St. Louis

Service Centers

North Side Center
4548 Dr. Martin L. King Drive
St. Louis, MO 63113
314-535-7484
Claudette Gibson, Area Coordinator

South Side Center
7714 S. Broadway
St. Louis, MO 63118
314-631-0019
Katrie Spink, Area Coordinator

North East Center
935 N. Vandeventer
St. Louis, MO 63108
314-631-2154
Dorothy Hunter, Area Coordinator

Wellston/North West Center
6356 Dr. Martin L. King Drive
Wellston, MO 63113
314-613-2311
Delores Haynes, Area Coordinator

Administrative Offices
929 N. spring Avenue
St. Louis, MO 63108
314-613-2200
Website: http://www.stlouis.missouri.org/hdc

> Community Action changes people's lives, embodies the spirit of hope, improves communities and makes America a better place to live. We care about the entire community, and we are dedicated to helping people help themselves and each other.

Charles Barge, Board Chairman   **Ruth A. Smith, President/CEO**

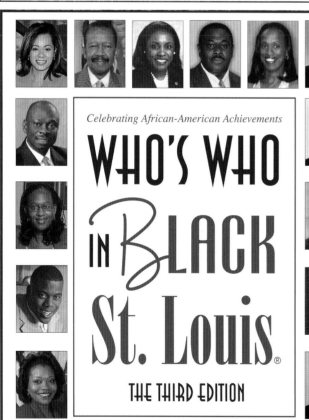

St. Louis'

MOST INFLUENTIAL

"One isn't necessarily born with courage, but one is born with potential. Without courage, we cannot practice any other virtue with consistency. We can't be kind, true, merciful, generous, or honest."

MAYA ANGELOU

AUTHOR AND POET

MOST INFLUENTIAL

Mark H. Anderson
Postmaster
City of St. Louis

Mark H. Anderson is the 42nd postmaster of St. Louis. He began his duties as the postmaster of St. Louis in December of 2001. In this position, he has administrative authority and operational oversight for the collection and delivery of mail to 490,000 business and residential customers. He is responsible for 33 stations and branches, nine finance units, and more than 2,300 employees.

A California native, Mark began his postal career in 1978 as a letter carrier in San Diego, where he spent the majority of his career. Prior to moving to St. Louis, he was the postmaster of Oceanside, California.

Mark developed and refined his expertise and knowledge in postal operations through a variety of positions of increased responsibility and accountability. These positions include supervisor of customer services; manager, delivery and retail operations; manager of customer services; station manager; manager, post office operations; and area manager. In addition, he assisted the Chicago Post Office with service improvement initiatives and served as the acting postmaster of Detroit.

Mark received his undergraduate degree in business administration from Lindenwood University in Missouri.

Thomas R. Bailey Jr.
President
Missouri Black Expo, Inc.

In October of 1991, Thomas R. Bailey Jr. founded Missouri Black Expo, Inc. in St. Louis, Missouri. He has been the president since its inception. The Missouri Black Expo is the second largest event of its kind in the United States.

Thomas also serves as the co-chair of national conferences and events for the 100 Black Men of America.

Bailey has been honored with numerous awards and recognitions. *The St. Louis Sentinel* newspaper selected him for their Yes I Can Award in 1985. He has received community service leadership awards from organizations including the St. Louis Black Accountants, The St. Louis Young Democrats, and *The St. Louis Argus* newspaper. Thomas has also been awarded the 100 Black Men of Metro St. Louis Trail Blazer Award, the 100 Black Men of America Wimberley Award, and the Mark of Excellence Award from MIX 97.1FM in St. Louis.

Bailey is married to the former Kathleen Graham of Tulsa, Oklahoma. They have three children, Graham, Shannon, and Sydney.

WHO'S *WHO*

Kenneth Bell is the project executive for an IBM contract at the State of Illinois. In this position, he manages the profit/loss and growth of an annual multimillion-dollar contract. His additional responsibilities include business development and management leadership development. In his 29 years at IBM, Kenneth has held positions in consulting, sales management and technical serviceability. He has received awards such as the 100% Sales Club and Technical Symposium. Additionally, he is president of the IBM Club Metro St. Louis and a member of the IBM St. Louis Black Networking Group.

A community volunteer, Kenneth serves on the board of Northside Community Center and is a member of the United Way Charmaine Chapman Leadership Giving Initiative.

He received a degree from the Missouri Institute of Technology in electronic technology, and has completed numerous IBM courses.

A St. Louis native, Kenneth is married to Dale Martin-Bell, and is the proud father of daughter D'Angela, sons Kenneth Jr., James, Bryant, and Michael, and great-niece Taylor. He also has a granddaughter, Hydeia, and three grandsons, DeAndris, Kenneth III and James Jr.

Kenneth G. Bell
Project Executive
Business Development Manager
IBM Corporation

Amber H. Boykins represents the 60th District in the Missouri House of Representatives and serves on the appropriations committee for transportation and economic development budget. She is the youngest African-American woman legislator in the history of the Missouri House. Boykins and her mother, a former state representative, are the only mother/daughter combination to serve in the Missouri House.

Boykins has received numerous awards including the Yes I Can Award from St. Louis Teachers – Local 420, the Cardinal Ritter Prep Leadership Award, Young Democrats Dedicated Leadership in Government, and the Making a Difference Order of the Eastern Star. *Essence* chose Boykins as one of 30 Women to Watch.

Boykins is a member of Women in Government, Delta Sigma Theta Sorority, Inc., NOBEL Women, The Links, Inc., the NAACP, the American Council of Young Political Leaders, and People for the American Way - Young Elected Officials Network.

A graduate of Cardinal Ritter College Prep and Columbia College, Boykins is pursuing a master of business administration degree and a juris doctorate. She lives in St. Louis with her husband, Shaun.

The Honorable
Amber (Holly) Boykins
Representative, 60th District
Missouri House of Representatives

MOST INFLUENTIAL

Maureen E. Brinkley
Director
U.S. Small Business Administration

M aureen Brinkley is the director of marketing and outreach for the U.S. Small Business Administration, St. Louis District. Her responsibility is to reach out to all markets, convey information concerning SBA programs, and increase distribution of SBA products to the small businessmen and women of America. A champion for women and minority business development, she has initiated projects to expand the use of SBA programs across the nation.

Brinkley is a dedicated employee serving in many capacities. Most prominently, she leads the Minority Enterprise Program and the One Stop Capital Shop Initiative, both becoming the model for the country. She was recently selected to assist the Portland, Oregon and Anchorage, Alaska districts.

Brinkley is the recipient of the 1996 SBA Minority Small Business Advocate Award and a *St. Louis Argus* Distinguished Citizen Award. She was a member of the Confluence St. Louis Minority Task Force, the Mayor's Small Business Advisory Council, the St. Louis Black Leadership Roundtable and Big Brothers/Big Sisters of Eastern Missouri.

Brinkley is most proud to be a member of First Baptist Church of Creve Coeur.

Gail A. Brown
President and Chief Executive Officer
Urban Planning and Development
Corporation of America, Inc.

G ail Brown is the president of a family of companies consisting of Urban Planning and Development Corporation (UPDC), Brown-Kortkamp Realty and Brown-Kortkamp Moving and Storage.

In 1990 Gail joined the family business founded by her father in 1961. With the passing of the baton in 1995, Gail now leads a team of real estate professionals providing traditional housing sales, development, land acquisition and relocation services. Under her leadership, UPDC has acquired more than 2000 parcels on behalf of clients for public and private developments. Brown-Kortkamp Realty markets new construction and government and bank-owned properties for several federal and private entities.

Gail holds a bachelor of arts degree from Macalester College in St. Paul, Minnesota and a master of business administration degree from St. Louis University.

A disciple of Central Baptist Church, Gail serves on the trustee ministry. In the community, Gail serves on boards of the YWCA, Better Family Life and Jefferson National Parks Association. She is president of the St. Louis Association of Real Estate Professionals as well as a state director for the Missouri Association of REALTORS®.

Shirley Brown, counsel in philanthropy, has 32 years of experience in fundraising campaign direction, meeting planning and events management. She specializes in creating and implementing fundraising campaigns, special events, and meeting planning for local and national nonprofit organizations, professional and business associations, educational institutions and the private sector.

Prior to starting her own business, Brown served as national executive director of Delta Sigma Theta Sorority, Inc. She also worked more than ten years for the United Negro College Fund as assistant national campaign director at the national headquarters in New York City, and as director of the Washington, D.C. and Birmingham, Alabama offices.

Brown was among the first group of fundraising executives and the first African American to be certified in fundraising by the Association of Fundraising Professionals. She is a member of the board of trustees at Talladega College in Alabama, and is a weekly society page columnist for the *St. Louis Argus* newspaper.

Brown received a bachelor's degree from Harris-Stowe State University, a master's degree from Southern Illinois University and lifetime teaching certification from the State of Missouri.

Shirley A. Brown
President & Chief Executive Officer
STL Campaigns and Events

Charles Bryson is the neighborhood development executive and senior policy advisor for St. Louis Mayor Francis G. Slay. In this position, Charles establishes polices, procedures and programs for the enhancement of neighborhoods throughout the city. This includes coordinating efforts of city departments, local elected officials, neighborhood groups, the police department and the St. Louis Federation of Block Units.

Charles also coordinates the mayor's board and commission appointments, and serves as a liaison with clergy and various ethnic groups.

Prior to working for the mayor, Charles worked in various public sector and nonprofit positions dealing with issues such as youth, the homeless and affordable housing.

A native of St. Louis, Charles is the son of the late Charles and Doris Bryson. He is married to Timberly McLeod Bryson (formerly of Peoria, Illinois), and is the proud father of two daughters, Bailey McLeod Bryson and Sydney McLeod Bryson.

Charles Bryson
Senior Policy Advisor
Office of the Mayor
City of St. Louis

MOST INFLUENTIAL

Dr. Gordon D. Bush
President
DALTAM, Inc.

Dr. Gordon D. Bush is the president of DALTAM, Inc., a national business development firm, and the publisher of *National Gaming Times* magazine. Previously, Bush served two terms as the mayor of East St. Louis, Illinois. In 1998 he brought the Casino Queen to East St. Louis, which initiated the biggest economic boom in the city's history.

A retired lieutenant colonel in the U.S. Army, Bush received the Presidential Citation from President Bill Clinton for 29 years of meritorious service. He received the Dr. Martin Luther King Leadership Award in 1995 from the State of Missouri and a Proclamation for Public Service from the State of Illinois. In 2003, a new school was named in his honor, Gordon D. Bush Elementary.

Bush was a featured speaker at the Million Man March in 1994. He also served as president of the National Conference of Black Mayors, and he is a life member of Kappa Alpha Psi and the NAACP.

He holds a bachelor's degree and a master's degree from Southern Illinois University and two honorary doctorate degrees.

A 33rd degree Mason, Shriner, Bush has been a member of Greater New Hope Baptist Church for 52 years. He is married to Brenda and they have two children, Tami and Dallon.

The Honorable
Anne-Marie Clarke
Family Court Commissioner
22nd Circuit of Missouri

Commissioner Anne-Marie Clarke has presided over family cases in St. Louis since January of 1986. Initially assigned to the juvenile division, she began her assignment in the domestic relations division in 2005.

Clarke received her bachelor's degree from Northwest Missouri State University in only three years. She followed her father, the late Thomas P. Clarke, into the legal profession, earning her law degree from Saint Louis University.

Clarke became the first black woman to serve on the St. Louis Board of Police Commissioners, appointed by the late Governor Mel Carnahan. She became the first woman president of the board with her unanimous election in April of 1994, serving until September of 1998.

Clarke is a life member of the National Bar Association and a board member of the NBA Judicial Council. She was the first black member of the board of governors of The Missouri Bar. She is a diamond life member of Delta Sigma Theta Sorority, Inc. Clarke is a member of St. Alphonsus "Rock" Catholic Church. She and her husband, Richard K. Gaines, love to travel.

William Lacy Clay was elected to the U.S. House of Representatives in 2000 and was chosen as president of the incoming Democratic freshman class. He serves on the Committee on Government Reform and several subcommittees.

A native of St. Louis, Clay moved to Washington in 1969 when his father, William Clay, was elected to the U.S. House of Representatives.

Clay was elected to the Missouri House of Representatives in 1983, and eight years later he won a seat in the Missouri Senate, where he served for nine years.

A member of the Congressional Black Caucus and the Progressive Caucus, Clay serves on the board of his father's William L. Clay Scholarship and Research Fund and the Congressional Black Caucus Foundation, Inc.

Clay holds a bachelor of science degree in government and politics from the University of Maryland. He also attended Harvard University's John F. Kennedy School of Government for senior executives in state and local government, and holds an honorary doctorate of laws from Lincoln University.

He and his wife, Ivie Lewellen Clay, have two children, Carol and William III.

The Honorable
William Lacy Clay
Representative, 1st District Missouri
U.S. House of Representatives

Stephen M. Coleman is the founder and majority shareholder of Daedalus Capital, LLC, an SEC registered investment advisor. He has served as chief investment officer since 1994 and is directly responsible for all client portfolios and the bottom line on performance. Daedelus Capital has received national honors for its success as an investor in publicly traded securities including recognition by *Pensions & Investments* magazine as the number one investment firm in the U.S. in 2000, 2003, and 2004.

Coleman's finance experience includes positions in corporate finance with Salomon Brothers, as president of S.M. Coleman & Company, as a portfolio manager with Prudential Securities, and as a general partner of ColJon Equity Partners, LP.

Some of Coleman's current nonprofit and civic involvements include serving as board president and chairman of the Annual Gala of the Wesley House, as governor of the Missouri Athletic Club, and as co-chair of the finance professionals sub-committee of the Charmaine Chapman Society Leadership Giving Initiative for the United Way of St. Louis.

He received his bachelor's degree from Amherst College and his MBA from Stanford University's Graduate School of Business.

Stephen grew up in Rock Hill, Missouri and married Judith Fagen Coleman; they have a 17-year-old daughter, Stevie Lynn.

Stephen M. Coleman
Founder & Majority Shareholder
Daedalus Capital, LLC

MOST INFLUENTIAL

Rodney Crim
Executive Director
St. Louis Development Corporation

Appointed by Mayor Francis G. Slay, Rodney Crim is executive director of the St. Louis Development Corporation, the economic development agency for the City of St. Louis.

Crim leads the agency's participation in business attraction, retention and growth. He is also responsible for financing and construction of multimillion-dollar commercial and residential development projects, all aimed at bringing people, jobs and investment to the city.

Crim's career reflects his passion for community and economic development. He has held executive management positions at major corporations and financial institutions in Chicago and Minneapolis. There, he also participated in numerous real estate and business development projects, creating partnerships that resulted in new jobs and new investment in underserved neighborhoods, retail shopping and industrial centers.

A graduate of the University of Minnesota, Crim has a master's degree in business administration from the University of St. Thomas in St. Paul, and is a certified public accountant.

A native of Chicago, Crim enjoys bicycling, sailing, racquetball, and family activities with his wife and two children.

The Honorable
Rita Heard Days
Senator, 14th District
Missouri Senate

Rita Heard Days was born in Minden, Louisiana in 1950. A graduate of Lincoln University, she was elected to the Missouri House of Representatives in 1993. In 2002 she was elected to the Missouri Senate where she currently serves the 14th District. She is a member of numerous committees including education, government accountability and fiscal oversight, small business insurance and industrial relations, transportation, terrorism, homeland security, Medicaid reform and others.

Days serves on many boards including the Children's Services Commission, the Juvenile Minority Overrepresentation Project, the Missouri Minority Business Advocacy Commission and the University of Missouri–St. Louis School of Social Welfare. She is a member of the Commission for the Future of Higher Education, Women Legislators of Missouri, the Missouri Legislative Black Caucus, the Normandy Township Democratic Club, the Kiwanis Club and Alpha Kappa Alpha Sorority, Inc.

A member of New Sunny Mount Church, Days has three children, Elliot, Natalie and Evelyn.

Kevin C. Dolliole is one of the most respected and renowned leaders in the airline industry. He is currently chair of the St. Louis Airport Commission and chief executive officer of Lambert-St. Louis International Airport.

Prior to joining Lambert, Kevin was aviation director for the City of San Antonio. He began his aviation career as a passenger service agent at Eastern Airlines in his hometown of New Orleans. He later secured management positions within the company that landed him in Atlanta, Georgia.

After 11 years in Atlanta, Kevin returned to New Orleans to serve as deputy director of aviation-facilities management, deputy director of operations and maintenance, deputy director of aviation – administration and finance, and acting director of New Orleans International Airport.

Kevin is a member of the American Association of Airport Executives policy and review committee, a nationwide compilation of senior management providing U.S. airports with security, safety and capacity guidance.

Kevin received a bachelor's degree in business administration from Xavier University of New Orleans, and a master of business administration degree from the University of New Orleans.

Kevin C. Dolliole
Chief Executive Officer
Lambert-St. Louis
International Airport

Charlie Dooley, county executive of St. Louis County, was unanimously elected by his fellow council members to succeed the late Buzz Westfall in the fall of 2003, and was reelected by voters in 2004. He was a member of the St. Louis County Council since 1994 when he became the first African American ever elected to the position.

Charlie's long, distinguished public service career began when he enlisted in the U.S. Army and fought in Vietnam as an army specialist from 1966 to 1968. Following his service, Charlie returned home and began serving his country on a local level. After serving as alderman for five years, Charlie was elected mayor of Northwoods in 1983.

During his time as mayor, Charlie served as president of both the St. Louis County Municipal League and the Missouri Chapter of Black Mayors. He was also a board member of the East-West Gateway Coordinating Council and an active member of the St. Louis County Economic Council. In addition to his public service, Charlie also worked at Boeing, retiring recently after 30 years.

The Honorable Charlie Dooley
County Executive
St. Louis County

MOST INFLUENTIAL

**The Honorable
George W. Draper III**
Judge
Missouri Court of Appeals
Eastern District

George W. Draper III was born August 5, 1953 in St. Louis. He was appointed to the Court of Appeals, Eastern District in 2000. He served as chief judge from July of 2004 to June of 2005. His term expires on December 31, 2014.

A graduate of Morehouse College, Draper earned a bachelor of arts degree in psychology. He received his juris doctorate from the Howard University School of Law.

Draper clerked for the Honorable Shellie Bowers, District of Columbia Superior Court. He also served as first assistant circuit attorney, and associate circuit judge for the 21st Judicial Circuit. He has been an adjunct professor at the Saint Louis University School of Law since 1996.

Draper belongs to Covenant Community Church. He is a member of the Mound City Bar Association; the Lawyers Association of St. Louis; the Bar Association of Metropolitan St. Louis; the Missouri Asian Bar Association; and the Prince Hall Free and Accepted Masons.

He is married to Judy P. Draper, associate circuit judge for the 21st Judicial Circuit Court. They have one daughter, Chelsea W. Draper.

**The Honorable
Judy Preddy Draper**
Associate Circuit Judge
21st Judicial Circuit Court

Judge Judy Preddy Draper was appointed associate circuit judge on April 13, 2004 by Governor Bob Holden.

Draper attended the University of North Carolina at Chapel Hill, receiving a bachelor's degree in labor relations in 1977. She received her juris doctorate from Howard University Law School in 1980 with law journal honors. After graduating from law school, she clerked for the U.S. Department of Labor, Office of Administrative Judges in Washington, D.C.

A former prosecutor for the City of St. Louis, Draper was an adjunct professor at Washington University in St. Louis School of Law. She clerked for the Honorable Clyde S. Cahill, federal district court judge, and was the first female general counsel for the Missouri Department of Corrections. Draper was in private practice in Clayton, handling criminal and civil cases. She also served as a municipal judge for the cities of Northwoods and Berkeley.

She is married to Judge George W. Draper III, the first African-American chief judge of the Missouri Court of Appeals, Eastern District. They have one daughter who is a freshman at Amherst College.

Tony O. Dukes is president and chief executive officer of The Dukes Group, construction managers and general contractors. He built the firm with the intent of tapping the vast potential of diversity offered in society in order to be competitive in professional construction services.

During his 28-year career, Dukes has served on several notable capital developments around the United States including the Disney MGM studio tour project; the St. Louis MetroLink light rail project; the American Airlines Arena, home of the Miami Heat; and the Lambert-St. Louis International Airport expansion.

Dukes is co-chair of the St. Louis Stemple Plan, representing the Associated General Contractors of America. He is a master mason and a member of the William H. Scott Military Lodge in St. Louis County.

Dukes received an associate degree in business administration from Southern Ohio College, and a bachelor's degree in communications from the University of Central Florida.

A native of Cincinnati, Dukes came to St. Louis in 1991. He is the proud father of his daughter, Aiesha Aila Dukes, currently attending Southern Illinois University.

Tony O. Dukes
President & Chief Executive Officer
The Dukes Group

The Honorable Jimmie M. Edwards was appointed circuit judge for the 22nd Judicial Circuit Court of Missouri in April of 1992.

A graduate of Saint Louis University, Edwards began a private law practice in St. Louis in 1981. He also held positions with Sabreliner Corporation as general counsel and Southwestern Bell Telephone Company.

Edwards has presided over many of the state's high-profile civil and criminal cases. He also served as a special Missouri Supreme Court judge, serving when any of the justices were unable to serve.

Edwards is a member of the executive council for all Missouri state judges and chairman of the Missouri Supreme Court records committee. He also serves on Missouri's civil law and habeas corpus committees. Additionally, Edwards is a professor at Saint Louis University and a visiting lecturer at the Washington University in St. Louis School of Law.

He is married to Stacy Edwards, and they have three children, Murphy, Ashley and John. Edwards is a member of Antioch Baptist Church, Omega Psi Phi Fraternity, Inc. and the Herbert Hoover Boys & Girls Club.

The Honorable
Jimmie M. Edwards
Judge
22nd Judicial Circuit
Court of Missouri

MOST INFLUENTIAL

Johnny Furr Jr.
Vice President
Urban Marketing & Community Affairs
Anheuser-Busch, Inc.

Johnny Furr Jr. is vice president of urban marketing and community affairs for Anheuser-Busch, Inc. In this role, Furr leads the development of objectives, strategies and action focused on sales in urban and African-American markets.

A native of St. Louis, Furr is a graduate of Sumner High School. He received a bachelor's degree in communications and marketing from Saint Louis University.

Furr has served as co-chair of the United Way of Greater St. Louis' Charmaine Chapman Society; chair of the National Council of Negro Women's Uncommon Height gala; and chair of the St. Louis American Foundation's Salute to Excellence in Education fund-raising dinner.

Furr is affiliated with numerous civic and community organizations including the Hip-Hop Summit Action Network, the Herbert Hoover Boys & Girls Club, the St. Louis Urban League and many others. He is a lifetime member of the NAACP and a member of Kappa Alpha Psi Fraternity, Inc.

Furr has received numerous awards including the Black Achievers in Industry Award from the YMCA of Greater New York.

Furr and his wife, Minga, have two daughters, Stacy and Jasmine.

Sherman George
Fire Commissioner & Chief
St. Louis Fire Department

On November 23, 1999, after 32 years of a distinguished career, Sherman George was named fire commissioner and chief of the St. Louis Fire Department. As the city's first African-American fire chief, George sits at the helm of one of the nation's top fire departments. There are 700 firefighters and support personnel, and 180 medical professionals in the department's bureau of emergency medical services. Established in 1857, the department provides citywide fire suppression and fire-prevention activities; hazardous materials, marine and cave-in incident taskforce deployment; and emergency medical services.

George earned his bachelor of science degree from Central Missouri State University. He is also a graduate of the Harvard University John F. Kennedy School of Government. He completed the executive development program at the Dillard University Carl H. Holmes Executive Development Institute, which prepares chief officers in the fire service.

George is a U.S. Army Vietnam veteran, having served in South Vietnam in 1966 and 1967. After receiving an honorable discharge, he continued reserve duty until 1987 when he retired as a sergeant.

Laurna Godwin is partner and co-founder of Vector Communications Corporation, a public involvement and communications consulting firm in St. Louis. Vector's core competencies include strategic planning and organizational development; meeting facilitation; event planning; media relations and communications planning; and video production.

At Vector, Laurna has received numerous national honors for her video production work. She has also been honored by the *St. Louis Business Journal* as one of the 25 Most Influential Businesswomen in St. Louis, and by Women of Achievement in the category of community leadership. She is a three-time Emmy Award-winning broadcast journalist.

Laurna serves on several corporate and civic boards including the Journal Register Company; the Greater St. Louis Community Foundation; the St. Louis Regional Chamber and Growth Association; the United Way of Greater St. Louis and the Girl Scout Council of Greater St. Louis, where she is board chair. She is also a commissioner on the City of St. Louis Downtown Economic Stimulus Authority.

Laurna received her undergraduate degree from Princeton University and her master's degree in journalism from Columbia University.

Laurna C. Godwin
Partner
Vector Communications Corporation

Jeanne Gore-Roberts has more than 15 years of experience in management and ownership in a variety of industries. Currently, she is a partner with BLL and Associates. Her responsibilities include managing the IT consulting and project management contract for the $1.2 billion Lambert-St. Louis International Airport expansion. Other clients include the State of Missouri, Texas Instruments and the Tier Corporation.

Gore-Roberts is a managing member of MJR Holdings. She has provided management oversight and analysis, and implemented acquisitions and dispositions of real estate properties in St. Louis and Malibu, California.

Gore-Roberts' numerous film and television credits include serving as co-executive producer of *Showtime at the Apollo*, and serving as a member of the judging committee for the *NAACP Image Awards*.

Gore-Roberts is a member of the Roberts Towers board of directors, the St. Louis Zoo Commission and the YWCA of St. Louis board of directors.

A lifelong St. Louis resident, Gore-Roberts is a graduate of Harris-Stowe State University. She is the mother of three daughters and one son, and has been married to Michael V. Roberts for 27 years.

Jeanne Gore-Roberts
Partner
BLL and Associates

MOST INFLUENTIAL

Samuel Gradford
President
National Black MBA Association, Inc.
St. Louis Chapter

Samuel Gradford is president of the National Black MBA Association – St. Louis Chapter. One of the premier African-American professional organizations in the U.S., the NBMBAA represents 100,000 African Americans with advanced business degrees. Sam joined the NBMBAA – St. Louis Chapter in 1992 and has served in a variety of positions since. His major accomplishments include the initiation and development of the St. Louis Chapter job fair.

Previously, Sam was director of workforce diversity for Metro, St. Louis' transportation agency. For 15 years he was responsible for diversity and equal employment opportunity programs. Prior to Metro, he spent ten years as a regional personnel manager for the Dial Corporation.

Sam is on the board of directors of numerous social and civic organizations. He is a member of the Urban League, the Human Resources Management Association and the Diversity Officers' Network of Civic Progress. He is a member of Union Missionary Baptist Church, where he serves on the board of deacons and as superintendent of Sunday school.

Sam holds a bachelor's degree and master's degree from the University of Missouri-Kansas City.

Shimmy Gray-Miller
Head Women's Basketball Coach
Saint Louis University

In the spring of 2005, Shimmy Gray-Miller became the sixth head coach in the 30-year history of the Saint Louis University women's basketball program.

A native of Flint, Michigan, 32-year-old Gray was an assistant coach at the University of Arizona for two seasons. During her stint in Tuscon, the Wildcats made it to the NCAA tournament each year. Gray led Arizona to a 20-12 overall record and an 11-7 mark in the Pacific-10 Conference.

Previously, Gray was an assistant coach at the University of Washington for three years. She helped the Huskies to the postseason every season, including two NCAA tournaments. In the 2000-2001 season, the Huskies reached the Elite Eight and finished the year ranked 14th in the polls.

Gray played at the University of Michigan and as a senior she served as team captain for the Wolverines. She was the 1994 Swish Club Award winner for leadership and dedication. After graduating from Michigan, she spent three years as a police officer in the cities of Ypsilanti and Ann Arbor, Michigan.

The Honorable Darlene Green is comptroller for the City of St. Louis, elected citywide. As chief fiscal officer for the city, she directs all of St. Louis' fiscal affairs with a budget of $800 million. Green also oversees the financing of some of the largest capital improvement projects in the St. Louis region including the St. Louis City Justice Center, the downtown Convention Center Hotel and the Lambert-St. Louis International Airport expansion.

Recently reelected for a third term, Green also holds the distinction of being the first woman ever elected to the position of comptroller in St. Louis. She was recently honored with the Gateway Classic Sports Foundation's Lifetime Achievement Award; the National Organization of Black Elected Legislative Women's Shining Star Award; and the *St. Louis Argus* newspaper's Distinguished Citizen Award.

A St. Louis native, Green earned a bachelor of science degree in business administration from Washington University in St. Louis. She is active in her community, both as an elected official and a citizen. A member of Antioch Baptist Church, she enjoys listening to spiritual and jazz music.

**The Honorable
Darlene Green**
Comptroller
City of St. Louis

Eric F. Harvey Sr. has been owner and chief executive officer of Carter Plaza for 23 years. He is also president of Flemming & Associates, Inc. Harvey created a construction design department within the commercial division of Flemming & Associates to design special programs for churches, schools and office building owners that would allow them to purchase their materials and pay for only labor.

As Flemming & Associates is a community-minded contracting service, Harvey instituted preventative maintenance, a program that assists in preserving the appearance of neighborhoods. The program administers quality repairs at an affordable cost and will create a plan to fit the particular needs of the customer.

A St. Louis native, Harvey graduated from Sumner High School and attended Saint Louis University's lead abatement program. He is chairman of the trustee board at his church and a board member of the African American Chamber of Commerce. He is married to Belinda Harvey and has a son, Eric Harvey Jr.

Eric F. Harvey Sr.
President
Flemming & Associates, Inc.

MOST INFLUENTIAL

Howard Hayes
Chairman
Land Reutilization Authority
City of St. Louis

Howard Hayes, chairman of the Land Reutilization Authority for St. Louis, was appointed to the commission by the St. Louis Public Schools. As chairman, he is responsible for leveraging millions of dollars in real estate for the development of residential and commercial projects. His proudest accomplishment is the creation of hundreds of homes dispersed throughout St. Louis' many neighborhoods.

Hayes is also a member of the St. Louis Development Corporation board, assisting 650 businesses and development projects in 2005. In his six-year tenure, more than $3 billion has been invested throughout St. Louis. He is pleased that the work to rebuild St. Louis' tax base has received attention from *USA Today* and *The New York Times*.

Currently, Hayes is the director of community engagement for the St. Louis Public Schools, serving as chairman of operations for the Academic Olympics, and as political director for the district's last $125 million bond issue.

A graduate of the St. Louis University Entrepreneurial Institute, Hayes also has a master of business administration degree. He and his wife, Toni, have two daughters, Morgan and Alexandra.

The Honorable
Esther Haywood
Representative, 71st District
Missouri House of Representatives

The Honorable Esther Haywood, a democrat, represents the 71st District in the Missouri House of Representatives. A retired teacher, Haywood taught math in East St. Louis for 30 years. She currently serves on the Normandy School board of directors.

Haywood worked with the Hospital Guild Charter to reopen Normandy Hospital. She is a charter member of Omicron Eta Chapter of Alpha Kappa Alpha Sorority, Inc., and a past president of the St. Louis County NAACP. Haywood is a recipient of the Yes I Can Award from the *St. Louis Sentinel* and a Lifetime Achievement Award from the St. Louis Teachers, Local 420. In 2004 she received the Ambassadors for Peace in the 21st Century Award.

Haywood attended Lincoln University and received a bachelor of science degree from Mississippi Industrial College. She also attended Saint Louis University and completed graduate studies at Memphis State University.

Born in Memphis, Tennessee, Haywood lives in Normandy with her husband, Edward Jay Haywood. They have two daughters, Angela Haywood Gaskin and Andreal Haywood Gray, and six grandchildren. She is a member of Murchinson Tabernacle CME Church.

D r. Madye Henson is president of Strategic Vision, focused on leadership and organizational development, strategic planning and diversity. She has led initiatives in the corporate, nonprofit, educational and governmental arenas.

Madye earned a doctor of management degree and a master of business administration degree from Webster University. She holds a bachelor's degree from the University of Missouri-Columbia.

Madye is vice chair of the St. Louis Black Leadership Roundtable and chair of its education committee, which released a five-year regional study on the elimination of the African-American achievement gap. She is a board member of the United Way of Greater St. Louis, and past chair of community investments, which oversaw the allocation of $67 million into the community. From 1995 to 2001, she was a member and officer of the SLPS Board of Education, serving as chair of the desegregation subcommittee.

An associate minister at West Side Missionary Baptist Church, Madye is founder of ACE-IT Middle School Enrichment Institute and co-founder of the Urban School Leadership Consortium. She is the proud mother of two sons, Kyle and Kristopher.

Dr. Madye G.J. Henson
President & Chief Executive Officer
Strategic Vision

T heodore "Ted" Hoskins is the state representative of Missouri's 80th District. He is also owner and chief executive officer of T&L Accounting Services, which specializes in taxes.

Hoskins has been involved in politics for more than 21 years, including 14 years of service for the City of Berkeley, where he was elected councilman and mayor.

A recipient of numerous awards for community involvement, political leadership and educational endeavors, Hoskins received the Making a Difference 2002 Award from the Order of the Eastern Star, the Flame 2002 Citizen of the Year Award and the Homer G. Philips Nurse Alumni Award for political leadership. A former national president of the National Shad Council and an auxiliary of Eta Phi Beta Sorority, Inc., Hoskins chairs the Missouri Legislative Black Caucus and its special committee on urban issues.

Hoskins holds a degree in business administration from the University of Missouri-St. Louis and conducted graduate studies in information systems and computer technology.

Hoskins is married to Lee Etta and they have three daughters, Rita, Pamela and Kelley, and one granddaughter, Taylor Harris.

The Honorable
Theodore Hoskins
Representative, 80th District
Missouri House of Representatives

MOST INFLUENTIAL

**The Honorable
Rodney R. Hubbard**
Representative, 58th District
Missouri House of Representatives

Rodney Hubbard, a democrat, represents the 58th District in the Missouri House of Representatives. He has sponsored and co-sponsored several pieces of legislation. He serves on the Appropriations, Public Safety and Corrections Committee, the Workforce Development and Workplace Safety Committee, the Corrections and State Institutions Committee, and the Job Creation and Economic Development-Interim Committee.

A native of St. Louis, Hubbard graduated from Mehlville High School and earned a bachelor of science degree in business administration from Lincoln University in 1999.

Following his graduation, Hubbard began his professional career in state government, where he remained for several years until his election to the Missouri House of Representatives in November of 2002.

Hubbard is a recipient of several awards for community service including the Yes I Can Award and the Lewis and Clark Statesman Award. He expresses his belief in today's youth by serving with the Taheed Youth Group, an anti-drug and violence taskforce.

He currently resides in St. Louis with his wife, Tarsha D. Hubbard, and three children, Ayana Amani, Rodney R. Jr. and Jabari Ali.

Barbara S. Jacob
President Emeritus
Girls Incorporated of St. Louis

Barbara S. Jacob is the consummate volunteer. Her work is exemplified by her service with Girls Incorporated of St. Louis, where she served as board president. She currently serves on the boards of St. Louis Variety, Forest Park Forever and the Jackie Joyner-Kersee Foundation. She also served on the board of The American Red Cross. As a board member of the United Way of Greater St. Louis, Barbara co-chaired the Charmaine Chapman Society and the Alexis de Tocqueville Society.

Barbara received the St. Louis Variety's 2001 Woman of the Year Award, the *Suburban Journals'* 2000 Woman of Achievement Award, the Faith House Angel Award, the *St. Louis Sentinel* Award and the Mathews-Dickey Sheer Elegance Award.

A member of the Gamma Omega Chapter of Alpha Kappa Alpha Sorority, Inc., Barbara also belongs to the Gateway Chapter of The Links, Inc.

Barbara received a bachelor of arts degree in accounting from Howard University in Washington, D.C.

Barbara is the wife of John E. Jacob, executive vice president of global communications for Anheuser-Busch. She is the mother of Sheryl Jacob-Desbordes.

Celerstine Briggs Johnson is assistant provost and director of student educational services at Saint Louis University. She leads student educational services in the provision of learning assistance activities for all students. Johnson is responsible for providing leadership for the retention management committee that develops and coordinates campus-wide retention strategies. She is responsible for developing proposals for continued funding of TRIO programs, and has received numerous university awards for her work.

Johnson holds a bachelor's degree in education from Harris-Stowe State University, a master's degree in the teaching of mathematics from Webster University, and a doctorate in higher education administration from Saint Louis University. She is nationally recognized for her work as a consultant and developer of educational opportunity programs. She previously served as president of the Council for Opportunity in Education in Washington, D.C.

Active in the community, Johnson serves in the education bureau for the Charmaine Chapman Fund of the United Way, and is a member of Delta Sigma Theta Sorority, Inc. She served as superintendent of Sunday school and chair of the worship committee at Christ Memorial Baptist Church.

Celerstine Briggs Johnson
Assistant Provost
Director of
Student Educational Services
Saint Louis University

The Honorable Connie L. Johnson represents part of St. Louis City (District 61) in the Missouri House of Representatives. She was named Minority Whip at the beginning of the 2005 legislative session. She is also a lawyer, employed at the law firm of Armstrong Teasdale, LLP.

Johnson's memberships include Delta Sigma Theta Sorority, Inc.; the Mound City, Metro St. Louis, National, and American Bar Associations; the Women Lawyers' Association; the American Council of Young Political Leaders; and the Missouri Association of Trial Attorneys. She is also a committeewoman for the 27th Ward in St. Louis, and a board member of Habitat for Humanity.

Some of Johnson's honors include the Champion of Justice Award from the Missouri Association of Trial Attorneys in 2004, the 2004 Community Service Award from the Mound City Bar Association, and an Outstanding Service Award from Lincoln University.

Johnson holds a bachelor of science degree from Bradley University (1991), a juris doctorate, and a doctor of medicine degree in health administration from Saint Louis University (1996).

The Honorable
Connie L. Johnson
State Representative, 61st District
Missouri House of Representatives

Morris F. Johnson III
President
St. Louis Community
College at Forest Park

Morris F. Johnson III has been president of St. Louis Community College at Forest Park since July of 2005. With an annual budget of $31.5 million, the urban campus at Forest Park serves approximately 7,500 credit and 3,400 noncredit students each semester.

An Arizona transplant, Johnson was vice president of student affairs and dean of student development services for 20 years at Phoenix College, one of ten colleges in the Maricopa Community College District. He also served as interim president in 2001. Prior to joining Phoenix College, Johnson served 12 years with Des Moines Area Community College.

Johnson holds a master's degree in psychiatric social work from the University of Iowa and a bachelor's degree in sociology from Dubuque University. He completed post-graduate coursework toward a doctorate in higher education administration at Iowa State University.

Johnson is an executive board member of the National Council on Black American Affairs, which presented him the 1998 Pioneer Award. He is a member of the St. Louis Black Leadership Roundtable and serves on the board of the Portfolio Art Gallery.

Dr. Charlene L. Jones
Assistant to the Superintendent
St. Louis Public Schools

Dr. Charlene Jones, assistant to the superintendent, has been employed by St. Louis Public Schools for more than 20 years. During her tenure, she has raised more than $500 million for the district in her role as campaign manager.

Jones has held several administrative positions in the district. She has also served as executive director of planning, and associate superintendent for personnel, while simultaneously managing the district's ballot issues.

Jones earned her bachelor of arts degree in political science from Rockford College in 1968. She earned her master's degree in political science from the University of Colorado at Boulder, and her doctorate in public policy analysis and administration from St. Louis University.

Jones is a member of the Black Leadership Roundtable and the Saint Louis University advisory council for the public policy doctoral program. She was awarded the 1988 Unsung Heroine Award by the Top Ladies of Distinction. In 1989 she was inducted into the Vashon Hall of Fame, and was named Top Educator of the Year by the *St. Louis Sentinel* in 2002. She has one son, Michael.

Darryl Jones is the managing partner for D&D Concessions, LLC and Jay Concessions, LLC in St. Louis. In this position, he oversees the operations of partnerships with HMS/Host and ARAMARK. In 2000 D&D received the Outstanding Small Business Award from Bank of America.

The ARAMARK/Jay Concessions partnership operates the food service program for the St. Louis Public School system. They implemented the One World Café concept to increase the number of students involved in the federal lunch program.

Darryl also owns TRI-TEC, Inc., a partner in America's Center Catering, which provides food service management for America's Center, the St. Louis Convention Center and the Edward Jones Dome.

Darryl is a graduate of Saint Louis University with a bachelor of arts degree in mathematics. In 1990 he was awarded his master of business administration degree in finance from Webster University.

A St. Louis native, Darryl is married with two sons, and he sits on several community boards including Our Little Haven, the Garden District Commission, Fontbonne University and Missouri State Bank. He is a member of Alpha Phi Alpha Fraternity, Inc.

Darryl T. Jones
Managing Partner
D&D Concessions, LLC

Richard L. King is chief executive officer of the Annie Malone Children and Family Service Center, one of St. Louis' oldest African-American child welfare agencies. It was established in 1888 and was supported for many years by Annie Turnbo Malone, the nation's first African-American woman millionaire.

In his position as CEO, Richard is responsible for the day-to-day operations of the agency, including, but not limited to, policy implementation, program planning and evaluation, personnel administration, budgeting and longterm strategic planning.

Richard received his undergraduate degree in sociology from the University of Nebraska-Omaha and his master of social work degree from the Saint Louis University School of Social Work. He is a graduate of the Leadership Center of St. Louis, as well as Leadership Winston-Salem. He has been a member of the Academy of Certified Social Workers since 1977.

A native of Omaha, Nebraska, Richard is married to Darlean (Cowan) and both are members of Westside Missionary Baptist Church. Richard is a member of Alpha Phi Alpha Fraternity, Inc. and serves on a number of nonprofit boards.

Richard L. King
Chief Executive Officer
Annie Malone Children and
Family Service Center

MOST INFLUENTIAL

Jennifer L. McCleary
Chiropractic Physician
Triad Sports & Family Chiropractic

Dr. Jennifer McCleary is the owner and physician at Triad Sports & Family Chiropractic. A board-certified chiropractor and acupuncturist, McCleary runs a family practice with a particular love for the care of athletes. She has experience with the world's most elite athletes at events including the U.S. Figure Skating National Championships, the Central American and Caribbean Games, and the U.S. Taekwando National Championships.

McCleary stays busy with patient care, community health lectures and working as a high school team physician. She is a member of Zeta Phi Beta Sorority, Inc., Urban League Young Professionals, the American Chiropractic Association and the Federation of International Sports Chiropractic.

McCleary earned a bachelor's degree in education from the University of Tennessee. She continued her studies at the Logan College of Chiropractic in St. Louis, graduating with a bachelor's degree in biology and a doctor of chiropractic degree. McCleary is dedicated to motivating people to reach personal goals. It is part of her mission to educate as many people as possible about the importance of chiropractic and health.

The Honorable
Donald L. McCullin
Judge
22nd Judicial Circuit
Court of Missouri

The Honorable Donald L. McCullin was appointed state circuit judge in the city of St. Louis in September of 1999.

McCullin attended public schools in St. Louis and earned a bachelor's degree from Southern Illinois University; a master's degree from Webster University; and a juris doctorate from the Saint Louis University School of Law. He is a member of the Missouri, Illinois and California bars.

McCullin has received numerous awards including the Bar Association of Metropolitan St. Louis President's Award; the Honorable Theodore McMillian Award; and in 2004, Region VIII of BLSA instituted the Donald L. McCullin Leadership Award, an annual award to a worthy student.

Active in the legal community, McCullin is a member of the Mound City Bar Association, the Bar Association of Metropolitan St. Louis, the National Bar Association and the American Bar Association. A former columnist for the St. Louis Lawyer newsletter, he wrote on minority issues in the legal profession. He served two terms as president of the Mound City Bar Association

McCullin has four children, Laurie, Cheryl, Donald Jr. and Renee; and eight grandchildren.

Michael McMillan is the alderman of the 19th Ward and license collector elect of the City of St. Louis. A graduate of Saint Louis University, McMillan previously served as committeeman of the 19th Ward and assistant to Mayor Bosley. He is chairman of the convention committee and a member of the budget, housing, personnel and utilities committees of the board.

McMillan is currently the treasurer of the Black Caucus and was previously the chairman and vice chairman. He is very active in revitalizing the 19th Ward with more than $1.2 billion in development including the MLK Plaza, four new schools, Saint Louis University, the Coronado Complex, Moolah Theatre & Lounge, Delta House, Kim's Kids and Blumeyer.

McMillan is a member of the board of the Clay Scholarship Fund, the Paula Carter Foundation and the Capital Committee. He is a former board member of the Urban League, the Missouri Local Records Board, the NAACP, the St. Louis Ambassadors and the JVL Initiative. He is a member of 100 Black Men, NBC-LEO, Urban League Young Professionals, Metropolis and other organizations.

**The Honorable
Michael McMillan**
Alderman
19th Ward

Leo Hezekiah Ming Jr. is vice president of human resources and administration for the St. Louis Convention & Visitors Commission. He directs the human resources functions at the America's Center convention center complex, including the Edward Jones Dome. He is also responsible for human resources and administration at the Commission's marketing office, which includes sales, services, publications, public relations and other support staff.

Leo holds a master's degree in human resource management from Webster University, and a bachelor's degree in labor management relations from the State University of New York.

Leo is very involved in the community and has served on the boards of Big Brothers Big Sisters, the Urban League of Metropolitan St. Louis and the St. Louis County Public Housing Commission. Additionally, he is an adjunct professor of human resources and hospitality management at Saint Louis University.

Leo is a member of the Society for Human Resource Management, the National Association of Black Meeting Planners and the National Black MBA Association. A former Marine, he received two Purple Heart medals, and is a member of Kappa Alpha Psi Fraternity, Inc.

Leo Hezekiah Ming Jr.
Vice President
Human Resources and Administration
St. Louis Convention &
Visitors Commission

MOST INFLUENTIAL

Sterling T. Moody Sr.
President
Supreme Consulting Group

Sterling Moody grew up in Kinloch, a small African-American community in St. Louis. In his youth, he was a grocery store bagger at just 15 years old, a job that proved to be the start of a long career in the grocery business.

A graduate of Kinloch High School, Sterling earned a degree in business administration from Southern Illinois University Carbondale. He then moved rapidly through the National Food Store Company to become its youngest store manager.

Entrepreneurship was as much a part of Sterling as management. In the 1980s he started the Supreme Car Care Center and Sterling's Marketplace, a 53,000-square-foot grocery store in St. Louis' African-American community.

Sterling took the idea of networking to a level that few have reached. His relationships in St. Louis brought many influential business and sports figures into relationships that have now become the Supreme Consulting Group. Not one to leave the grocery business behind, Sterling has also developed the increasingly powerful Allstar Beverage Company.

Teri A. Murray, Ph.D., R.N.
Director
Saint Louis University
School of Nursing

Dr. Teri A. Murray is director of the Saint Louis University School of Nursing. She provides administrative oversight of the baccalaureate, master's, and doctoral nursing education programs. She holds a bachelor's and master's degrees in nursing, a master's degree in education, and a doctor of philosophy degree in higher education administration.

Murray was appointed by Governor Holden and reappointed by Governor Blunt to serve on the Missouri State Board of Nursing. She currently serves as president of the Missouri State Board of Nursing, which oversees all nursing practice within the state. She also serves on the Missouri Minority Health Advisory Committee, which designs, implements and evaluates community-driven strategies to eliminate health disparities in minority populations.

Murray is published in areas related to health promotion, risk reduction and disease prevention in vulnerable populations. She was named a fellow in the prestigious 2006 Robert Wood Johnson Executive Nurse Fellows Program, which provides leadership development for nurses who aspire to lead and shape the U.S. healthcare system. She is married to Bruce Murray.

Following a prestigious career in network and systems software spanning more than 20 years, Brenda Newberry founded The Newberry Group, Inc. in 1996. Her award-winning IT business and technical expertise is utilized in daily client interactions, as well as in the classroom and the community. An associate professor at Washington University since 1987, Brenda serves multiple civic and charitable organizations.

Brenda has received numerous awards including being named one of the 2006 Most Influential Business Women, the 2006 Scott-St. Louis Chapter AFCEAN of the Year Award, the 2006 Athena Leadership Foundation Award, and the 2005 SBA Missouri Small Business Person of the Year Award.

Brenda serves on the boards of several organizations including the Missouri Small Business Development Center, United Services for the Handicapped, the St. Louis Economic Council, the St. Louis Regional Chamber and Growth Association, Focus St. Louis, SSM Healthcare, Innovate St. Louis and the United Way of Greater St. Louis. She is a member of the Regional Business Council.

Brenda and her husband, Maurice, have been married 34 years and have two daughters, Yasmin and Cherie.

Brenda Newberry
Chairman & Chief Executive Officer
The Newberry Group, Inc.

Vickie Newton joined KMOV Channel 4 in January of 2002 as a weekday anchor and reporter for *News 4 St. Louis*. In 2003 she won an Emmy Award for best anchorperson.

Before coming to KMOV, Vickie worked as an anchor for CNN Headline News reporting from the network's headquarters in Atlanta. Vickie also worked as an anchor for Atlanta's WSB-TV. She has worked at WDIV in Detroit, KMBC and WDAF in Kansas City, and KATV in Little Rock.

Vickie takes pride in her community involvement. She serves on the St. Louis board of directors for the YWCA and the Alzheimer's Association. She also serves on the board of directors for the National Association of Black Journalists.

Vickie spearheaded the formation of a partnership to promote literacy. She was recognized by bi-state literacy organizations with a grant named in her honor.

Vickie received her master's degree in journalism from the University of Detroit. In her spare time, she is a concert pianist. She hopes to start a consortium of piano teachers who will offer free lessons to children.

Vickie Newton
Anchor & Reporter
KMOV/CBS-4

MOST INFLUENTIAL

M. Bernadette Officer
President & Chief Executive Officer
Officer Funeral Homes

M. Bernadette Officer, president and chief executive officer of the Officer Funeral Homes, is a funeral director and embalmer licensed in Illinois and Missouri. She oversees the day-to-day operations of the corporation.

Bernadette is a graduate of Fisk University in Nashville, Tennessee with a bachelor of arts degree in psychology. She also earned a master of arts degree in education from George Washington University in Washington, D.C., and a degree in mortuary science from the Worsham College of Mortuary Science in Wheeling, Illinois.

Bernadette holds membership in the St. Clair County Funeral Directors Association, the Missouri Funeral Directors Association, the International Order of the Golden Rule (past board member), and the International Cemetery and Funeral Association. Her civic and social involvement includes Diamond Life membership in Delta Sigma Theta Sorority, Inc., the Smart Set and the Sunday Jams. As a devoted member of St. Luke A.M.E. Church, her spiritual goal is to deepen her relationship with God. Professionally, Bernadette is dedicated to continuing to provide excellence in funeral service.

The Honorable Carl E. Officer
Mayor
City of East St. Louis

In 1979 the Honorable Carl E. Officer became the youngest mayor in the country when he won the office in his hometown of East St. Louis, Illinois. He served as mayor until 1991. After a 12-year hiatus, Officer was reelected as mayor and returned to office in May of 2003. He was ordained as an elder in the AME Church in 2001. He is also vice president of the Officer Funeral Homes.

Officer earned a bachelor of science degree in political science at the former Western College, now Miami University in Oxford, Ohio. He is also a graduate of the John F. Kennedy School of Government at Harvard University. He received a degree in mortuary science from Southern Illinois University in Carbondale, Illinois, and he is a licensed funeral director and embalmer in Illinois and Missouri.

Officer holds membership in the Illinois, St. Clair County, and National Funeral Directors Associations; the International Order of the Golden Rule; and Kappa Alpha Psi Fraternity, Inc. A 33rd degree Mason, he is the father of one daughter.

harlotte VM Ottley is a personal and professional market development strategist whose career spans more than 30 years. An educator, award-winning media executive and on-air talent, Ottley has won four Emmy Awards through productions with CBS and NBC stations. Additionally, she headed her own business in New York with affiliates in 11 cities. She has represented the nation's top financial corporations during the height of mergers and acquisitions. Professional individuals, including corporate, political and civic leaders, as well as celebrities from the stage, sports and media, all benefit from her services during major transitions in their career development.

Her accomplishments have been recognized nationally in *Fortune* magazine, *Time* magazine and numerous other publications including *Crain's New York Business*. She is a contributing author in Donald Trump's *The Way to the Top, The Best Business Advice I Ever Received.*

A native of East St. Louis, Ottley recently returned to the St. Louis area. Her client list includes the late Katherine Dunham's board and estate; National Baseball Hall of Famer Lou Brock; St. Louis Rams linebacker Michael Jones; and other legendary figures.

Charlotte VM Ottley
Market Development Strategist

---

alerie E. Patton serves as executive director of the St. Louis Business Diversity Initiative, a private business collaboration funded by Civic Progress. In this position, she develops strategies, solutions and programs for member companies and large nonprofit organizations in the St. Louis region in the area of workforce diversity (recruitment, retention and advancement of talented people of color).

Prior to accepting this position in April of 2002, Valerie held numerous positions at Southwestern Bell and Bank of America in the areas of information systems, process management, accounting, and project and product management.

Valerie has received numerous awards and distinctions. She is community-focused and engaged, serving on the board of directors for Fortitude Foundation, the Black Leadership Roundtable, YWCA Metro St. Louis, and the Downtown-Marquette YMCA. Valerie is a member of Delta Sigma Theta Sorority, Inc. and The Links, Inc.

Valerie holds degrees from Howard University, Webster University and Washington University. Additionally, she has done postgraduate studies in business management. She enjoys spending time with family and friends, traveling, reading, photography, sports, and helping others realize their fullest potential.

Valerie E. Patton
Executive Director
St. Louis Business Diversity Initiative

MOST INFLUENTIAL

Aaron Phillips
Vice President
Regional Operations Manager
Regions Bank

Aaron Phillips is vice president and regional operations manager for Regions Bank. In this capacity, he is responsible for providing coaching and feedback to 22 branch managers and their operations staff regarding compliance issues and policy and procedure. Aaron also chairs the local bank's diversity council that address various issues related to and promoting diversity.

A native of St. Louis, Aaron received a degree in finance from Saint Louis University. He has also attended several other banking-related schools including the Commercial Lending School in Oklahoma. Aaron is a member of the 1979 Class of Leadership St. Louis.

Aaron serves on several boards and chairs the board of the Annie Malone Children & Family Service Center. He is a board member of the St. Louis Metropolitan Urban League, and the Catholic Charities of St. Louis. Aaron is a member of the Executive Leadership Institute for the University of Missouri-St. Louis.

Cheryl D. Polk
Executive Vice President
United Way of Greater St. Louis

Cheryl D. Polk, executive vice president and chief operations officer of the United Way of Greater St. Louis, serves the fifth-largest United Way in the nation. Previously, Cheryl led the turnaround of the $100 million American Red Cross Missouri-Illinois Blood Services Region and brought blood collections and revenues to record highs during her tenure. She also created the Charles Drew Community Blood Donation Campaign, benefiting children with sickle cell disease.

Cheryl serves on various committees and boards for organizations including Grand Center, The St. Louis Minority Roundtable, the Metropolitan Association for Philanthropy, the St. Louis Art Museum Friends, KETC Channel 9, A World of Difference, The St. Louis Forum, the Missouri Historical Society and the President's Council of the Girl Scouts. She was appointed to the State Library Council by the secretary of state.

Cheryl has raised millions of dollars for nonprofit organizations and is the recipient of numerous awards. She was recognized as one of the Most Influential Business Women, making her the go-to person for making things happen in the region.

Steven C. Roberts is one of St. Louis' most dynamic entrepreneurs. Educated in the St. Louis Public Schools, he worked his way through college at Clark University and law school at Washington University in St. Louis. With his brother, Michael, Roberts has worked to bring jobs and economic opportunity to the African-American community from which he came. His endeavors over the last 29 years have created thousands of jobs and entrepreneurial opportunities, increased economic activity and enhanced the quality of life for the African-American community.

A St. Louis alderman from 1979 to 1993, Roberts specialized in developing legislation for the city's major redevelopment projects, including St. Louis Union Station, St. Louis Centre, Cervantes Convention Center expansion and the new sports stadium. His broad range of professional knowledge and experience encompasses the application of innovative financing strategies for large public projects, public-private sector development negotiation strategies and successful management techniques for urban commercial properties.

The Roberts Companies consist of real estate development, wireless communication site development and construction, television stations and the largest MBE/WBE consulting firm in the United States.

Steven C. Roberts
President & Chief Operating Officer
The Roberts Companies

Michael V. Roberts Jr. is vice president of business development for The Roberts Companies. His sole responsibility is to expand the asset and net worth of the family-owned, 63-company business. Michael monitors all legal transactions involving real estate and commercial development projects. Prior to his current employment, he practiced corporate law at Armstrong Teasdale, LLP.

Michael is a co-founder of Gateway Live, LLC, a concert, lifestyle marketing and sponsorship acquisition company, and Sho-Town Entertainment, LLC, a sports and entertainment management company. He is also a co-founder of Roberts Twins & Associates, an entertainment consulting firm. Michael is co-producer of the *Mike and Jeanne Show* on UPN, starring his twin sister, Jeanne, and himself. He co-founded the Gateway Young Democrats and served as the first elected president.

Michael received a bachelor of arts degree, cum laude, from Morehouse College. In 2004 he received his juris doctorate degree from Pepperdine School of Law. He holds membership in Kappa Alpha Psi Fraternity, Inc. and is active in freemasonry.

Michael V. Roberts Jr., J.D.
Vice President, Business Development
The Roberts Companies

MOST INFLUENTIAL

Michael V. Roberts Sr., J.D.
Chairman & Chief Executive Officer
The Roberts Companies

A classic American entrepreneur, Michael Roberts Sr. is chairman and chief executive officer of The Roberts Companies. The Roberts Companies' business assets include the Roberts Broadcasting Company, Roberts Aviation, the Roberts Mayfair Hotel, the Roberts Tower Company and Roberts Plaza, LLC.

Roberts has a broad range of professional knowledge and experience as a business owner and public official, having served on the St. Louis Board of Aldermen from 1977 to 1985.

Throughout his career, Roberts has maintained a strong commitment to the African-American community. His endeavors have created thousands of jobs and entrepreneurial opportunities, raised the level of economic activity and enhanced the quality of life for the African-American community.

In addition to serving on the board of directors for Alamosa PCS Holdings, Inc., Roberts was selected to participate in President Bill Clinton's People to People Ambassador Program as a delegate on an economic development mission to China.

Roberts was educated in St. Louis Public Schools and worked his way through college. He earned a juris doctorate from Saint Louis University and is now one the city's leading businessmen.

Will Ross, M.D.
Associate Dean for Diversity
Washington University in St. Louis
School of Medicine

Dr. Will R. Ross is associate dean for diversity at Washington University in St. Louis School of Medicine and a senior fellow at the Center for Health Policy. Ross oversees diversity affairs and directs clinical outreach programs that promote community-based healthcare.

As a public health and healthcare policy expert, Ross focuses on improving the public health infrastructure and resolving healthcare disparities. A leading kidney specialist, he was named one of America's Top Physicians by the 2005 Consumer Research Council.

Ross is a charter member of the St. Louis Regional Health Commission. He is vice chairman of the board of the Missouri Foundation for Health and a healthcare consultant for the *St. Louis American Newspaper*.

Ross earned a bachelor's degree from Yale University in 1980. He received his medical degree and fellowship in kidney diseases at Washington University in St. Louis. In 2005 he received the Ethic of Service Award from Washington University and the Distinguished Community Service in Medicine Award from the Missouri State Dr. King Celebration Commission.

He is married to Arlene Moore and has two daughters, Merris and Naima.

Sid S. Shurn is president of The Shurn Group, LLC (TSG). In 1989 he started TSG, a full-service human resources staffing firm specializing in information systems. He began with only two employees. Today he has ten in-house employees and more than 350 temporary or contract employees. Sid has more than ten years of corporate experience in the management information systems field, and more than 20 years in the search, staffing and recruitment field.

TSG has been recognized as one of the Top Ten Minority-Owned Companies in the *St. Louis Business Journal's Book of Lists,* and as one of the Top 25 African American Businesses in St. Louis by *The St. Louis American,* the St. Louis Regional Chamber and Growth Association, and the Urban League of Metropolitan St. Louis.

Sid serves as a board member on the Workforce Development Board and CHIPS. He is also a mentor with Junior Achievement.

Sid earned his bachelor of science degree in business administration from Lindenwood University.

A St. Louis native, Sid has one daughter, Nikole. In his spare time, he enjoys fishing, roller-skating and reading.

Sid S. Shurn
President
The Shurn Group, LLC

Ruth A. Smith is president and chief executive officer of the Human Development Corporation of Metropolitan St. Louis. As the first female president and CEO, she is the catalyst for their mission of "helping people, changing lives." She supervises a network of programs that assist more than 100,000 St. Louis area residents annually. These programs help residents to attain self-sufficiency and achieve their full potential.

Smith is an immediate past president of the St. Louis Metropolitan Chapter of 100 Black Women and an executive committee member of the St. Louis NAACP. She is a board member of the St. Louis Gateway Classic Sports Foundation. She is involved with a number of organizations including the Citizens for Missouri's Children, the Missouri Association for Social Welfare, the National Council of Negro Women and Delta Sigma Theta Sorority, Inc.

Smith is the recipient of the Clergy's Martin Luther King Jr. Award, the Missouri Legislative Black Caucus Gwen Giles Award, and has a star in the St. Louis Gateway Classic Sports Foundation Walk of Fame.

Smith earned a degree in management from Maryville University.

Ruth A. Smith
President & Chief Executive Officer
Human Development Corporation
of Metropolitan St. Louis

MOST INFLUENTIAL

David L. Steward
Founder & Chairman
World Wide Technology, Inc.

World Wide Technology, Inc. (WWT) was founded in 1990 by David Steward to distribute computer hardware, software and services to the federal government. Today, WWT and affiliate company, Telcobuy.com, are the leading electronic procurement and logistics companies in the information technology and telecommunications industry.

In 2001 WWT was ranked 14th in the *St. Louis Business Journal*'s list of privately held companies. *Black Enterprise* magazine named WWT the number one African American-owned business in the United States in 2004. During 2000, WWT earned national honors from *Federal Computer Week* and *Washington Technology* as the top minority technology contractor. Recently, Steward was recognized by *Ebony* magazine as one of The 100 Most Influential Black Americans.

Steward serves on numerous committees and boards including Civic Progress of St. Louis, the Missouri Technology Corporation and the St. Louis Science Center. Additionally, he is the author of *Doing Business by the Good Book, Fifty-Two Lessons on Success Straight from the Bible.*

Steward grew up in Clinton, Missouri and graduated from Central Missouri State University. He and his wife, Thelma, have two children, David and Kimberly.

Dr. Donald M. Suggs
President
The St. Louis American Newspaper

Dr. Donald M. Suggs is president and publisher of *The St. Louis American Newspaper.* He has been an advocate and patron of African and African-American cultural expression for more than 40 years.

Suggs graduated with a doctor of dental sciences degree from Indiana University. He completed post-graduate work at Washington University in St. Louis. He served as chief of oral surgery at Dover Air Force Base, and was the first African American to serve as an associate clinical professor at Saint Louis University Dental School.

Suggs served as chairman of the 1968 Poor People's March on Washington. He founded the African Continuum to bring African-American art to St. Louis. Currently serving on the St. Louis Art Museum board of commissioners, he was president of the Alexander-Suggs Gallery of African Art.

Suggs holds honorary doctorate degrees from the University of Missouri-St. Louis, Harris-Stowe State University and Saint Louis University. He was the first African American to serve as president of the Convention & Visitors Bureau of St. Louis.

He is the father of Donald M. Jr., Dawn Marie and Dina Margaret.

WHO'S *Who*

D r. Jean-Alfred Thomas Sr. has served the St. Louis community for more than 25 years as an obstetrician and gynecologist. A medical pioneer, he helped introduce the laparoscopic hysterectomy technique to the St. Louis area.

In 2006 Thomas was one of six physicians out of 1,600 hospitals to receive 99th percentile patient satisfaction. He was promoted to the rank of associate clinical professor of obstetrics, gynecology and women's health at Saint Louis University. In 2004 he was presented the Resident Teaching Award from the graduating class.

A fellow of the American College of Obstetrics and Gynecology, Thomas is a recipient of the *St. Louis American* Salute to Excellence in Healthcare award. He is a member of the Association of Haitian Physicians Abroad, the National Medical Association, and the Mound City Medical Forum.

Thomas received his medical degree in Port-au-Prince, Haiti. He completed his residency training at Homer G. Phillips and Saint Louis University Hospitals, graduating as chief resident.

He is married to Mary H. Thomas and is the proud father of two sons and one daughter.

Photo © L.D. Ingram Gallery & Studio

Dr. Jean A. Thomas Sr.
Physician
Women's Health Ob-Gyn

L arry Thomas began his career in 1977 as an intern at Edward Jones, while working toward a bachelor's degree in business administration at Washington University in St. Louis. Since then, Thomas has held many roles within Edward Jones. He is currently responsible for distributing newly issued corporate notes.

Thomas sits on the board of the St. Louis Children's Hospital, the Herbert Hoover Boys & Girls Club, the St. Louis Zoo, Forest Park Forever, the Bond Market Association and the Bond Market Foundation.

Thomas also serves on Washington University's board of trustees and is a member of the board of governors. He sits on the national advisory council of the John M. Olin School of Business and is a member of its executive alumni association.

Thomas earned his master of business administration degrees from Lindenwood University and Northwestern University's Kellogg School of Management.

Larry Thomas
Principal
Edward Jones

MOST INFLUENTIAL

Betty L. Thompson
Community and Resource
Development Coordinator
Human Development Corporation

A former Missouri state representative, Betty L. Thompson serves as community and resource development coordinator for the Human Development Corporation. She was also the first African-American female elected in University City and the first African-American female elected to Women in Municipal Government.

Thompson is involved with several organizations including the NAACP, the Dr. Martin Luther King Jr. St. Louis Support Group, Women in Municipal Government, the National Coalition of 100 Black Women and the Kwame Foundation, where she is president. She served on the University City Council for 18 years.

Thompson has received numerous awards for community involvement including the 2006 Leadership Award from the St. Louis Gateway Classic Sports Foundation and the 2006 Dr. Martin Luther King University City Council and University Schools Award.

A 1958 graduate of Sumner High School, Thompson received a certificate of business from Hubbards Business College and a certificate of managerial management from Washington University in St. Louis.

Thompson resides in University City with her husband, Jack. They attend Northern Missionary Baptist Church, and have four children, Anthony, Tyrone, Sonja and Kwame.

Mary A. T. Tillman, M.D.
Pediatrician

Dr. Mary A. T. Tillman is a pediatrician with a private practice in St. Louis. She is an attending physician at St. Louis Children's Hospital; professor at the Washington University School of Medicine; diplomat of the American Board of Pediatrics; and fellow of the American Academy of Pediatrics.

Tillman is the first woman president of the Mound City Medical Forum. She is president of the Annie Malone Children & Family Service Center and a national officer and local president of Zeta Phi Beta Sorority, Inc. She is active is many professional associations. Tillman is a recipient of the Howard University College of Medicine Distinguished Alumni Award, the Women in Medicine Award from the National Medical Association, and numerous other honors.

A graduate of Howard University, Tillman holds a bachelor's degree and a doctor of medicine degree. She completed her internship and residency at the Homer G. Phillips Hospital.

A native of Bristow, Oklahoma, she is married to Judge Daniel Tillman. She is the mother of two, Dana Tillman Chee and Dr. Daniel Tillman Jr., and the grandmother of three.

D r. James M. Victory was appointed superintendent for the School District of University City on July 1, 2005. He has been in public school education for more than 28 years. Victory has been a teacher, junior high school assistant principal, elementary principal, middle school principal, high school principal, executive director for middle schools and executive director for high schools. Prior to accepting his current position, he was employed in Virginia with Portsmouth Public Schools, Hampton City Public Schools and Norfolk Public Schools.

Victory received his bachelor's and master's degrees from Norfolk State University in Norfolk, Virginia. He received his certificate of advanced graduate studies and doctorate in educational administration from Virginia Polytechnic Institute and State University in Blacksburg, Virginia. He is a member of Omega Psi Phi Fraternity, Inc.

His wife, Deborah, is also involved in education. They are the proud parents of two daughters and three grandchildren.

Dr. James M. Victory
Superintendent
School District of University City

D r. Candace T. Wakefield is the owner and practicing pediatric dentist of Children's Dental Zone! She is passionate about helping children maintain healthy and beautiful smiles by establishing a positive attitude towards dentistry.

Wakefield graduated from the University of Missouri-Columbia in 1995. She attended Southern Illinois University School of Dental Medicine and earned her doctor of dental medicine degree in 2000. She continued her dental education at Howard University in Washington, D.C. Wakefield was elected chief resident in the department of pediatric dentistry and received her specialty certificate in pediatric dentistry in 2002. She is also an adjunct faculty member at Southern Illinois University School of Dental Medicine.

Wakefield is an active member of the American Academy of Pediatric Dentistry, the American Dental Association, the Missouri Dental Association and the Greater St. Louis Dental Society. She has volunteered her dental services to meet the needs of children in Nicaragua and Jamaica.

Dr. Candace T. Wakefield
Pediatric Dentist
Children's Dental Zone!

MOST INFLUENTIAL

**The Honorable
Juanita Head Walton**
Representative, 81st District
Missouri House of Representatives

Democratic Representative Juanita Head Walton represents the 81st District in the Missouri House of Representatives.

Walton is the Democratic committeewoman of Ferguson Township. She is the former director of the Grace Hill Women's Business Center. She also served as a trainer for St. Louis Community College, instructor at Alabama State University and administrator for Maritz Performance. She is currently a licensed realtor.

Walton is a member of Alpha Kappa Alpha Sorority, Inc., Gamma Omega Chapter, the Archway Chapter of The Links, Inc. and the National Foundation of Women Legislators (NFWL). President-elect of the National Order of Women Legislators, Walton chairs the business and finance committee for the National Black Caucus of State Legislators. She is president of the Missouri Black Caucus Foundation.

Walton is the recipient of the NFWL Policy Chair Award and the 2002 Wetterau Award.

Walton received her bachelor of science degree in business administration from Lincoln University, and a master's degree in corporate communications from Lindenwood College.

She is married to Attorney Elbert Walton and they have two sons, Elbert III and Johnathan.

James Webb
President & Chief Executive Officer
St. Louis Minority Business Council

James Webb has been a leader in the St. Louis community for more than 30 years. Currently, he is president and chief executive officer of the St. Louis Minority Business Council. During his six-year tenure as head of the council, he has significantly increased corporate participation and visibility of minority-owned business enterprises (MBEs). As a result, major corporations in the St. Louis area are awarding a greater share of their business to MBEs.

Prior to joining the council, James held management positions at Southwestern Bell and AT&T. He serves on the board of several universities and is on the board and executive committee of the National Minority Supplier Development Council. He is a member of the St. Louis Black Leadership Roundtable and the Mayor's Taskforce on Minority Business Development.

James is a graduate of Lincoln University, and continued his studies at Washington University and the Wharton School of the University of Pennsylvania. A native of St. Louis, James is married to Margaret, and is the proud father of Ann.

Kelvin Westbrook is the founder, president, and chief executive officer of Millennium Digital Media, LLC, a privately held company in the business of providing cable television, high speed and traditional internet access, and other broadband telecommunications services.

Prior to founding Millennium Digital Media in 1997, Westbrook founded and served as the president and chairman of LEB Communications, Inc., which, in affiliation with Charter Communications, managed and operated cable television systems in various parts of the U.S. Prior to founding LEB in 1993, he was a partner in the national law firm of Paul, Hastings, Janofsky & Walker in New York City where he specialized in corporate matters including mergers and acquisitions and corporate finance.

Kelvin is a director of Archer Daniels Midland Company, Angelica Corporation, the National Cable and Telecommunications Association, the National Cable Satellite Corporation (C-SPAN), Christian Hospital Northeast-Northwest, the St. Louis Internship Program, and Chesterfield Day School. Additionally, he is a member of the American Bar Association.

He received an undergraduate degree in business administration from the University of Washington in 1977 and a juris doctorate from Harvard Law School in 1982.

Kelvin has lived in St. Louis since 1994. He is married and has three children.

Kelvin R. Westbrook
President & CEO
Millennium Digital Media, LLC

Dr. Consuelo Hopkins Wilkins is an assistant professor in internal medicine and geriatrics at Washington University. She combines an active clinical practice with a research career in Alzheimer's disease. She also serves as medical director of Barnes Jewish Extended Care.

Wilkins graduated magna cum laude, Phi Beta Kappa, with a bachelor of science in microbiology from Howard University in only three years. She continued at Howard University and received her doctor of medicine degree. Wilkins then completed a residency in internal medicine at Duke University Medical Center and a fellowship in geriatrics at Washington University.

Wilkins was named Best Physician in Region V of the National Medical Association and one of America's Top Physicians. She received the prestigious Beeson Award for Aging Research and has presented and published her research both nationally and internationally. Wilkins has served as president of the Mound City Medical Forum and is an advocate for eliminating health disparities.

She is married to Dr. Kenneth L. Wilkins II. They have a daughter, Elise, and a son, Kenneth (Trey).

Consuelo H. Wilkins, M.D.
Assistant Professor of Medicine
Washington University

MOST INFLUENTIAL

Larry C. Williams
Treasurer
City of St. Louis

As treasurer of the City of St. Louis, Larry Williams serves as custodian of the city's fiscal assets and chief investment manager. He has held this position for more than 23 years. Some of his responsibilities include selecting bond trustees and paying agents for the city's financial borrowing of cash funds and leasehold payments, and he serves as chairman of the funds and banking committee, the parking commission, and the Community Reinvestment Act.

Williams' duties imposed by the Missouri State Statute include serving as custodian of the police and firefighter retirement systems funds and supervising the city's parking operations.

Williams is a member of numerous boards and commissions including the Government Finance Officers Association of the United States and Canada, the Municipal Treasurers Association, the International Parking Institute, the Land Clearance for Redevelopment Authority, Planned Industrial Expansion Authority, the Downtown Now Board, the Downtown St. Louis Community Improvement District, and the Marshall Faulk Foundation.

A St. Louis native with a degree in business administration, Larry is married to JoAnn Williams and is the father of six children.

Earl Wilson Jr.
President & Executive Director
St. Louis Gateway Classic
Sports Foundation

Since 1994, Earl Wilson Jr. has served as president and executive director of the St. Louis Gateway Classic Sports Foundation. The organization has donated millions of dollars to charitable organizations, underwritten youth athletic programs and awarded scholarships to young men and women.

After graduating from Lincoln University in 1956, Wilson served on active duty with the U.S. Army Corps of Engineers, where he rose to the rank of captain. In 1963 he was hired by IBM as a sales representative, retiring in 1988 as one of the highest-ranking black employees.

Wilson served as vice president of marketing for the U.S. Olympic Festival in St. Louis, and in 1994 he helped to found the St. Louis Gateway Classic Sports Foundation. He has received numerous honors for his work with IBM and his involvement in the community.

Wilson is president of the Lincoln University board of curators and has received honorary doctorates from Lincoln University, Harris-Stowe State University and the University of Arkansas-Pine Bluff.

He is married to Billie Wilson. He and his deceased wife, Margie, have three daughters, Denise, Stacey and Kimberly.

Ida Goodwin Woolfolk served the St. Louis Public Schools for more than 38 years as counselor, teacher and superintendent. She is a nationally recognized consultant and speaker in the areas of diversity, stress management and communications. She presently serves as a consultant to several companies and agencies.

A 1993 Woman of Achievement honoree, Ida has received outstanding citizen awards from *The St. Louis Argus* and the *St. Louis Sentinel.* She was honored by the National Association for Equal Opportunity in Higher Education. She is an alumna of Harris-Stowe State College and Saint Louis University.

Ida serves as board chair of the Hopewell Health Center, chair of the national legacy committee for The Links, Inc., and director of education for the Churches of God in Christ-Eastern Missouri. A former president of the Urban League Guild, she is a member of the St. Louis Symphony's community outreach board and Delta Sigma Theta Sorority, Inc.

Born in Dallas, Texas, Ida is very proud of her family, which includes her daughter, Sarah, son-in-law, Chris Edwards, and two magnificent grandsons, Chris and Caleb.

Ida Goodwin Woolfolk
National Consultant &
Retired Administrator
St. Louis Public Schools

John A. Wright, Fulbright scholar, author and retired administrator, is an adjunct instructor at Fontbonne University. He has served in various educational roles including teacher, superintendent, school board member and community college trustee.

One of John's seven books on African-American history in St. Louis, *Discovering African American St. Louis – A Guide to Historic Sites,* was voted the second best paperback book in St. Louis in 1994. He is chairman of the board for the Missouri Humanities Council and the African American Heritage Association.

John is the recipient of numerous awards including the St. Louis American Foundation's Lifetime Achievement Award, the Black World History Museum Griot Award, the National Daughters of the American Revolution Community Service Award and the Harris-Stowe University Excellence in Education Award.

John received his bachelor of arts degree in elementary education from Harris-Stowe State University, and his master's degree and doctorate in educational administration from Saint Louis University.

A native of St. Louis, John and his wife, Sylvia, are the proud parents of John Jr., David and Curtis. They have nine grandchildren.

John A. Wright
Adjunct Instructor
Fontbonne University

MOST INFLUENTIAL

Dr. Katie Harper Wright
Education & Personal
Development Consultant

Dr. Katie Harper Wright is an educator and writer who does consultant work in the areas of educational and personal development. She writes for *The St. Louis Argus* newspaper, and The Dr. Katie Harper Wright Papers are archived at the University of Missouri-St. Louis.

Wright is a longtime member of MENSA, the High IQ Society, where she serves as proctor. She is a recipient of more than 150 awards and honors for her community service, professional education, and journalism. She has many professional involvements including the United Way, the East St. Louis Financial Authority, and the St. Clair County Mental Health Board.

A product of St. Louis Public Schools, Wright graduated with high honors from Vashon High School, and she holds a bachelor's degree and a master's degree from the University of Illinois at Champaign-Urbana. She earned a doctorate in special education and political science from Saint Louis University.

Katie is married to Marvin Wright and they have one daughter, Virginia Jordan, and one granddaughter, Diana Kaye Jordan. She is also an elder at First United Presbyterian Church.

The Honorable
Robin Wright-Jones
Representative, 63rd District...
Missouri House of Representatives

Robin Wright-Jones represents the 63rd legislative district of the Missouri General Assembly. She was elected to fill an unexpired term in March of 2002 and has served as chair of the House Democratic Caucus since 2003. Wright-Jones spent ten years as a classroom and substitute teacher for the St. Louis Archdiocese and St. Louis Public Schools.

Wright-Jones worked in the real estate industry, public housing administration and the private sector from 1980 to 2002. She has been an ardent community volunteer and political activist for more than 36 years. A member of Delta Sigma Theta Sorority, Inc., she belongs to St. James AME Church.

Wright-Jones has received the 2003, 2004 and 2005 RCGA Lewis and Clark Statesman Award for outstanding leadership and devotion to a cause. In 2003 and 2005 she received the *St. Louis Business Journal*'s Legislative Leadership Award. On September 22, 2006, she was awarded the Crystal Wagon Award from the board of governors of SSM Cardinal Glennon Children's Medical Center for her work in championing children's issues.

National City®

CORPORATE SPOTLIGHT

National City

Reginald P. Scott
Vice President & Executive Director
National City Community
Development Corporation

Monica Settles-White
Vice President
Human Resources Consultant
National City Bank

Reggie Scott is the community development officer for National City's Community Development Corporation, whose mission is to facilitate the revitalization of low- and moderate-income areas. Scott is responsible for equity investments in community redevelopment projects in the St. Louis area.

Previously, Scott was a residential developer with the Bank of America Community Development Corporation and the director of St. Louis County's Office of Community Development where he managed federal block grant programs. These included the Community Development Block Grant (CDBG) and the HOME Investment Partnership Program (HOME).

Scott received a bachelor's degree in business administration from Rockhurst University, a master's degree in public policy from the University of Michigan, and a professional certification in real estate development from the National Development Council. He received a Sloan Fellowship from the Institute for Public Policy Studies at the University of Michigan and the John F. Kennedy School of Government at Harvard University.

Scott serves on numerous boards and committees, including the board of trustees for the St. Louis Home Builders Association and the board of directors of St. Louis Black Repertory.

Monica Settles-White is vice president and human resources consultant for National City Bank. In this position, she manages the human resources strategy and execution for the St. Louis market. In 2006 she played a key role in the annual Excel Awards, the Pioneer Bank merger and the United Way campaign.

Monica received a bachelor's degree from the U.S. Military Academy and a master's degree from George Washington University. She spent nine years as an army engineer officer in various positions, including assistant professor of military science at Norfolk State University. In 1998 Monica was honored in *Who's Who Among America's Teachers*.

After military service, Monica joined GE's human resources leadership program. She then joined the Illinois Department of Human Services as a labor relations liaison. In 2005 she returned home to the St. Louis metropolitan area to join National City.

Monica is a member of Holy Trinity Church and the West Point Society. She is the daughter of Lionel and Jacquline Settles and the mother of Angelina White.

WHO'S WHO

John Shivers is senior vice president and district sales executive for National City Bank. A native of St. Louis, Shivers has been part of the local banking arena for more than 20 years. During his banking career, he has focused on retail banking, business development, consumer and small business lending and community relations.

As a district sales executive, Shivers is responsible for more than $275 million in deposits and managing the retail, investment and small business opportunities for nine of National City's branches.

Shivers serves on the board of directors for the Gateway Classic Sports Foundation, Mathews-Dickey Boys' and Girls' Club, Payback, Inc., The St. Louis Minority Business Council Mentorship Committee, and the economic development board of the Grace Hill Neighborhood Association. Shivers is also an advisory director for MOKAN and a member of the United Way's Charmaine Chapman Society. He is the past vice chair of St. Louis' Tax Increment Financing Commission.

Shivers holds a bachelor's degree in business administration from Truman State University and recently completed the National City University Leadership Development Program.

John R. Shivers III
Senior Vice President
District Sales Executive
National City Bank

Celebrating African-American Achievement

Harris Stowe State University New Residence Hall

Rev. Dr. William G. Gillespie Residence Hall & Student Center

Rooted in our community, KAI charts a new path in the road to the educational experience. Strategically delivering high quality services for urban facilities is our hallmark.

w w w . k a i - d b . c o m

KAI
Design & BUILD

One Metropolitan Square
St. Louis, MO 63102
314.241.8188

Specializing in Residential & Commercial Real Estate

Looking to sell or purchase property?
Our professional sales representatives can help you.

We pride ourselves in giving our clients the best service possible

Customer **appreciation** and customer **satisfaction** is our main focus

"Giving You the Respect You Deserve"

Linda M. Wash Real Estate, LLC
Residential and Commercial Real Estate

303 North Union Boulevard, Suite 210
Corner of Union and Pershing
St. Louis, Missouri 63108
Office: (314) 361-3900
www.LMWash.com

Linda M. Wash, Broker Associate

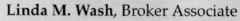

WHO'S *Who*

St. Louis'

CORPORATE BRASS

"We will either find a way or make one."

HANNIBAL

AFRICAN GENERAL

CORPORATE BRASS

Kirwyn Adderley
Director of Site
Resource Management
Center Operations
Express Scripts, Inc.

Kirwyn Adderley is director of the site resource management center for Express Scripts, Inc. He is responsible for nine contact center sites. The resource management group oversees strategic planning, staffing, scheduling, the management of daily volumes and service performance for the contact centers. Kirwyn established the company's national command center, which is the hub for around-the-clock contact center monitoring. He also played a key role in the business continuity/disaster recovery planning.

Kirwyn enjoys giving back to the community. His primary civic focus is on youth and those in need. He uses sports to develop, nurture and mentor young athletes to become model citizens. He has assisted many student athletes with getting into college and obtaining scholarships.

A two-time NCAA All-American wrestler, Kirwyn received a bachelor of science degree from Norfolk Sate University. He later obtained his Six Sigma Green Belt certification.

A native of Philadelphia, Pennsylvania, Kirwyn and his wife, Dawn, are the proud parents of two children, Austin and Kiara.

Terease Baker-Bell
Business Partner Territory Manager
IBM Corporation

Terease Baker-Bell is a business partner territory manager for IBM Corporation, where she manages the overall software business partner engagements within the central region. Her business unit was the top-performing region in the country in business partner sales in 2004.

Terease has been awarded multiple performance awards during her tenure at IBM. She has conducted forums on women with families and how to cope with corporate America. She is co-founder of the Who Am I When Nobody's Looking Women's Retreat, an event of introspection and self-awareness.

In her spare time, Terease is an aspiring children's literature author. She volunteers in church activities and offers marketing assistance to S.A.L.T., a faith-based organization that supports Haiti. She assists in scholastic fundraising as secretary of the Howard University Alumni Organization, and she is a member of Delta Sigma Theta Sorority, Inc.

Terease received her bachelor of arts degree from Howard University, and her MBA in marketing management from George Washington University.

A St. Louis native, Terease is a proud mother of two girls, Trinity and Selah, and the wife of Latham Bell.

Carla Bell is a senior Oracle I/T specialist for IBM Global Services. She is responsible for all aspects of Oracle database management. She interviews and recommends candidates for Oracle positions and represents IBM in client meetings. Furthermore, she mentors personnel and is the co-founder of the CICS Application Users Group at McDonnell Douglas.

In addition to receiving numerous awards from IBM and their clients, Carla has spearheaded and led teams that have received quality awards. She holds a bachelor's degree, and Oracle master's degrees in database and in network administration.

Carla serves on the board of directors for Metro Theater Company. She is a member of the IBM St. Louis Black Network Group, which works with Turner Magnet and Cardinal Ritter Preparatory Schools during Black Family Technology Awareness Week. Likewise, she works with the Black Expo and the Ementorplace at Northeast Middle School.

Carla serves on several community organizations including Parkway Dialogue Network, the Bellerive ways and means committee, and Alpha Kappa Alpha Sorority, Inc.

The wife of Sanford Bell Jr., Carla is the mother of Sanford III and Kelley.

Carla R. Bell
Senior Oracle I/T Specialist
IBM Corporation

Justine Blue is the director of manual claims operations at Express Scripts, Inc., headquartered in St. Louis, Missouri. In her current role, Justine is responsible for overseeing the day-to-day operations of claims departments in St. Louis and Bloomington, Minnesota. Her departments process nearly eight million manual prescription claims per year for both private and commercial sector businesses.

With nearly 6,000 employees, Express Scripts recognized Justine as an "Employee of the Quarter" last year. Less than 50 employees in the entire company have ever received this honor.

Currently enrolled at Saint Louis University, Justine is pursuing a master's degree in public administration. She is expected to graduate in 2009.

Justine and her husband, John, were born and raised in St. Louis where they currently reside with their son Justin.

Justine Blue
Director
Manual Claims Operations
Express Scripts, Inc.

CORPORATE BRASS

Nicholette Booker
Director
Project Management Office
& Estimation
Express Scripts, Inc.

Nicholette Booker is the director of the project management office (PMO) for Express Scripts, Inc. The PMO is the center of excellence for infrastructure project delivery capabilities.

Nicholette has more than 20 years of experience in developing information technology investments in the financial services, energy and manufacturing industries. During her career, she has built several consulting practices for a big five consulting company, managed complex international projects and established a program management office.

Nicholette has volunteered with the Leukemia Society, served as a trustee of her former church and participated in fundraisers for muscular dystrophy. Additionally, she is a recipient of several awards including the Ernst & Young Project Excellence Award and the Lyondell Epic Award.

Nicholette received a bachelor of science degree in industrial management from Purdue University. She minored in computer science and accounting.

In her spare time, Nicholette enjoys traveling, especially to the United Kingdom where she lived for three years, photography and scuba diving.

Lorenzo M. Boyd
Vice President & Managing Director
Investment Banking
A.G. Edwards & Sons, Inc.

Lorenzo Boyd joined the public finance department of A.G. Edwards & Sons nine years ago and is currently a vice president and managing director of investment banking. During his tenure in public finance where he specializes in K-12, fire district and local government financings, Boyd has completed more than 100 financings with a par amount exceeding $4.4 billion.

Prior to joining A.G. Edwards, Boyd served four years of active duty in the U.S. Navy from 1988 to 1992. While in the Navy, Boyd earned the Kuwait Liberation and Navy Commendation medal for his involvement in Desert Shield/Desert Storm.

Boyd earned a bachelor of science in business administration degree from Lindenwood University. In the last five years, he has obtained numerous securities licenses including the municipal securities representative (series 52), the general securities NYSE/NASD registered representative license (series 7), and uniform securities state agent license (series 63).

Lorenzo Boyd and his wife, Sheila, reside in St. Louis with their two daughters, Keyana and Jaelyn.

Teresa Bryce is senior vice president and director of legal and corporate affairs for Nexstar Financial Corporation. She manages all legal issues along with regulatory compliance, quality assurance, and credit policy. Teresa received the 2004 Most Influential Women in Business award from the *St. Louis Business Journal,* and the 2001 Distinguished Service Award from the American Association of Residential Mortgage Regulators. In 2002, Teresa was inducted into the Mortgage Banker's Legion.

Teresa is active in the mortgage industry as a member of the board of directors of the Mortgage Bankers Association of America, and the Residential Board of Governors. She is the chair of the board of trustees of the Research Institute for Housing America as well as a member of the Fannie Mae National Advisory Council.

Teresa holds a bachelor of arts degree from the University of Virginia (UVA), and a juris doctorate from Columbia University. She is a member of the board of directors of the Shakespeare Festival of St. Louis; chair of the Ridley Scholarship Fund at UVA; and a member of the UVA board of managers.

Teresa Bryce
Senior Vice President
Nexstar Financial Corporation

Alonzo Byrd Jr. is director of corporate relations for Enterprise Rent-A-Car. He is responsible for the development and execution of the company's corporate citizenship initiatives nationwide. Byrd develops and enhances initiatives that demonstrate the company's social responsibility and involvement with national groups and organizations. He also works with Enterprise operating groups nationwide to cultivate and maintain close ties between Enterprise and community leaders, nonprofit organizations, and multicultural media groups.

Prior to joining Enterprise, Byrd was a vice president at Fleishman-Hillard, Inc., a leading international public relations agency. At Fleishman-Hillard, Byrd managed a wide range of media relations, community relations, and diversity related issues for Fortune 500 clients. He counseled nonprofit organizations including the United Negro College Fund, the Tiger Woods Foundation, and Paraquad.

A native of East St. Louis, Byrd has also worked as director of public relations for the St. Louis Bi-State Chapter of the American Red Cross. As a journalist, Byrd has worked for the *Kansas City Times*, the *Oakland Press* in Pontiac, Michigan, and the *Belleville News Democrat* in Illinois.

Byrd is married and has one child. He graduated from Southern Illinois University at Edwardsville with a bachelor's degree in journalism in 1981.

Alonzo Byrd Jr.
Director of Corporate Relations
Enterprise Rent-A-Car

CORPORATE BRASS

S. Wray Clay
Vice President,
Community Investment
United Way of Greater St. Louis

S. Wray Clay has worked with the United Way of Greater St. Louis since 1984. In 1990, she was appointed vice president of allocations/agency relations, where she managed a department team and more than 400 volunteers with the annual responsibility to distribute more than $42 million to support health and human services. Currently vice president for community investment, Wray is responsible for developing special initiatives and community partnerships in line with United Way's strategic vision.

Wray has been a member of the Edwardsville School Board since 1997. She works with the St. Louis Children's Hospital's Healthy Kids at Play Initiative, and the Susan B. Komen Grants Committee. Wray was a participant in Leadership St. Louis and also volunteered with the St. Louis Zoo Friends Association. Additionally, she is a member of St. Peter's AME Church, the NAACP, and Delta Sigma Theta Sorority, Inc.

Wray attended Southern Illinois University Edwardsville, where she obtained a bachelor of science degree in human services and a master of science degree in public administration. She is the mother of Justin and Jihan.

West Ewing
Division Manager
Schnuck Markets, Inc.

West Ewing is a division manager for Schnuck Markets, Inc. The St. Louis-based grocery company operates more than 100 stores in the Midwest.

Ewing joined Schnucks in 1979 and worked his way up through the ranks. In 1991, he became a store manager, and in 1995, he was promoted to division manager. He is currently responsible for 1,800 associates and 12 full-service supermarkets.

A 1973 graduate of Vashon High School, Ewing attended Forest Park Community College and is currently pursuing a bachelor's degree at the University of Missouri-St. Louis.

Ewing remains committed to community outreach. He is an active supporter of the United Way, and a leadership contributor and proud member of the Charmaine Chapman Society. In 1992, Ewing was honored with *The St. Louis Sentinel*'s Yes I Can award, and in 1997, he was inducted into the Vashon Hall of Fame.

Ewing and his wife, Ora, reside in O'Fallon, Missouri and have three children, Jason, Anisha, and Lawrence. The family attends Mt. Zion Missionary Baptist Church in St. Charles, where Ewing is chairman of the deacon board.

Theodore "Teddy" Foster Jr. is the director of human resources and corporate development for the Human Development Corporation. In this role, he manages recruitment, performance management, training, compensation, benefits, safety, development, grant monitoring, evaluation and reporting functions. He coordinates an award-winning community leadership program, Step Up To Leadership, and directs the youth enrichment and mentoring program, Young Scholars Academy. He is also the 2006 recipient of the coveted Winnie Brown Memorial Award for executive leadership.

Teddy is engaged in several civic endeavors. He is an active volunteer with the National Conference for Community and Justice, and Parents of African-American Students. He also offers community leadership by serving on several boards including the Lutheran Family and Children Services of Missouri and Vestry of All Saints Episcopal Church.

Teddy received a master of business administration degree and bachelor's degree from Lindenwood University. He is a graduate of the Institute for Educational Leadership's fellowship program.

A native of St. Louis, Teddy is the loving husband of Farida Foster and the proud father of three children, Fouzia, Zachary and Zarina.

Theodore Foster Jr.
Director of Human Resources &
Corporate Development
Human Development Corporation

Lisa Gates-Norwood is currently assistant vice president and branch manager of Gateway Bank of St. Louis, one of the first and oldest minority-owned banks in the country. In this role, she oversees customer service operations as well as marketing and advertising. Lisa began her career with Gateway Bank in 1998.

Prior to her current position at Gateway, Lisa was involved in the start-up of one of the most successful minority beer distributorships in St. Louis. She held positions in operations, marketing and sales, and finance for Lismark Distributing Company.

Lisa attended Rosati-Kain High School, California College of Arts and Webster University.

Lisa is involved in many civic and charitable organizations in the St. Louis area including the Mathews-Dickey Boys' & Girls' Club, the Myrtle Hilliard Davis Comprehensive Health Center, and the Seventh District Police Neighborhood Association. Lisa has also given the gift of life as a kidney donor.

She is married and is the proud mother of a teenage daughter.

Lisa Gates-Norwood
Assistant Vice President
Gateway Bank of St. Louis

CORPORATE BRASS

Courtney Gibson
Divisional Vice President
Diversity and Community Affairs
Macy's Midwest

Courtney Gibson is the divisional vice president of diversity and community affairs for Macy's Midwest. In her role, Courtney works closely with key management to ensure that the company embraces diversity as a strategic business priority, provides a work environment that celebrates differences and ensures respect for all associates. In addition, she works closely with community organizations in each market to determine the best way to direct charitable giving and community service efforts.

Courtney is a graduate of the University of Southern California (USC) with a bachelor of science degree in business administration. She began her career at Robinson's May, the Los Angeles affiliate of the May Company, and has held several positions over the past 12 years.

A native of Denver, Colorado, Courtney lived in Los Angeles for 16 years and relocated to St. Louis in February of 2006. She is on the board of the United Negro College Fund and the Make-A-Wish Foundation. In her spare time, Courtney enjoys watching football, snow skiing and scuba diving.

M. Lee Glasper
Accredited Customer
Relationship Representative
IBM Corporation

Lee Glasper is an accredited customer relationship representative for the IBM Corporation. In this position, she is responsible for ensuring client satisfaction and responsiveness; transaction handling, which optimizes revenue potential; and solid collaboration and teamwork, demonstrating personal leadership and execution of excellence. She is the administrative liaison for IBM's internal and external clients, and she manages administrative end-to-end processes of IBM customer fulfillment operations for the central region.

Lee has served as chairperson of the IBM Women's Network Group and is a member of the IBM Black Network Group, the IBM Mentor of St. Louis Program, and the IBM regional and accreditation councils. Furthermore, she is the IBM coordinator of the Annual St. Louis City/County Schools Career Awareness Fair, and actively participates in other IBM Community on Demand services.

Lee has a bachelor of science degree in business education with certifications in Illinois and Missouri.

An Edwardsville, Illinois native, Lee is the wife of Lawrence Glasper and is the proud mother of twin daughters, Rebecca Lynn and Rachael LeAnn. She is a member of the Shalom Church (City of Peace).

Rhonda Gray recently joined the United Way of Greater St. Louis as a member of the allocations staff in the community investment division. Rhonda is responsible for the investment of community dollars and United Way resources to a system of nonprofit agencies.

Rhonda has been recognized for her extensive experience in youth development, leadership development and diversity. She has served as a keynote speaker, workshop facilitator and trainer for corporate, academic, religious and nonprofit organizations. Rhonda's insights about individual, social and organizational change have grown out of her years of working with organizations dedicated to community revitalization and educational reform.

Rhonda is the recipient of the Dale Carnegie Highest Award for Achievement, and the Dean's Award for Outstanding Service to Children from the University of Missouri-St. Louis. She has served as a mentor and volunteers on several community and educational advisory boards.

A native of St. Louis, Rhonda obtained a bachelor's degree in English and business from Alabama A&M University. She has a master's degree in counseling from the University of Missouri-St. Louis.

Rhonda Gray
Allocations Panel Staff
Community Investment Division
United Way of Greater St. Louis

Ernest E. Green III is deputy police chief for the University City Police Department. He has authored four notable law enforcement related publications. He is a deputy commander for the St. Louis Metropolitan major case squad.

Ernest is a member of the Ferguson Heights Church of Christ, regional vice president for the National Organization of Black Law Enforcement (NOBLE), and a member of 100 Black Men, the FBI National Academy Association, and LEO (Law Enforcement Executives Organization). He is a board member for the University City Education Foundation. He was also a 2005 University City High School Hall of Fame inductee.

Ernest graduated from the FBI National Academy in Quantico, Virginia. He holds a master of arts degree in management and human resource development from Webster University and a bachelor of arts in business administration and personnel management from Truman State University.

Ernest and his wife, Alicia, are the proud parents of two sons, Ernest IV and Ellis.

Ernest E. Green III
Deputy Chief of Police
University City Police Department

CORPORATE BRASS

Geoff Green
Director of Talent Acquisitions
Brown Shoe Company

Geoff Green is director of talent acquisitions for Brown Shoe Company. In this position, Geoff manages domestic and international recruiting for Brown Shoe's offices, distribution centers and more than 1,300 specialty retail footwear stores. The primary focus of his role is to bring top talent to the organization.

Geoff has nearly 20 years of experience in the retail industry, with past positions including manager of recruiting for a chain of 700 apparel stores, and district sales manager for groups of eight to 15 footwear chain stores.

Geoff was featured in the *St. Louis Business Journal*'s prestigious 40 under 40 list in 2004. He is very active in the St. Louis community and serves as a board member for St. Louis Artworks, and a member of the local chapter of the National Black MBA Association. He holds a bachelor of science degree in communications from Ohio University.

Geoff and his wife, Val, have four beautiful children, Jasmyn, Jenae, Gino and Jordan.

Theresa E. Hassler
Director of Political Consulting &
Government Relations
The Maverick Group, LLC

Theresa E. Hassler is the director of political consulting and government relations for The Maverick Group, LLC. In this position, she serves as an advisor for elected officials, business leaders and nonprofit organizations. As a registered lobbyist with the State of Missouri, Theresa has advocated for private and public sector organizations, both in Missouri and in Atlanta.

Theresa previously served as the director of boards and commissions for the Office of the Lieutenant Governor in the state's capitol, also serving as the liaison for economic development policy. She has held senior staff positions in two statewide political campaigns.

Theresa is founder and executive director of C.R.E.A.T.E., Inc. (Community Resources Ensuring Access to Everyone), a nonprofit organization that coordinates services for senior citizens living in affordable housing developments.

A strong advocate for continuity in non-partisan political education among minorities, Theresa has been a conference speaker during the Missouri Association for Blacks in Higher Education conference. She is a member of the National Alumni Council for Southeast Missouri State University where she earned her bachelor's degree in art in 2002.

Sonya Henry manages the business partner advocate team, which consists of 11 technical business partner (BP) advocates who work with distributors and partners throughout the United States. Sonya's team ensures that these partners and selected providers have the right skills, resources and tools to help them exceed their sales objectives in pSeries, iSeries, and total storage IBM hardware products, which represents a more than $1.6 billion territory. The goal is to assist BPs by ensuring solution provider enablement on IBM technologies, act as an advocate when required and encourage strong focus on solution assurance.

Sonya has more than 21 years of experience in the computer industry providing education, sales and technical support. She received a bachelor of arts degree in public relations, with a minor in computer science, from Howard University, and has studied business at the University of Oslo in Norway. She is a board member of Confluence Academy, a charter school sponsored by Rolla University.

Sonya is a St. Louis native, a Normandy High School graduate, and the proud mother of Robert F. III, Kahla and Sonjay Henry.

Sonya Henry
Manager, Business
Partner Advocate Team
IBM Corporation

Betty Hopkins is student development coordinator for the University of Missouri-St. Louis, the largest university in the St. Louis metropolitan area. In this position, she works with a diverse population of students whose majors fall under fine arts and communications and the college of arts and sciences. She advises students on selecting a degree and implementing an action plan for completion.

Betty has received several recognitions for providing services to students with disabilities and other special needs. She is widely recognized for her ability to relate to students on campus.

Betty received a bachelor of science degree from Saint Louis University. In 2002 she was awarded a master of education degree in counseling from the University of Missouri-St. Louis.

A native of St. Louis, Betty is the proud mother of Andrea and Larry Jr. She has one grandchild, Raekwon.

Betty A. Hopkins
Student Development Coordinator
University of Missouri-St. Louis

CORPORATE BRASS

Mark P. Hughes
Director, Guest Safety/Transportation
President Casino

Mark Hughes is the director of guest safety and transportation on the President Casino. His responsibilities include enforcing all state and federal gaming regulations, providing a safe environment for guest and employees, and overseeing transportation and parking amenities. He was involved in security awareness development for the Port of St. Louis with the United States Coast Guard.

Mark has received several designations and certifications including workplace violence prevention specialist (NASP) in 2006, and certified Homeland Security Level III designation in 2006. In August of 2006, he started a security solutions business located in St. Louis County.

His memberships include the American College of Forensic Examiners Institute; the Area Maritime Security Committee (AMSC), steering committee member; and the American Society for Industrial Security (ASIS), member of the National/St. Louis chapter.

While continuing his education, he has received a certification in information systems from OIC in 1986, and an associate degree in automotive/diesel technology from Bailey Technical Institute (ITT Tech) in 1987. A lifelong St. Louis resident, Mark is the father of four children, and has been happily married for 17 years.

Donn Johnson
Director of Communications
Missouri Historical Society

As director of communications for the Missouri Historical Society, Donn Johnson is responsible for establishing and maintaining positive relationships with the community. He creates and oversees the public relations and promotional aspects of all exhibits and programs.

A St. Louis native, Donn holds a bachelor's degree in media studies, magna cum laude, from Webster University. In 2003 he was named Outstanding Alumnus of the Webster University School of Communications. He received a 2004 Emmy Award for his commentary for KETC-TV. He is also the recipient of three awards for Excellence in Radio and Print from the Greater St. Louis Association of Black Journalists.

Donn served three years as vice president of the American Federation of Radio and Television Artists and is a member of the NAACP. He is also a board member of the African American Heritage Foundation.

Donn produced the educational series *A Place In Time* in conjunction with HEC-TV. The program has won seven Telly Awards for excellence in cable television.

Donn lives in West St. Louis County with his wife, Earlene, and his daughter, Lauren.

Michael Johnson was named vice president of urban services for the YMCA of Greater St. Louis in May of 2005. He is responsible for the day-to-day administration of the Monsanto Family YMCA, its early childhood education center, the YMCA Boys Choir and the Performing Arts Center. He is also responsible for the management of programs coordinated within 12 schools. The programs administered by the vice president of urban services impact more than 7,000 children and their families in the greater St. Louis area.

Prior to his appointment in St. Louis, Johnson served as special assistant to the CEO of Philadelphia Public Schools and was responsible for their community outreach, faith-based programs, after-school programs and facilities management. He also held management positions at the Boys and Girls Clubs of Chicago and the Chicago Public Schools.

Johnson holds a master of business administration degree and a bachelor's degree in business education from Chicago State University. He is a board member for the St. Louis Chapter of the NAACP, and a member of the Washington University School of Medicine African American advisory board.

Michael Johnson
Vice President of Urban Services
YMCA of Greater St. Louis

Robyn Johnson is the director of pharmacy operations for Express Scripts in St. Louis. In this position, she is responsible for the production of prescription orders. With her previous experience in the financial industry, she continues to expand her horizons within the healthcare industry.

Robyn received a bachelor of science degree in business administration from North Carolina A&T State University. She is a member of Delta Sigma Theta Sorority, Inc., and is a faithful member of Church on the Rock in St. Peters, Missouri.

One of her many passions is working in the community. She received the 2004 Annual Volunteer Award from the O'Fallon Boys' and Girls' Club.

A Native of Greensboro, North Carolina, Robyn is the wife of Tony Johnson and the proud mother of one daughter, Brittanie, and one son, Christian. Robyn and her family reside in Lake St. Louis.

Robyn Johnson
Director, Pharmacy Operations
Express Scripts, Inc.

CORPORATE BRASS

Rosalind Johnson
Regional Sales Manager
American Eagle Outfitters

Rosalind Johnson is a regional sales manger for American Eagle Outfitters. In this position, which she has held for the past four years, Rosalind is responsible for leading a team of seven district managers and profitably operating, staffing and merchandising more than 70 American Eagle stores in nine states. Additionally, she is a board member of the American Eagle Outfitters Foundation, which donates time and financial support to charitable organizations in the communities in which they operate. Most recently, Rosalind has taken a leadership role in her company's diversity initiative.

Over the past 19 years, Rosalind has held various positions in both department and specialty store organizations, including Macy's New York, Federated Department Stores' Abraham & Straus division and Gap, Inc.

A native of Newark, New Jersey, Rosalind received a bachelor of arts degree from Rutgers University. Rosalind is the wife of Lee Johnson and the mother of three daughters, Bahja, Lea and Sana.

Adella Jones
Director of Communications
Metro

Adella Jones is the director of communications for Metro, the public transportation company of the St. Louis region. She is responsible for overseeing the development and implementation of communications and community relations programs and activities, which are designed to enhance public awareness through media coverage and interaction with community and business groups and the general public.

Previously, Adella served as St. Louis press secretary for Missouri's Third District Congressman Richard A. Gephardt. She has also served as director of communications and chief spokesperson for the St. Louis Metropolitan Police Department and as community relations manager for the St. Louis Convention and Visitors Commission.

Adella is a member of the Greater St. Louis Association of Black Journalists and is education chairperson and coordinator of the Minority Journalism Workshop. In 1998, she was named one of *St. Louis Business Journal's* 40 Under 40.

Jones is a graduate of Southern Illinois University at Edwardsville and holds a bachelor's degree in radio and television communications with a minor in print journalism and government. She resides in St. Louis, Missouri.

Michael B. Kennedy Jr. is vice president of sales and marketing for KAI Design & Build, the innovative award-winning firm behind projects such as the St. Louis City Justice Center, Cochran Gardens and Harris-Stowe State University's Gillespie Hall. Michael has accomplished great changes in his seven years at the 26-year-old Missouri and Texas-based firm.

Michael is also owner of Jabez Development, a company established in 2004. In early 2006, Michael completed a $2.2 million residential project in Gaslight Square. He was also featured in the *St. Louis Business Journal's* 30 under 30 in 2004.

A Hampton University graduate with a degree in business, Michael is setting the precedent for young African-American men. He attributes his success to his faith and commitment to a strong community. Michael is an active member of the BJC Children's Hospital development board, the St. Louis Association of Realtors affordable housing taskforce and the Downtown St. Louis Partnership housing and marketing committees.

A St. Louis native, Michael is married to Billye Kennedy. They are both avid St. Louis Cardinals and Rams fans.

Michael B. Kennedy Jr.
Vice President of Sales & Marketing
KAI Design and Build

Jim Killion is vice president of sales for Maritz Inc., the world's largest source of integrated performance improvement, incentive travel and marketing research services. In his role as leader in the office of professional selling, he is responsible for the development of sales professionals, as well as the development and re-engineering of strategic sales tools, processes and sales strategies.

Killion joined Maritz in 2001 as division vice president of sales planning. Previously, he was national sales director of strategic accounts for GE Capital Information Technology Solutions. His extensive sales management experience also includes more than 20 years of various senior management positions with Xerox Corporation.

In addition to his business endeavors, Killion is involved with various professional, academic and charitable organizations, including the Black MBA Association, Destination Manhood, the Wesley House Association and the Time-to-Read Literacy Program.

A native of Alton, Illinois, Killion holds a bachelor of science degree in business administration from Southern Illinois University–Carbondale. He and his wife, Darla, live in northwest St. Louis County.

James H. Killion III
Vice President, Sales Office
of Professional Selling
Maritz Inc.

CORPORATE BRASS

Johnny Little Jr.
Executive Director, Communications
St. Louis Public Schools

As executive director of communications in the St. Louis Public Schools district (SLPS), Johnny Little Jr. steers the communications functions of Missouri's largest school district.

Little majored in television production at Rust College in Mississippi. There, he began his professional television career in 1995 as a news producer at WJTV, CBS' affiliate in Jackson. The following year, after a stint as a news producer for an ABC station in Birmingham, Alabama, Little came north to St. Louis, where he has remained ever since.

From late 1996 to 2002, Little was a news producer at St. Louis' FOX affiliate, KTVI. He then returned to the CBS fold as an executive producer at KMOV. In 2004 he took on his present position at the SLPS. In this capacity, Little advises the superintendent, the school board president and other key officials on myriad issues relating to district public relations.

Little received a master's degree in business management from Webster University in 1998.

Timothy M. McClure
Director of Merchandise Planning
Macy's Midwest

Timothy McClure is the director of merchandise planning for the fashion accessories division at Macy's Midwest. In this position, he manages the financial sales plans and receipt flows for retail sales totaling $160 million annually. He also manages the allocation and distribution of accessories merchandise for more than 80 Macy's locations throughout the Midwest region.

Timothy has held several positions in his ten-year retail career at Famous Barr/Macy's, including buyer for Nine West shoes, buyer for costume jewelry and buyer for fashion watches/small leather goods, for which he was named Buyer of the Year in 2003.

Timothy received a bachelor of arts degree in psychology from Morehouse College in Atlanta, Georgia.

A native of St. Louis, Timothy is married to the former Jennifer Thornhill, and is the proud father of two daughters, Camryn and Kennedi.

Eric Mitchell
Director, Management
Information Systems
President Casino

Eric Mitchell has worked in the casino industry since its inception in the St. Louis market. He is currently director of management information systems (MIS) at the President Casino located on the St. Louis Riverfront. In this role, he participates in the leadership and management of the MIS department while helping to envision future information technology direction and goals.

Eric has had the opportunity to work with the Gateway Classic Sports Foundation and other positive organizations in the St. Louis region. These interactions put him in touch with many smart and talented people, and their ideas and opinions helped him become a better leader.

Eric has undergraduate and graduate degrees in business. Before his current position at President Casino, he had the opportunity to plan and assist in the opening of another casino in the St. Louis market. He has also served as a systems engineer for a major slot machine company.

Eric has been married to his lovely wife, Terry, for ten years. They have two children, Riley and Oliver. Eric is the son of Warren and Sylvia Mitchell.

Tommie Monroe
Vice President, Corporate Affairs and
Minority Business Development
Adam's Mark Hotels & Resorts

As vice president of corporate affairs and minority business development for Adam's Mark Hotels, Tommie Monroe oversees community affairs, advertising, charitable donations and diversity initiatives.

Adam's Mark Hotels recently received the top ranking on the NAACP's 2006 Lodging Industry Report Card. During Monroe's tenure at Adam's Mark, the company has improved its position each year, but this marks the first time since its inception that the company has achieved the highest rating. Additionally, he has repositioned the company to highlight its commitment to diversity and the minority community.

Monroe is a member of the National Coalition of Black Meeting Planners, and serves as co-chair of the corporate advisory council of the International Association of Hispanic Meeting Professionals. He has been featured as one of the Top Blacks in Lodging by *Black Meetings & Tourism* magazine.

Raised in East Harlem in New York City, Monroe received a nomination to the U.S. Air Force Academy from Congressman Charles Rangel. He earned a bachelor's degree in psychology from Mt. Mercy College in Cedar Rapids, Iowa.

CORPORATE BRASS

Cheryl Muniz
Vice President & Market Officer
ProLogis

Cheryl Muniz is vice president and market officer for ProLogis, the largest global provider of distribution facilities. She is responsible for the development, acquisition, leasing and management of a three million-square-foot portfolio.

Prior to joining ProLogis, Cheryl spent six years with Paragon Group's office in retail and multifamily portfolios and was awarded District Manager of the Year.

Cheryl sits on the board of CoreNet and the Earth City board of trustees. She is a member of the Society of Industrial and Office REALTORS, Commercial Real Estate Women and the National Association of Industrial and Office Properties. She is pursuing her CCIM designation.

A native of St. Louis, Cheryl received a bachelor of arts degree from Webster University and mentors through Mathews-Dickey's Rainbow program.

Emily R. Pitts
Principal, Banking Services
Edward Jones

Emily R. Pitts is a principal in the banking services area of Edward Jones. Emily began her career with Edward Jones as an investment representative in Atlanta, Georgia. She relocated to St. Louis in January of 2004 when she was invited to become a general partner of the firm. Emily is responsible for the Edward Jones credit card and Edward Jones Mortgage Services nationwide. She also manages the current vendor relationships for these services with MBNA and Wells Fargo. Emily has worked in the brokerage industry for several financial institutions for more than 23 years.

Emily is a member of Alpha Kappa Alpha Sorority, Inc., The Links, Inc., and she serves on the board of the Hope House in St. Louis. A graduate of Clark Atlanta University, she holds the AAMS certification from the College of Financial Planning.

Emily's husband, Richard, is an investment representative with Edward Jones. She also has three stepdaughters and four step-grandchildren all located in Atlanta.

Kevin Riggs serves as director of Illinois government affairs for the St. Louis Regional Chamber & Growth Association. He leads their lobbying and public policy initiatives in Springfield, Illinois.

Kevin brings varied public policy and governmental affairs experience to his position. Previously, he served as a senior appropriations budget analyst for the Illinois General Assembly; a regional supervisor in special population and decennial counts for Illinois, Indiana and Wisconsin for the Census Bureau; and manager of community development for the East-West Gateway Council of Governments.

Kevin serves on numerous boards, including the St. Louis United Way government relations committee, Kappa Alpha Psi Fraternity, Inc., the Leadership Council of Southwestern Illinois, the St. Louis Downtown Partnership legislative affairs committee, and the Urban League of St. Louis employment committee.

Kevin holds a bachelor's degree in political science from Southern Illinois University at Carbondale and a master's degree in public administration from Southern Illinois University at Edwardsville. Currently, Kevin resides in O'Fallon, Illinois with his wife and family.

Kevin Riggs
Director, Illinois Government Affairs
St. Louis Regional Chamber &
Growth Association

Shuntaé Shields Ryan is the marketing and public relations manager for the Downtown St. Louis Partnership, the organization most active in the revitalization of downtown St. Louis. Her responsibilities include managing the marketing, communications and public relations activities of the organization.

Ryan serves as host and producer of the television program, *Talk About Downtown*, on City TV-10. Under her leadership, the Partnership launched its first comprehensive advertising campaign, creating a Web site and a host of marketing materials to promote downtown.

The marketing department has received various awards under Ryan's leadership, including the Missouri Downtown Association Downtown Excellence Award for marketing and communications; the MDA Award for image marketing; and the Excellence in Redevelopment Award for image promotion.

As a way of giving back to the community, Ryan has served as the public relations instructor for high school students participating in the Greater St. Louis Association of Black Journalists workshop and as the marketing director for her church, Greater Grace.

She has been married to Lydell Ryan for seven years and is the mother of a four-year-old son, Jordon.

Shuntaé Shields Ryan
Marketing & Public Relations Manager
Downtown St. Louis Partnership

CORPORATE BRASS

Kimberly Smith
Channels Territory Manager
IBM Corporation

Kimberly Smith is a channels territory manager for IBM Corporation. She manages the largest sales territory in the central region for the channels organization. Kim's responsibilities include implementing long term sales strategy and preparing successful marketing plans to support and drive sales quota. In her past 12 years with IBM, she has held positions in sales, human resources and consulting services. She has received such honors as a leadership award, High Flyer of the Year and the 100 Percent Club. Kim is a member of several organizations within IBM, the St. Louis Black Networking Group, Women's Networking Group and the IBM Club, where she is vice president.

Active in the community, Kim is a board member for Mentor St. Louis and the YWCA of Metropolitan St. Louis, and a member of the Charmaine Chapman Society of the United Way and Alpha Kappa Alpha Sorority, Inc.

Kimberly has a bachelor's degree in marketing and a master's degree in business management.

She is married to Herman Smith III and is a proud mother of two daughters, Lauren and Kennedy, and one son, Jackson.

Elaine Harris Spearman, Esq.
Legal Advisor & Chief Staffing Officer
City of St. Louis Comptroller's Office

Elaine Harris Spearman, Esq. is the legal advisor and chief staffing officer for the Comptroller's Office. In this position, she coordinates the overall functions of the Comptroller's Office. Elaine served as director of human services in the administration of the city's first African-American mayor.

She has received an array of awards including the Association of Elected Officials 2005 Comptroller Employee of the Year Award, the Coalition of 100 Black Women's Outstanding Legal Services Award, and the Top Ladies of Distinction Humanitarian Award.

Elaine is a member of the Mound City and National Bar Associations, the Bar Association of Metropolitan St. Louis, and the Missouri and Illinois Bars.

She received a bachelor of arts degree in social administration from Tennessee A&I State University and a doctorate of jurisprudence from Saint Louis University School of Law.

Elaine is a member of Washington Metropolitan AME Zion Church, where she has served as vice president of the board of trustees and is currently serving as the church's attorney. Her hobbies are gardening, interior design and cooking.

Leah Reynolds Stoddard is a vice president and treasury management sales officer for the central region of Bank of America. She has been in banking for 17 years, and with Bank of America for 12 years. Leah advises clients in the commercial and higher education segments on the management of their working capital assets. She has also held the positions of banking center manager and manager of recruiting.

An alumna of the INROADS program, Leah earned her bachelor of arts degree in business administration from Stephens College in Columbia, Missouri. She is certified by the Association for Financial Professionals as a certified treasury professional.

Leah serves on the advisory board of the American Red Cross Charles Drew program. She is a member of Delta Sigma Theta Sorority, Inc., Jack and Jill of America, Inc., and Unity Lutheran Church.

A native of St. Louis, Leah is the proud mother of one son, Graham.

Leah Reynolds Stoddard
Vice President
Global Treasury Services
Bank of America

Kim Tubbs-Herron is Microsoft area general manager of the small and midmarket solutions and partners (SMS&P) group for the North Central region. Based in St. Louis, Kim leads Microsoft's sales, marketing and support teams for SMS&P in a seven-state area that includes Missouri, Kansas, Minnesota, Iowa, North Dakota, South Dakota and Nebraska.

Kim is responsible for business leadership, strategy, orchestration, sales execution, and aligning and connecting programs with customers and partners. Her other responsibilities involve developing strategic plans, directing business solutions and platform sales teams, and building and developing Microsoft's people, processes and solutions.

Kim's distinguished career includes ten years at Microsoft Corporation, 13 years at Digital Equipment Corporation and five years at Polaroid. She holds a bachelor of science degree in business from the University of Maryland. She is a board member and marketing chairperson for the Information Technology Senior Management Forum.

When Kim is not in the office or traveling, she can be found on the golf course with her husband, Terrance Herron. Kim is the mother of two daughters, Kira and Nikiya.

Kim Tubbs-Herron
Area General Manager
Microsoft Corporation

CORPORATE BRASS

Barbara A. Washington
Vice President
Public Relations and Special Events
Mathews-Dickey Boys' & Girls' Club

A 20-plus year industry veteran, Barbara A. Washington is the vice president of public relations and special events for the Mathews-Dickey Boys' & Girls' Club, a St. Louis-area youth organization serving more than 40,000 young men and women annually. In this capacity, Washington serves as the official spokesperson and directs and manages communications with key audiences, including members, parents, staff, volunteers, alumni, corporate sponsors, funding institutions, and local and national media.

Washington established and annually oversees several community-wide fund-raisers that generate nearly $1 million for Mathews-Dickey, and have included such notables as U.S. Secretary of Commerce Don Evans. Her efforts as a counselor, mentor and friend have earned her the affectionate, unofficial title of "club mom." Washington is a Press Club board member and United Way of Greater St. Louis committee member and volunteer.

A certified special event professional, Washington studied journalism and communications at Fontbonne College in St. Louis, and the Maryland Extension University in Nuremberg, West Germany. A native of Arcola, Mississippi, Washington has two sons and four grandsons.

Herschel A. West
Director of Food and Beverage
Forest Park Golf Club

Herschel A. West is the director of food and beverage for the Forest Park Golf Club, a subsidiary of the American Golf Corporation. In this position, he manages more than 60 employees. He is responsible for all menu development and costing, and he oversees all catering sales operations for the golf club, as well as Ruthie's Grill, which is located on the grounds.

Herschel handles all labor management and controls, and purchases all food and beverages. Likewise, he oversees all in-house training, and he is currently in the general manager's training program for American Golf Corporation. Herschel is responsible for ensuring that all catering sales goals are met, totaling in excess of $2 million annually.

Herschel's initial training in the hospitality industry began with Marriott Corporation in March of 1989 as an hourly associate. Through a lot of hard work and perseverance, he was able to rise through the ranks from hourly to supervisory to management positions during a span of 11 years.

A native of St. Louis, Herschel is a graduate of California State University-Dominguez Hills.

Ericca Willis
Director of Minority
Business Development
St. Louis Development Corporation

Ericca Willis was hired as the director of minority business development for the St. Louis Development Corporation on July 8, 2002. She serves as the minority business owner advocate with the task of increasing the success of minority-owned businesses in St. Louis. Through the use of seminars, conferences, workshops, and symposiums, targeted firms are provided opportunities and services to help foster growth and development.

Previously, Willis was area director of the Department of Economic Development, and manager of loan administration and financial services for the St. Louis Minority Business Council.

A St. Louis native, Willis attended Berkeley Senior High School but graduated from McAteer High in San Francisco, California. In 1992, she received a bachelor of arts degree from the University of California-San Diego. She went on to receive her paralegal certificate from the University of San Diego.

In 1994, Willis relocated to Los Angeles and worked for Wherehouse Entertainment, Inc., where she utilized her paralegal training. In 1998, she returned to St. Louis with her daughter. She is now married to Keith Antone Willis, publisher of *Who's Who in Black St. Louis*®, and has two sons.

Lori Elbert Willis
Director of Communications
Schnuck Markets, Inc.

Lori Elbert Willis is the director of communications for St. Louis-based Schnuck Markets, Inc. Schnuck Markets ranked 80th on *Forbes* magazine's listing of the nation's Largest Private Companies. Since joining Schnucks in 2001, Willis has been responsible for developing internal and external communications. She is the spokesperson and media liaison for the company, which includes more than 100 combination food and drug stores throughout the Midwest.

In 2003, Willis coordinated the communications efforts of the Greater St. Louis Food Employers Council, a labor-relations partnership between the area's largest union grocers that oversees the interests of more than 13,000 store associates. Over the years, she has been instrumental in developing longterm communications strategies for nonprofit, public, and private companies.

Willis graduated from Jefferson City High School in 1978 and earned a degree in mass communications from Lincoln University of Missouri in 1982.

Willis and her husband, Mick, have three children, Ryan, Taryn, and Paige. They all reside in Ballwin, Missouri and attend the First Baptist Church of Chesterfield. She is active in local United Way efforts and currently serves as chairperson of the Ballwin Board of Adjustments.

●●● MENTOR ST.LOUIS

BY. making a DONATION, you will be SUPPORTING A better world and helping to create a different future that affects us all

BUSINESS UNUSUAL

If your company sees itself as an integral part of the world, and if your company employees are the sort who want to make a difference in their own community then they many benefits of corporate participation can be yours.

Mentor St. Louis can provide all the tools you need to tell the story around your offices. One easy start is to send company-wide emails with a passionate call to action, perhaps a company-matching program or incentive and one web link: www.mentorstlouis.org

INDIVIDUAL BELIEFS

- Gain personal satisfaction from making a difference in the life of a child.
- Meet and work with a diverse group of people.
- Help to strengthen and improve our community

CORPORATE BELIEFS

- Helps build employee self-esteem.
- Instills pride in each participating employee.
- Promotes camaraderie among employees.
- Creates a positive ripple effect when actively promoted and publicized in the workplace.
- Demonstrated the company's commitment to a better community.

www.mentorstlouis.org
(314) 531-2570
Mentor St. Louis
4236 Lindell Blvd., Suite 105
St. Louis, MO 63108
Fax: (314) 531-3385

WHO'S *Who*

St. Louis Rams

Victor Adeyanju
94
Defensive End

Alex Barron
70
Offensive Tackle

Ray Agnew
Director, Player Development
and Team Pastor

Ron Bartell
24
Cornerback

Jon Alston
57
Linebacker

Adrian E. Bracy
Vice President, Finance

Oshiomogho Atogwe
21
Safety

Fakhir Brown
34
Cornerback

Brian Baker
Defensive Line

Isaac Bruce
80
Wide Receiver

Joe Baker
Defensive Quality Control,
Linebackers

Tony Bryant
92
Defensive End

Jerametrius Butler
23
Cornerback

Dick Daniels
Scout

Dominique Byrd
86
Tight End

Stephen Davis
48
Running Back

Dwaine Carpenter
27
Safety

Henry Ellard
Wide Receivers

Jerome Carter
42
Safety

Marshall Faulk
28
Running Back

Corey Chavous
25
Safety

Tony Fisher
30
Running Back

Dexter Coakley
52
Linebacker

Travis Fisher
22
Cornerback

La'Roi Glover
97
Defensive Tackle

Steven Jackson
39
Running Back

Marques Hagans
15
Wide Receiver
(Practice Squad)

Jimmy Kennedy
73
Defensive Tackle

Keith Harris
Sponsorship Services
Coordinator

Duane Lewis
Director, New Media

Tye Hill
26
Cornerback

Leonard Little
91
Defensive End

Brad Holmes
Scout

Ken Mayweather
Facilities

Torry Holt
81
Wide Receiver

Lawrence McCutcheon
Director, Player Personnel

Shaun McDonald
84
Wide Receiver

Fred Russell
36
Running Back
(Practice Squad)

Ron Milus
Assistant Secondary

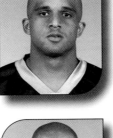

Tim Sandidge
71
Defensive Tackle
(Practice Squad)

Wayne Moses
Running Backs

Paul Smith
31
Running Back

Rosalind Oglesby
Executive Assistant,
Accounting

Raonall Smith
56
Linebacker

Orlando Pace
76
Offensive Tackle

Tony Softli
Vice President,
Player Personnel

J.R. Reed
32
Safety

Claude Terrell
75
Guard

Dominique Thompson
17
Wide Receiver
(Practice Squad)

John David Washington
35
Running Back
(Practice Squad)

Larry Turner
63
Guard/Center

Will Witherspoon
51
Linebacker

Artis Twyman
Assistant Director,
Football Media

Claude Wroten
99
Defensive Tackle

Bob Wallace
Executive Vice President and
General Counsel

Michael Yarbrough
Manager, Community Outreach
and Youth Football Programs

St. Louis'

COUNSELORS AT LAW

"The only way to get equality is for two people to get the same thing at the same time at the same place."

THURGOOD MARSHALL, 1908-1993

U.S. SUPREME COURT JUSTICE

COUNSELORS AT LAW

Eric Kendall Banks
Partner, Attorney at Law
Thompson Coburn LLP

Eric Kendall Banks is a partner with Thompson Coburn LLP. He is a trial lawyer, primarily representing management with labor and employment issues. He is licensed in Missouri and Illinois and has been admitted to practice before the United States Supreme Court and a number of federal circuit and district courts.

Banks is a member of the Missouri, American, National and Mound City Bar Associations, as well as the Bar Association of Metropolitan St. Louis. He has litigated cases throughout the United States. Prior to joining Thompson Coburn, Banks was the city counselor.

Banks is a member of the Missouri Athletic Club, the Noonday Club and Transfiguration Lutheran Church.

As a result of his community service, Banks has received numerous awards. He was a 2003 recipient of the Equal Justice Award, presented by Legal Services Corporation of Eastern Missouri to long-standing advocates for equal justice. He was also selected as a Missouri/Kansas Super Lawyer for 2005 and 2006.

Banks is the father of two teenagers, Brittany and Bryson.

Richard E. Banks
Attorney at Law
Banks & Associates

Richard E. Banks is one of St. Louis' premier personal injury attorneys. His long list of winning cases includes a $12.2 million award in a wrongful case and a $7.7 million verdict against the transit authority. He is currently taking on one of the nation's largest trucking companies in multimillion-dollar litigation. Banks & Associates recently relocated to the downtown historic St. Louis Union Station.

Banks is licensed to practice law in Missouri and Illinois. He serves on many boards including the St. Louis Gateway Classic Sports Foundation and the Urban League of Metropolitan St. Louis. Additionally, he is a partner in the Black Family Channel Cable Network.

Banks is a recipient of the coveted Ashly Award from Legal Services of Eastern Missouri, the governor's MLK Outstanding Business Award and many others. He has been featured in several publications for his accomplishments in and out of the courtroom.

Banks is a product of Howard University and Texas Southern University School of Law. A St. Louis native, he lives with his two children, Jessica and Richard Jr.

Jacqueline Blocker, a senior litigation associate at Greensfelder, Hemker & Gale, devotes the majority of her practice to the oil and gas industry, with an emphasis in environmental law. She is a member of the firm's diversity committee and summer mentor program.

Blocker earned her bachelor's degree, cum laude, from Harvard College. While at Harvard, she was the co-founder and vice president of In Sports, Inc., a nonprofit organization that encourages student athletes to volunteer in programs for underprivileged children. She received her juris doctorate from the University of Missouri-Kansas City and served as the information campaign manager for the Greenwood Reparations Coalition.

Blocker is a member of the St. Louis Harvard Club, the Bar Association of Metropolitan St. Louis, and the American Bar Association's environmental, energy and resource section. She is a participant in Read Across America and the Angel Tree Project. She was an executive board member of the Simon Estes Educational Foundation.

A native of Tulsa, Oklahoma, she is the proud daughter of Jackie and Mildred Blocker, and the proud granddaughter of the late Dr. Ione T. Morrison.

Jacqueline L. Blocker
Senior Litigation Associate
Greensfelder, Hemker & Gale, PC

Steven N. Cousins is the first African-American partner with the law firm Armstrong Teasdale, LLP. He is the founder and practice group leader of its bankruptcy department and a member of its executive committee.

Cousins has been involved in national cases such as Enron, Kmart and TWA. He assisted the national office of the NAACP in restructuring its affairs, and he also served as expansion counsel for the Lambert-St. Louis International Airport.

Cousins was recognized in *The Best Lawyers In America* and in *Black Enterprise* magazine. He serves on the boards of the St. Louis Art Museum, BJC Health System, and The PrivateBank. Additionally, he serves on the board for the St. Louis Children's Hospital, the St. Louis Internship Program and the St. Louis Public Schools Foundation. He is general counsel for the St. Louis Regional Chamber and Growth Association.

Cousins received his juris doctorate from the University of Pennsylvania School of Law in 1980, and his bachelor of arts degree from Yale University in 1977.

He is an author and speaker at numerous national bankruptcy conferences.

Steven N. Cousins
Partner, Attorney at Law
Armstrong Teasdale, LLP

COUNSELORS AT LAW

Larry L. Deskins
Member, Attorney at Law
Lewis, Rice & Fingersh, L.C.

Larry L. Deskins is a member of Lewis, Rice & Fingersh, L.C. The St. Louis practice focuses on banking, mergers and acquisitions, securities, closely held businesses, partnerships and joint ventures. Larry received his law degree from Washington University in St. Louis School of Law in 1977, where he currently serves on the Tyrell Williams lecture committee. He received his bachelor of arts degree from Allegheny College in 1974.

Banks is a member of the Missouri and Illinois state bars. Additionally, he serves on the board of directors for the Automobile Club (AAA) of Missouri and The Repertory Theatre of St. Louis.

Larry has three children, Maya, Larry and Logan. He enjoys golfing and is a member of Norwood Hills Country Club. He is also a member of the Missouri Athletic Club and thc Noonday Club.

Jovita Foster
Senior Associate
Armstrong Teasdale LLP

Jovita Foster is a senior associate at Armstrong Teasdale LLP, one of St. Louis' largest law firms. She is a trial attorney with considerable experience in the area of commercial litigation. She has successfully tried numerous cases to conclusion in the city and county of St. Louis, as well as before the federal court. She is licensed to practice law in Missouri and Illinois.

Jovita serves as a commissioner for the Credit Union Commission of Missouri. She is a member of the Bar Association of Metropolitan St. Louis and serves on AIM High's board of directors.

Jovita earned a bachelor of arts degree from the University of Missouri-Columbia in 1997. She earned a juris doctorate from Washington University in St. Louis in 2000. She received the American College of Trial Lawyers Medal for Excellence in Trial Advocacy in 1999 and the Milton F. Napier Trial Award for excellence in trial advocacy in 2000.

A native of St. Louis, Jovita is the wife of Darius Foster. She is the proud mother of Kaitlyn.

Connie McFarland-Butler is a partner at Armstrong Teasdale LLP, one of St. Louis' largest law firms. Connie is a trial attorney practicing in all facets of litigation including appeals, personal injury, complex torts, product liability and medical malpractice claims. She is licensed to practice in Missouri and Illinois.

Connie is a member of the International Association of Defense Counsel, the Defense Research Institute, the National Association of Railroad Defense Counsel, the Missouri Bar Association, the Illinois State Bar Association and the Bar Association of Metropolitan St. Louis. She has served as a board member for Shelter the Children, and on the 2001 campaign steering committee for the Washington University in St. Louis School of Law.

Connie received a bachelor of arts degree from Washington University in St. Louis in 1991, and a juris doctorate in 1996. Connie currently serves as an adjunct professor in trial practice at the law school.

A native of West Point, Mississippi, Connie is the wife of Waymon Butler III, and the proud mother of five children, Waymon, Laurence, Jordan, Jonathan and Jasmine.

Connie McFarland-Butler
Partner, Attorney at Law
Armstrong Teasdale LLP

Pamela J. Meanes is a partner with Thompson Coburn LLP, St. Louis' largest law firm. As a partner in the firm's litigation and public law practices, Pam represents clients on a wide range of matters including land use, eminent domain and contract disputes, employment and personnel issues, administrative law and many others.

Pam attended Monmouth College, where she obtained her bachelor's degree in 1990. There, she recognized a shortage of African-American professors and decided to become a professor, earning her master's degree from Clark Atlanta University in 1993. She then decided that becoming a lawyer would be the best way to create change in her community, so she earned her juris doctorate from the University of Iowa in 1996.

Pam began her career at Thompson Coburn later that year and was elected partner in 2005. In addition to her work at the law firm, Pam is president of the Mound City Bar Association, the oldest African-American bar association west of the Mississippi. She is active in her church and is a member of the NAACP and the Urban League.

Pamela J. Meanes
Partner, Attorney at Law
Thompson Coburn LLP

COUNSELORS AT LAW

Shirley A. Padmore
Member, Attorney at Law
Husch & Eppenberger, LLC

Shirley Padmore is a member of the law firm of Husch & Eppenberger, LLC, a 315-lawyer firm. Shirley began her career with Husch in 1995 as an associate in the general business litigation practice group. In 2003 Shirley became a member of the firm and served as chair of the firm's hiring committee. Her practice areas include general business, commercial, construction and products liability litigation.

Active in her community, Shirley is a member of the African Refugee and Immigrant Service. She is also a member of Women's Support and Community Services, and a volunteer for Junior Achievement of St. Louis and the Volunteer Lawyers Program. In 2004 Shirley was featured in the *St. Louis Business Journal*'s 40 Under 40.

In 1995 Shirley received her law degree from the Washington University in St. Louis School of Law, where she was the executive notes editor of the *Journal of Urban and Contemporary Law*. In 1991 she received a bachelor of arts degree in political science from the University of Pennsylvania.

Shira Truitt
Counselor
Mental & Emotional Wellness, LLC

A native of Baton Rouge, Louisiana, Shira Truitt earned her undergraduate degree in psychology from Southern University and A&M College. While attending Washington University in St. Louis, she earned her master's degree in social work and a law degree.

Truitt is a licensed clinical social worker in Missouri and Louisiana, and a licensed attorney in Missouri and Illinois. She practices law in association with a small firm in St. Louis and enjoys a small private practice, Mental & Emotional Wellness, where she offers counseling.

A member of several professional and social organizations in St. Louis, Truitt is an ardent community volunteer. She assists various charitable organizations in meeting the needs of vulnerable and at-risk populations in the St. Louis metropolitan area.

Thank You, St. Louis

for helping us to empower communities & change lives

Helping our neighbors in the St. Louis region…
survive, climb out of poverty & change lives.

Urban League
of Metropolitan St. Louis, Inc.
Empowering Communities. Changing Lives.

he Urban League of Metropolitan

The Urban League of Metropolitan St. Louis supports and guides our neighbors in the St. Louis region who struggle in poverty and need our community's help. The organization provides social services and programs for African Americans and others. The Urban League partners with other community organizations, businesses and individuals. It is a member of the United Way of Greater St. Louis and an affiliate of the National Urban League.

The League's priorities are to help clients gain economic empowerment, basic needs and educational excellence/equality. The Urban League is built on an 89-year history of delivering quality services to our clients.

Economic Empowerment

The Economic Empowerment Initiative provides resources to strengthen individuals, families, and communities by improving and climbing the economic "ladder" to a better quality of life. Programs include:

- Urban Youth Empowerment Program
- Foreclosure Prevention (National Urban League Initiative)
- Business Training Center
- Jobs for Missouri Graduates
- Employment Services
- Workforce Investment Act (WIA) for youth
- Money Smart Financial Literacy

Helping Young Adults Prepare for Jobs that Matter

The Urban League of Metropolitan St. Louis is the exclusive youth service contractor for the Workforce Investment Act (WIA) in St. Louis County. It provides a variety of both in-school and out-of-school services and training to prepare youth for productive employment. It partners with 13 county school districts to serve over 600 youths, ages 14-21. The program is funded by the US Department of Labor through the St. Louis County Department of Human Services.

Education Quality & Equality

The Education Initiative encourages and enables participants to apply learning to everyday situations, to embrace technology and to achieve academic excellence.

- Head Start
- Scholarships
- Vaughn Cultural Center

Helping Kids Get a Real Head Start

The Urban League of Metropolitan St. Louis' Head Start program provides multiple developmental services at four fully licensed centers for St. Louis City low-income, pre-school children (ages three to five) and social services for their families. Specific services for children focus on education, socio-emotional development, physical and mental health, and nutrition.

Meeting Basic Needs

The Meeting Basic Needs Initiative provides clients in need with food, clothing and other life necessities while strengthening families and helping people become self-sufficient.

- Food/Clothing
- HUD Housing Counseling
- Utility Assistance
- GED
- Weatherization

Helping Homeowners Survive & Save Energy

The Urban League of Metropolitan St. Louis' Weatherization program helps low to moderate income families and elderly/disabled homeowners to reduce their utility bills by making repairs to their homes that will reduce energy consumption, energy costs, correct health/safety hazards and substandard living conditions. Weatherization kits were provided to 250 residents through the St. Louis City and St. Louis County offices in partnership with AmerenUE.

Tara Rhodes

Tara Rhodes is a victim of Hurricane Katrina who has relocated to St. Louis from Mississippi. Ms. Rhodes had lost everything and had been trying to stabilize life for herself and her two children, ages 11 and 15. She worked with Urban League Family Service Worker Anetra Chapman and had one of her children enrolled in the Head Start program at the Jennings location.

During the holiday season, a donor was interested in making a donation to one of our Katrina families. Cases were submitted to the President's office and the donor selected the recipient. Ms. Rhodes was selected and was awarded $2,000 towards items listed in her letter.

Tara Rhodes

Ms. Rhodes was able to purchase items necessary in rebuilding her home here in St. Louis. Today, she is employed as a full-time family service worker at the Urban League of Metropolitan St. Louis in the Head Start program.

> *"I am thankful for the help of the Urban League and other charities with stabilizing my family financially and emotionally. They truly motivated me to not get comfortable but to strive for self-sufficiency."*
>
> — *Tara Rhodes*

*E*ach year, the Urban League of Metropolitan St. Louis serves more than 66,000 individuals.

70% – Female head of household

74% – Under $9,999 annual income

95% – African American

20% – 55 and older

More than **740** youth are enrolled in our WIA school-to-work programs.

More than **800** children attend Head Start.

Antoine

Antoine had been a participant in the Urban League's Workforce Investment Act (WIA) program since 2000. He started out working with Urban League case manager LaWanda Powell through Jennings School District. He worked a variety of jobs through the summer employment activity and received year round services to help him to graduate. Through a series of unfortunate events, Antoine found himself no longer able to attend school at Jennings.

It was at this point that Ms. Powell enlisted the help of fellow case manager Brad Tillis to help get Antoine back on track to graduate. Through the support of both Mr. Tillis and Ms. Powell and the countless hours the two of them put in counseling and mentoring Antoine, he successfully attained his High School Diploma.

Antoine's struggles were not over with the completion of his Diploma and neither was Brad and LaWanda's job working with him. They continued to maintain close contact with Antoine and he began to volunteer at the North Oaks location of the Missouri Career Center. He averaged 30-35 hours/week dong whatever was asked of him. In December of 2005, his months of dedicated and diligent service finally paid off and Antoine was offered a 6-month work experience assignment as a Maintenance Aide at the Missouri Career Center.

Helping our neighbors in the St. Louis region ... survive, climb out of poverty & change lives.

Membership

Membership in the Urban League of Metropolitan St. Louis offers community news, special events and other opportunities. In addition, membership in the **John T. Clark Honor Society** presents valuable social leadership and business contacts.

— AUXILIARY ORGANIZATIONS —

Urban League Guild

The Urban League Guild of Metropolitan St. Louis are community volunteers who are dedicated to improving the quality of life for

African Americans and others in need in the St. Louis region. The Guild also helps to support the League's efforts to reach out and address the economic, social and health needs of minorities, elderly, youth and disadvantaged persons within our region.

Federation of Block Units

The Federation of Block Units is a volunteer organization focused on helping residents of St. Louis communities improve their neighborhoods and quality of life. Block Units work to improve neighborhoods, educate citizens on their responsibilities and encourage teamwork to use all available resources. They also facilitate cooperation among citizens, government, voluntary organizations and other stakeholders.

Young Professionals

The Urban League Young Professionals (ULYP) of Metropolitan St. Louis engage and develop future leaders for the Urban League movement.

The group consists of African Americans and others between the ages of 21-40. Young Professionals organize fundraising events, personal/professional development seminars and professional networking parties.

V olunteer.
Donate.
Join.
Get involved.

What interests you? What experience can you share with neighbors struggling in poverty? The Urban League of Metropolitan St. Louis offers many ways for you to get involved as a member, volunteer, contributor, sponsor or partner.

Lee Lewis, Community Relations Manager at Enterprise Rent A Car; **James H. Buford**, Urban League President; **Dwight Miller**, General Manager of Enterprise Rent A Car; and **Rolandis Nash**, VP of the St. Louis City Division of the Urban League.

Sponsorship Opportunities

The Urban League of Metropolitan St. Louis welcomes the involvement, partnerships and support from individual citizens, corporations and other organizations located in the St. Louis region. The mission and services of the organization provide collaborative opportunities for the Urban League to partner with other organizations and individuals in the St. Louis region.

United Way
of Greater St. Louis

For more information
on how you can get involved, contact
Urban League of Metropolitan St. Louis
3701 Grandel Square • St. Louis, MO 63108
(314) 615-3600
www.urbanleague-stl.org

Urban League
of Metropolitan St. Louis, Inc.
Empowering Communities. Changing Lives.
#1 Ranked Affiliate of the National Urban League

St. Louis'

MEDIA PROFESSIONALS

"Lots of people want to ride with you in the limo, but what you want is someone who will take the bus with you when the limo breaks down."

OPRAH WINFREY

PUBLISHER, PRODUCER & ENTERTAINER

MEDIA PROFESSIONALS

Marcus "Ma'at" Atkins
Freelance Writer & Theatre Director

Marcus "Ma'at" Atkins is an award-winning journalist in the St. Louis area. Currently, Marcus contributes to the *West End Word*, the *St. Louis Argus* and KDHX FM 88.1. He also writes a weekly entertainment column, "Out Town" on his own popular Web site. He has written for the *Suburban Journals*, *The St. Louis American*, *Upscale Magazine* and *Flipside Newszine*.

Marcus is a regional Emmy Award-nominee and the recipient of the National Association of Black Journalists Award. He was a featured poet with the Eugene B. Redmond Writers Club at the 2002 National Black Arts Festival in Atlanta. Marcus co-authored the 1998 book, *Visible Glory: Million Man March*. In theatre, he has directed community stage plays since 1999.

Marcus received a bachelor of science degree and a master's degree in mass communications from Southern Illinois University Edwardsville. At SIUE, he helped to form the literary organization, The Black Literary Guild, and the award-winning poetry series, Public Poet. In 1995 he was named Student of the Year at his alma mater.

Marcus is a native of East St. Louis.

Leamon "Bill" Beene
Entertainment Editor
The St. Louis American

Leamon "Bill" Beene is entertainment editor, a photojournalist and a general assignment reporter for *The St. Louis American*. As entertainment editor, Bill is responsible for planning, writing and delegating content for the award-winning paper's Living It section. As a photojournalist, Bill shoots nightlife, concerts, book-signings and other entertainment-related events. In addition, he shoots photographs for new stories. In his capacity as general assignment reporter, he writes community, soft and hard news stories.

Bill has won local, national, individual and collective awards during his nearly ten-year tenure at *The St. Louis American*. His success as a journalist has won him spots on local radio stations.

Bill grew up in the inner city of North St. Louis and attended Sumner High School. During high school, an assignment to write a short story introduced Bill to his gift of creative writing. Without higher formal education, he taught himself to write. With friends he wrote scripts, directed and stage-managed four sketch comedy shows. A year later, he won a six-month, entry-level creative writing program job at D'Arcy ad agency.

WHO'S *Who*

MEDIA PROFESSIONALS

Pamela L. Bolden
Director, Marketing & Public Relations
YWCA Metro St. Louis

Pamela L. Bolden, a public relations professional, has practiced her craft in the nonprofit sector for more than 15 years. She is currently director of marketing and public relations for the YWCA Metro St. Louis. She has successfully increased the visibility and value of other large organizations that also have national brand affiliations, from the Urban League of Metropolitan St. Louis to the United Way of Greater St. Louis. Pamela was also a profile writer/contributor for the third edition of *Who's Who In Black St. Louis*®.

Her experiences include project management, media relations, special events and brand management. During her Urban League tenure, Pamela established the popular "Summer Sojourns."

Pamela earned a communications degree from Illinois State University. She is a member of the Public Relations Society of America and the Greater St. Louis Association of Black Journalists, where she has held numerous positions, including president. Pamela is a lifelong member of Mt. Zion Missionary Baptist Church in East St. Louis, Illinois, where she sings with the Voices of Zion and provides public relations for many church activities.

Wendi Brown
Morning Show Producer/Co-Host
WHHL Hot 104.1

Wendi Brown is the morning show producer/co-host for *Craig Blac & The Hot Morning Show*. Her responsibilities include booking guests for the show, generating publicity, daily preparation of the show, reviewing proposals and assisting the program director.

Brown is originally from Prince George's County, Maryland and spent two years studying abroad in Bolivia and Venezuela. Upon her return, she attended Clark Atlanta University in Atlanta, Georgia with a focus in international studies.

Her career in radio began in Columbus, Ohio with a privately-owned radio station, Z103.1, and quickly transitioned to a larger arena with Radio One. Brown's meteoric rise in radio is due largely in part to her superior radio skills.

She is single and has no children.

MEDIA PROFESSIONALS

Elliott Davis
Anchor
KTVI FOX 2

Elliott Davis has distinguished himself as the investigative reporter for FOX 2's *You Paid For It.* The popular ongoing investigations look into government waste in the St. Louis area. Elliott has questioned officials from mayors to governors in search for answers. He also co-anchors evening newscasts on FOX 2 News on Fridays and Saturdays. His diverse career path led him to FOX 2 in May of 1980, when he joined FOX 2 News as a weekend writer and editor. Previously, Elliott worked in advertising for the *Suburban Journal* newspaper.

Elliott's *You Paid For It* series has made him a champion of the underdog in the area. His hard-hitting investigations have made him a lightning rod of controversy in the St. Louis area's political and bureaucratic arena.

Elliott won an Emmy Award in 2002 for Best Investigative Report, and the St. Louis Black Journalism awards for Best Television Series in 2001, 2002 and 2003. He is a past winner of the Illinois Broadcasters Award and the National Association of Black Journalists award for Best Television Series.

Howard D. Denson
Publisher & Chief Executive Officer
St. Louis Black Pages

Howard D. Denson is publisher and chief executive officer of the *St. Louis Black Pages*, an annual empowerment magazine and business directory that has served the St. Louis African-American community for 18 years.

An honors graduate of Hampton University and Harvard Business School, Howard is an advocate for children and is resolute in his community service. He is a founder of RESPOND, Inc., which recruits and supports adoptive and foster care families in the St. Louis community. He is involved in urban educational reform initiatives and serves on many boards.

Howard has received numerous awards including the National Adoption Advocate Award from the North American Council on Adoptable Children; the Annie M. Pope Turnbo Malone Award from Annie Malone Children's and Family Services Center; the Achievement Award for Contributions to Business Development from Better Family Life, Inc.; and, with his wife, the Salute to Excellence in Education Stellar Performer Award from the St. Louis American Foundation.

Howard and his wife, Vickie, are exceptionally proud of their daughters, Yolanda, Adrienne and Kimberly; their son-in-law, Christopher Lehman; and their granddaughter, Imani.

Vickie Mathis Denson is president of *St. Louis Black Pages*, an annual empowerment magazine and business directory that has served the St. Louis African-American community for 18 years.

An honors graduate of Herbert H. Lehman College, Vickie has an indefatigable commitment to volunteer service. She is a founder and board president of RESPOND, Inc., which recruits and supports adoptive and foster care families. She is board vice president and housing committee member of Congregations/Offender Partnership Enterprise, Inc., which mentors, houses and aids ex-offenders upon their re-entry into society.

Vickie is president of the Blackberry Hill Neighborhood Association, and the Washington Metropolitan AME Zion Church deaconess board. She chairs the church's nursery ministry.

Vickie is a recipient of the prestigious National Adoption Advocate Award from the North American Council on Adoptable Children. She, with her husband, received the Salute to Excellence in Education Stellar Performer Award from the St. Louis American Foundation.

Vickie and her husband, Howard, are the proud parents of Kimberly, Adrienne and Yolanda. They have one son-in-law, Christopher Lehman, and one granddaughter, Imani.

Vickie M. Denson
President
St. Louis Black Pages

Ruth Ezell is a producer for *Living St. Louis*, an Emmy Award-winning magazine show on St. Louis' public television station. Her feature stories take viewers across the region, providing insightful perspectives on the people and places that define St. Louis area culture.

Ruth is also co-host of the Saturday edition of *Total Information AM* on radio powerhouse KMOX. Over the course of her career, she has worked at several Midwest radio and television stations as a reporter, producer, and anchor.

Ruth attended Olivet College, the University of San Francisco, and the University College of Washington University.

A native of Detroit, Michigan, Ruth's father, Dr. William Ezell (now deceased) was the first minority to be licensed in the state as a veterinarian, and was a former chairman of Michigan's Veterinary Medical Board of Examiners.

Ruth Ezell
Producer
KETC-TV

MEDIA PROFESSIONALS

Marilyn Reece Parker
Editor & Publisher
Sparkman Your Christian
Classified Publication

Marilyn Reece Parker is the editor and publisher of *Sparkman Your Christian Classified Publication*, the leading Christian publication in the region. She and her mother, Dr. Bessie L. Reece, own the publication, named in honor of Marilyn's grandmother, the late Ida M. Sparkman.

The company offers the Sparkman Lecture Series, "How to Succeed on Your Job According to Biblical Principles," which began in 2004. This series presents a unique job maintenance program for the community.

Before beginning her career in media, Marilyn was employed with Washington University in St. Louis. She worked at *Limelight* newspaper, the *St. Louis Sentinel* and the *North Star Magazine*.

Marilyn is a member of Greater Faith Missionary Baptist Church, where she serves as a licensed minister and a community outreach servant leader whose focus is on employment.

Marilyn and her husband, Larry, have three children. LaTaunia Scott, son-in-law Andrew and Larry Jr. reside in St. Louis, and MaDonna Young and son-in-law Toney live in South Dakota. Marilyn has two grandchildren, Amal Parker-Scott and Toney Akeem Young Jr.

Rev. Yvonne Samuel
Education Reporter
St. Louis Post-Dispatch

Rev. Yvonne Samuel is a 28-year veteran news reporter for the *St. Louis Post-Dispatch*. During her tenure, she has written numerous news and feature articles on housing, education, religion, politics, social issues and African Americans. For several years, Samuel worked as the community outreach coordinator for the *Post-Dispatch* newsroom, a job she created. In this capacity, she wrote a column and coordinated neighborhood community forums and community discussions with international journalists. As a change agent and diversity trainer for the *Post-Dispatch*, she designed and facilitated two-day diversity awareness sessions for 1,500 *Post-Dispatch* employees. On the academic level, Samuel is an adjunct professor of English for St. Louis Community College at Forest Park.

She holds a master of divinity degree from Union Theological Seminary of New York and a bachelor of journalism degree from the School of Journalism at the University of Missouri-Columbia. She has served as senior pastor of five churches and has won numerous awards and fellowships throughout her distinguished career.

Samuel is single and lives in University City. Her motto is: Preaching, Teaching, Reaching, Communicating.

WHO'S *Who*

St. Louis'
MEDIA PROFESSIONALS

Robin Smith
Anchor & Reporter
KMOV Channel 4

Robin Smith is an Emmy Award-winning news anchor and reporter at the St. Louis CBS affiliate, KMOV Channel 4.

Smith has received numerous awards for her work. In 2000 she was inducted into the Hall of Fame by the Greater St. Louis Association of Black Journalists. Alpha Kappa Alpha Sorority, Inc., Gamma Omega Chapter presented her with the Diamond Achiever Award in television media. In 1981 she won an Emmy Award for her coverage of the "First Day of Desegregation" and in 1978 she received the Outstanding Young Woman of the Year award from the National Association of Colored Women's Clubs, Inc.

Since 1988, Smith has hosted the Variety Club telethon for physically disabled children and the United Negro College Fund telethon since 1986. She is a spokesperson for A World of Difference, a religious, ethnic and cultural prejudice reduction campaign of the Anti-Defamation League.

Smith makes numerous appearances in the community to make St. Louis a better place to live. She earned a bachelor's degree from Lindenwood University and an executive master's degree in international business from Saint Louis University.

Lou Thimes, J.R.
Radio Personality
1490 WESL

Lou Thimes, J.R., better known as "The Real J.R.," can be heard every weekday afternoon on 1490 WESL on *The Real Afternoon Show*. For 25 years, J.R. has become a mainstay in St. Louis radio. His trademark cowboy hat and boots have become just as popular as J.R. himself.

He was first introduced to television and radio as the anchor of his school's news broadcast at Cupples Elementary School. From there, he went on to Sumner High School, where he was the official master of ceremonies at nearly every school event as well as the deejay for any and every school dance. J.R. went on to become the first African-American announcer at KBCT in Newton, Kansas.

J.R. had early exposure to personality radio in St. Louis under the guidance of his still ever-so-popular father, the legendary "Lou Fatha Thimes." His career has taken him from Baltimore to Wichita, Peoria, Los Angeles, St. Louis and beyond. He has been a television news anchor/reporter, done television commercials and still enjoys his work today as much as or more than his beginning.

MEDIA PROFESSIONALS

Dianne White
Special Assistant to the Mayor
City of St. Louis

Currently the special assistant to Mayor Francis Slay, Dianne White is known as a pioneer in breaking down racial barriers in St. Louis. She was the first African-American model in major St. Louis department stores, including Stix-Baer & Fuller and Saks Fifth Avenue. In 1962 Dianne became the first African-American weathercaster in the nation at NBC affiliate Channel 5.

As a 40-year veteran of St. Louis television and radio, she has demonstrated wide-ranging skills in reporting, anchoring, producing, writing and public speaking. Dianne's career at KSDK-TV spanned more than 26 years, from features to hard news. She has received many honors including Woman of the Year, the St. Louis Black Journalism Hall of Fame, the St. Louis NATAS Silver Circle and numerous others.

Dianne freely gives of her time to many community projects and has opened 11 Dianne White Girls Clubs throughout the city. Until April of 2002, she could be seen on Charter Communications' weekly television program *Shades of Success*.

Dianne is also a proud mother of one son, Chip, and is an archeology and history teacher.

St. Louis'

ACADEMIA

"To know nothing is bad...To learn nothing is worse."

African Proverb

ACADEMIA

Andrew Bailey
Educator
East St. Louis School District 189

Andrew Bailey is a special education teacher in East St. Louis School District 189. He has taught in several elementary grade levels from second through fifth, participated in an annual MECCA summer school program and worked in the gifted program in the district. Bailey served in the Church of God in Christ as Sunday school teacher, district superintendent, and in the national church as sectional leader during the National Convocation.

Bailey is a life member of Omega Psi Phi Fraternity, Inc. In this organization, he received the 2000 Man of the Year Award and the Stanley Douglas Editors Award.

Andrew has received the Homer Randolph Community Involvement Award from Alpha Phi Alpha Fraternity, Inc., and was selected by Iota Phi Lamba Sorority, Inc. to receive the 2004 Distinguished Service Award. He received the Dedicated Service Award from the American Red Cross.

Andrew earned an undergraduate degree in elementary education and special education from Southern Illinois University Edwardsville. In addition, he was awarded a master's degree in elementary education and completed the education administrative program.

Luke Bobo
Assistant Dean for Training Ministries
Covenant Theological Seminary

As assistant dean for training ministries at Covenant Theological Seminary, Luke Bobo provides oversight for the Francis Schaeffer Institute, the Youth in Ministry Institute, and field education for two degreed programs. Luke is also an adjunct professor at Lindenwood University.

An ordained associate minister at First Baptist Church of Chesterfield, Luke teaches, preaches, facilitates workshops, provides premarital counseling and substitutes for the pastor.

Luke has published articles on topics including technology, obesity, bioethics, stem cell research and rap music. He and his daughter, Briana, traveled to Cape Town, South Africa, where he lectured at the University of Cape Town and preached at area churches. Luke also helped lead an educational tour through Europe. He enjoys volunteering with several nonprofit organizations.

Luke earned a bachelor's degree in electrical engineering from the University of Kansas, a master's degree in electrical/computer engineering from the University of Missouri-Columbia, and a master of divinity degree from Covenant. He is pursuing a doctorate in adult education from the University of Missouri-St. Louis.

Luke and his wife, Rita, are the proud parents of Briana and Caleb.

Stephanie Clintonia Boddie is an assistant professor at the Warren Brown School of Social Work at Washington University in St. Louis and the African and African-American studies program. She is a faculty associate at the Center for Social Development and Center on Urban Research and Public Policy. She is a senior fellow at Rouse & Hoyt Urban Revitalizers and at the University of Pennsylvania's program for research on religion and urban civil society, and the program for religion and social policy research.

Stephanie is co-author of *The Newer Deal, The Invisible Caring Hand, The Other Philadelphia Story, Way to Give* and 30 other publications. She is currently lead investigator of the black churches component of the Mapping the Du Bois Philadelphia Negro Project. In 2005 she received the Association for Community Organization and Social Administration's emerging scholar award for her scholarship on black congregations, community development and asset building.

Stephanie received her bachelor's degree from Johns Hopkins University, and a master's degree and doctorate from the University of Pennsylvania.

A native of Baltimore, Maryland Stephanie loves music, art and African violets.

Stephanie Clintonia Boddie
Assistant Professor
Washington University in St. Louis

Dr. Thomas B. Cason has served as principal of Soldan International Studies High School for seven years. During this time, there has been an improvement in test scores, attendance rate and graduation rate.

A recipient of the 2004 Ambassadors in Education Principal Leadership Award, Cason was one of ten principals in the U.S. recognized by the MetLife Foundation and Nation Civic League. The Urban League of Metropolitan St. Louis and the National Council of Negro Women have also recognized him.

Cason presides on the University of Missouri-Columbia governing board and the University of Missouri Operations Council for Educational Renewal Partnership. He is a senior partner with The Principals' Partnership of Union Pacific Railroad.

Cason received his bachelor of science and master of science degrees from Southern Illinois University at Edwardsville. He obtained his educational specialist and doctor of education degree from Saint Louis University.

A native of East St. Louis, Cason has one daughter, Tania, and two sons, Ryan and Derron. He is a member of Pi Lamda Theta International Honor Society and Kappa Alpha Psi Fraternity, Inc.

Thomas B. Cason
Principal
Soldan International
Studies High School
St. Louis Public Schools System

ACADEMIA

Renee M. Cunningham-Williams, Ph.D.
Visiting Associate Professor
Brown School of Social Work
Washington University in St. Louis

Dr. Renee Cunningham-Williams is a visiting associate professor of social work at Washington University in St. Louis. Formerly, she served on the medical school faculty for nearly 12 years. She conducts research in health/mental health disparities, disordered gambling and addictions.

Renee's research is published in scientific journals with international readership. An award-winning NIH-funded researcher, she has been recognized by the Society for Addiction Medicine, the American Psychopathological Association and National Public Radio. A member of Alpha Kappa Alpha Sorority, Inc. she is on the board of Provident.

Before the age of 30, Renee earned a bachelor of social work degree from Howard University, master's and doctoral degrees from the Brown School at Washington University, and a master's degree in psychiatric epidemiology and biostatistics from the Washington University in St. Louis School of Medicine, where she completed post-doctoral training.

A Cardinal Ritter College Prep alumna and former Blumeyer Housing project resident, Renee's accomplishments are testaments that "through God, all things are possible." Renee is married to Benjamin E. Williams Jr. and is the proud mother of Benjamin III and Courtney Danielle.

Alexander Harris Jr., O.D.
Director of Externships
University of Missouri-St. Louis
College of Optometry

Dr. Alexander Harris Jr. is director of externships, a clinical assistant professor and minority affairs advisor at the University of Missouri-St. Louis College of Optometry. In his administrative role, he places and monitors externs at hospitals, clinics and private optometric offices in the U.S. and abroad. He sees limited private patients at Overland Eyecare Associates.

Harris was the first African-American president of the St. Louis Optometric Society, and received *The St. Louis American*'s Salute to Excellence in Education. He is also a recipient of the University of Evansville African-American Alumni's Apex Award for community service.

Harris holds a bachelor's degree from the University of Evansville in Indiana, a master's degree from Washington University in St. Louis, and a doctor of optometry degree from the University of Missouri-t. Louis.

A St. Louis native, Harris graduated from Beaumont High School. He was formerly married to Lisa Harris and they have two children, Carmen and Damon.

D r. John Ingram is an affiliate associate professor in the division of educational leadership and policy studies at the University of Missouri-St. Louis. He teaches graduate level classes to master's, specialist and doctoral candidates. He also serves as co-director of the Career Transition Certification Program.

Previously, Ingram worked in the St. Louis Public Schools for 39 years, holding a variety of positions including teacher, principal, assistant superintendent and associate superintendent.

A product of St. Louis Public Schools, Ingram graduated from Vashon High School and Harris Teachers College. He is a member of the Vashon Hall of Fame and is a Harris-Stowe State University Distinguished Alumni. Ingram received his master's degree, specialist certificate and doctorate from the University of Wisconsin-Madison.

Ingram is a member of Washington Tabernacle Baptist Church and a life member of Kappa Alpha Psi Fraternity, Inc.

A native of St. Louis, he is married to Irma J. Agnew Ingram and is the proud father of three children, Lamont, Scott and Catherine. Ingram has one son-in-law, Nigel Graham, and one grandson, Darren.

Dr. John Ingram
Affiliate Associate Professor
University of Missouri-St. Louis

G ina Washington is currently the vice principal at the Construction Careers Center charter high school in St. Louis. She has been with the school since it first opened and is responsible for all student activities. Gina also assists in managing teachers and is responsible in assisting in the everyday operations of the school. She has a passion for youth ministry.

Gina has been recognized by *Who's Who Among America's Teachers*. She received her bachelor of science degree in education at Lincoln University in Jefferson City, Missouri, and her master's degree in secondary administration from the University of Missouri-St. Louis. She has experience teaching at Gateway Christian High School and as an adjunct faculty member at Harris-Stowe State University. She is a member of Delta Sigma Theta Sorority, Inc.

Gina lives in O'Fallon, Illinois and has one daughter, Vivian Faith. She has been married to her husband, Don Washington, for 11 years.

Gina Washington
Vice Principal
Construction Careers Center

St. Louis'

ACADEMIA

Ann Chism Williams, Ph.D.
Dean of Students
East St. Louis District 189

Ann Chism Williams, Ph.D., dean of students in East St. Louis School District 189, is a tireless volunteer in her community. She was recently appointed by the mayor and aldermanic council of Creve Coeur to serve on the historical preservation committee. She has also served on the park board and as a commissioner of the ethics board.

Ann completed the Women in Leadership training program by the Coro Foundation and is a past president of the Pi Lambda Theta honor and professional association at Saint Louis University. In 2004 Mayor Francis Slay and the Board of Aldermen presented a resolution to recognize and honor Ann as a distinguished member of the community.

A member of Alpha Kappa Alpha Sorority, Inc., Ann is committed to scholarship, volunteerism and community service.

Ann received a bachelor of science degree in English from Tuskegee University, a master of science degree in special education from Southern Illinois University and a doctor of philosophy degree in educational psychology from Saint Louis University.

Ann is the wife of Hiram Williams.

Renee Thomas Woods
Communications Instructor
St. Louis Community College

Renee Thomas Woods is a communications instructor at St. Louis Community College at Florissant Valley. She also taught at the school's Forest Park campus and at Saint Louis University.

Prior to teaching at the collegiate level, Woods founded a business, Communiqué Public Relations. She worked in public relations with AT&T and Lucent Technologies in Murray Hill, New Jersey and Chicago, Illinois.

Woods currently serves on the board of directors for the Annie Malone Children and Family Service Center, as well as the marketing committees for the St. Louis African Arts Festival and the Joe Torry "Giving Back the Love" Foundation.

Woods received a bachelor's degree from the Missouri School of Journalism and a master's degree from Saint Louis University. Woods and her husband, Henry, have four children.

40% of allocated dollars
$19.8 million
26% of 400 volunteers

The numbers speak for themselves: Charmaine's legacy of leadership and giving continues—stronger than ever.

The Charmaine Chapman Society is the premier philanthropic organization for African Americans in the St. Louis metropolitan area. The Society recognizes African Americans who contribute $1,000 or more to the annual United Way of Greater St. Louis campaign, which helps support 200 health and human service agencies in 16 Missouri and Illinois counties. Members of the Charmaine Chapman Society gain a significant return on investment:

In 2006, United Way will invest more than **40% of allocated dollars**—approximately **$19.8 million**—to agencies that primarily serve African Americans. What's more, African Americans comprise **26% of the more than 400 volunteers** who decide how contributions are disbursed. For additional information or to become a member, please call 314.539.4191, e-mail ccs@stl.unitedway.org or visit PledgeUnitedWay.org.

charmaine chapman
society

african american leadership giving

United Way
of Greater St. Louis

PledgeUnitedWay.org

Anheuser-Busch, Inc
Partnering A Global Community

A diversified international corporation whose primary products are beer, beer packaging and family entertainment parks, Anheuser-Busch produces the Budweiser label of beverages, and its subsidiaries include Metal Container Corporation and Busch Entertainment Corporation, which operates nine theme parks in the United States.

At Anheuser-Busch, we take our role as a corporate citizen seriously. Whether it is through supporting community groups across the U.S., protecting the environment, observing the highest ethical standards in all our business dealings, a commitment to diversity in our hiring, or promoting the responsible use of our products by adults, Anheuser-Busch has always believed that doing good by the public and doing well as a company go hand-in-hand.

Anheuser-Busch Is Not Just In The Community, We Are Of The Community

For more than 100 years, Anheuser-Busch has partnered with local and community organizations to address community issues and celebrate the significant contributions African-Americans have made across the nation and throughout the world. We accomplish this through philanthropic and programmatic efforts that include promoting education, economic development, youth initiatives and health and wellness. In fact, Anheuser-Busch has provided a legacy of leadership in these areas for most of the company's history.

Education

Anheuser-Busch has long supported education as the single best way to create opportunity for all. By investing in education, we hope to improve the outlook for individuals within our communities, while also strengthening the fabric of our communities as a whole. Of course, no one can accomplish these goals acting alone. That's why Anheuser-Busch works in partnership with local organizations across America to help increase access to educational opportunities - because these partner organizations are often in the best position to understand and serve local needs. We are proud of what we've accomplished over the decades helping raise more than $175 million to support educational opportunity at the nation's historically black colleges and universities, to our own Budweiser Urban Scholarship Program, which provides scholarship funds to community partners to enable individuals to pursue their higher education goals.

Economic Development

It is a part of Anheuser-Busch's operating philosophy that doing business with minority- and women-owned business is good business. Through our Partners in Economic Progress Program, Anheuser-Busch and it's subsidiaries have been able to significantly increase the number of minority and women supplier we purchase goods and services from, as well as the volume of those goods and services purchased.

By providing opportunities for these companies to develop into stronger business enterprises, Anheuser-Busch contributes to the economic development of communities across the country. Partners In Economic Progress reflects our belief that positive benefits can accrue for businesses that participate, which today numbers at more than 9,000 vendors and more than $309 million annually in business conducted with these firms.

St. Louis'

COMMUNITY LEADERS

"When the water starts boiling it's foolish to turn off the heat."

NELSON MANDELA

STATESMAN AND CIVIL RIGHTS ACTIVIST

SPONSORED BY

Anheuser-Busch, Inc.

ONE OF THE ANHEUSER-BUSCH COMPANIES

Malik Ahmed
President & Chief Executive Officer
Better Family Life, Inc.

Malik Ahmed is the national president and chief executive officer of Better Family Life, Inc. (BFL), a community development organization he founded in 1983. Headquartered in St. Louis, BFL has more than 70 employees and an annual budget exceeding $5 million.

A native of New York City, Ahmed holds a bachelor's degree in economics from Herbert H. Lehman College and a master's degree in public administration/policy analysis from Southern Illinois University. He spent three years working as an urban planner in Mali as a Peace Corps volunteer.

Ahmed is the recipient of numerous awards, including the Notable Award from Neighborhoods, USA. Under his direction, BFL has received awards for community service and local government.

On June 29, 2005, BFL became the owner of the historic Emerson School building on Page Boulevard. Ahmed is spearheading a campaign for a $4.5 million renovation of Emerson School to convert it into the Better Family Life Cultural Center and Museum.

Ahmed is committed to rebuilding St. Louis' West End community and the exaltation of the African-American community and preservation of its culture.

Gerald S. Brooks
Director of Marketing &
Public Relations
St. Louis Public Library

Gerald S. Brooks is the director of marketing and public relations for the St. Louis Public Library. In this capacity, he oversees the day-to-day operations of the marketing department and supervises all aspects of the library's public relations, media relations, and community relations.

Active in the St. Louis community for the last three decades, Gerald serves on a number of boards and committees. His memberships include the 100 Black Men of Metropolitan St. Louis and the Missouri Library Association. In 1999, he was appointed to the Missouri Library Marketing Task Force, and in 2001, he was chosen as a member of the Missouri Legislative Committee for Libraries.

For his community efforts, Gerald has been honored with many awards from various organizations. He is also profiled in best-selling author Gail Sheehy's book, *Understanding Men's Passages*, and is a contributing author to *Missouri Libraries: Your Lifetime Connection*, a marketing manual for Missouri library staff and trustees.

Gerald holds a bachelor's degree in business administration from Tarkio College and resides in St. Louis with his wife, Estella. They have two daughters, Lisa and Latonya.

Stephanie Brown is assistant deputy chief U.S. probation officer for the U.S. Probation Office, Eastern District of Missouri. In this administrative position, she manages more than 80 employees. Her primary focus is the expeditious handling of investigative work for the courts, institutions, parole authorities and other agencies. She is also responsible for the operations of the satellite office in Cape Girardeau, Missouri.

Stephanie is a member of the American Correction Association, the Association of Women Executives in Corrections and the Federal Probation Officer Association. She is a board member with the National Organization of Black Law Enforcement Executives. She is also a member of Alpha Kappa Alpha Sorority, Inc.

Stephanie received a bachelor of science degree in corrections from Illinois State University in Normal, Illinois, and a master of science degree in criminal justice administration from the University of California at Long Beach. She is a graduate of the Federal Judiciary Leadership Development Program and Coro's Women in Leadership program.

Stephanie is the proud mother of one daughter, Sydney.

Stephanie Brown
Assistant Deputy Chief
Probation Officer
U.S. Probation Office
Eastern District of Missouri

Alicia Buck, outreach and early awareness regional coordinator for the Missouri Department of Higher Education, is responsible for implementation of the Gaining Early Awareness & Readiness for Undergraduate Programs (GEAR UP) grant.

GEAR UP is a federal grant with the objective of devising interventions to engage, educate, motivate and propel middle and high school students toward higher education options. Alicia strengthens the team that supports this effort, comprised of district administration, academic teams, parents, and community and higher education partnerships. She also provides leadership within the St. Louis Public School District, impacting more than 2,500 students. She is dedicated to exposing and directing people to life sustaining opportunities.

Alicia earned her undergraduate degree from the University of Missouri St. Louis and is currently pursuing a master of education degree. She has volunteered with several social service organizations that offer assistance and support to families and children in crisis. She was featured in the *St. Louis Post Dispatch* and on Channel 9 community awareness programs for related human service issues. Alicia's passion is spending time with family and skating.

Alicia D. Buck
Outreach & Early
Awareness Specialist
Missouri Department of
Higher Education

Tara Leigh Buckner
Executive Director
Greater St. Louis Regional
Empowerment Zone

Tara Buckner is the executive director of the Greater St. Louis Regional Empowerment Zone. She directs management of a multimillion-dollar HUD grant, which supports business and community development projects in St. Louis City and County, Missouri, and East St. Louis and Centreville, Illinois. An urban planner, Tara has worked on a variety of planning issues in Detroit, Minneapolis and St. Louis. She is a member of the American Institute of Certified Planners and serves on the executive board of the St. Louis section of the American Planning Association.

Tara is a volunteer for the United Way and the Girl Scouts of America, and is active in Jack and Jill of America, Inc. She is a member of Alpha Kappa Alpha Sorority, Inc., and a life member of the National Alumni Association of Spelman College. She also belongs to Pilgrim Congregational UCC.

Tara holds a bachelor of arts degree from Spelman College and a master of public administration from Wayne State University.

Born in Kansas and raised in Minnesota, Tara is married and the mother of two daughters.

James R. Clark
Vice President
Community Outreach
Better Family Life, Inc.

James Clark is the vice president of community outreach for Better Family Life, Inc. (BLF). In this capacity Clark oversees BFL's magazine, *Under the Arch*, Neighborhood Alliance and Beyond the Walls. He also oversees recruitment for the MET Center, the region's premiere job training center located in Wellston.

Additionally, Clark coordinates one of the largest festivals in the metropolitan area. Family Week is BFL's weeklong celebration of family. Taking place during the summer, Family Week consists of activities, workshops and lectures targeting the family. A traditional component of Family Week is the Who's Who in Black St. Louis Celebrity Softball Classic.

As a consultant, Clark has coordinated some of the areas most effective political and outreach campaigns. He is the husband of PeChaz Clark, chief executive officer of Ultimate Aerobics, and has two children, Leo Adams of the Show Me Squad and LeNetria Adams, a junior at Cardinal Ritter College Prep.

George Cotton Sr. is the executive director of REACH St. Louis, a St. Louis-based HIV/AIDS advocacy, education and testing center. He is also a nationally recognized motivational speaker, lecturer, trainer and owner of George R. Cotton, Sr. & Associates, Inc. Additionally, he serves as an adjunct instructor of political science and communications at Lakes College in Illinois. With more than 15 years of experience as a community activist, program director and business owner, Cotton has lectured and trained more than 10,000 participants through his workshops and seminars.

Cotton is the former two-term president of the board of education in University City. He also served as a member of University City's City Council.

His accomplishments include serving as editor and chief of *A-MAGAZINE*, executive director of the Greater East St. Louis Community Fund and facilitator of professional development for the St. Louis Public Schools.

Cotton holds a master's degree in political science and a bachelor's degree in fine arts from Arkansas State University.

He is married and the father of two sons and one daughter.

George R. Cotton Sr.
Executive Director
REACH St. Louis, Inc.

Joycelyn Farmer is the cultural health initiatives director for the American Heart Association, St. Louis division of the Heartland Affiliate. In this position, she strives to establish priorities and strategies to educate and motivate minority populations to reduce heart disease and stroke disparities. She uses programs, messaging, media, advocacy and partnerships that reach out to and empower underserved communities to live healthier lifestyles.

Joycelyn has been recognized for her dedication and outstanding community involvement. She was awarded the American Heart Association's Achievement Award in 2004 and 2006. She is also the 2006 recipient of the Heartland Affiliate Program Integration Award of the Year.

A native of South Carolina, Joycelyn earned her bachelor of science degree from South Carolina State University. She is the wife of Lieutenant Colonel Samuel Farmer Jr. and the proud mother of one son, Daryl. Her hobbies are attending Daryl's soccer games, reading and volunteering. Her favorite book is *I Know Why the Caged Bird Sings* by Maya Angelou.

Joycelyn Farmer
Cultural Health Initiatives Director
American Heart Association

COMMUNITY LEADERS

Sponsored By Anheuser-Busch, Inc.
ONE OF THE ANHEUSER-BUSCH COMPANIES

Alan K. Green
Executive Assistant
Highways & Traffic & Public Works
St. Louis County

Alan K. Green is the executive assistant for St. Louis County's Highways and Traffic and Public Works Department. He represents programs, policies and issues to the other departments in county government, outside agencies and individuals to implement the policies and procedures of the department.

Alan has received awards and recognition from the U.S. Attorney for the Eastern District, the White House, Zeta Phi Beta Sorority, Inc., the Black Child Development Institute, the CBS *Sunday Morning* show, *The Wall Street Journal*, the *St. Louis Post-Dispatch* and many other organizations.

Alan earned a bachelor of science degree in criminal justice with a minor in American diplomacy from the University of Texas at Tyler. He holds a master of management and development of human resoureces degree from National Louis University, and a master of business administration degree from Lindenwood University. He also attended the St. Louis Metropolitan Police Academy and the American Express Financial Advisors Leadership Academy.

A native of Michigan, Alan is married to Toni Green and they have four children, Tiffany, Alan Jr., Garrett and Trevor.

© ROSCOE CRENSHAW

Jerome "Scrooge"
Michael Harris
Director
Institute for the Advancement of
Jazz Study and Performance

In September of 2005, Jerome "Scrooge" Michael Harris' dream became a reality with the Institute for the Advancement of Jazz Study and Performance. The Institute is under the direction of Jerome, a world-class percussionist and bassist with more than 30 years of musical experience. Located at the Community Women Against Hardship Family Support Center, the Institute is an innovative, after-school music and education mentoring program intended to elevate the self-discipline and self-esteem of its students.

Jerome's musical career includes membership in the Black Artists' Group; service as an adjunct faculty member at Webster University; and scintillating performances as an ensemble player with numerous local, national and international artists. He excels as both a leader and sideman, and sustains a remarkable synergy with arresting vocalists and exciting instrumentalists alike in a variety of formats.

Under his direction, the Institute serves as an important cultural and educational resource in the community, providing invaluable experience for area youth.

James Ingram is the program manager for Provident Counseling's Shreve Neighborhood Center, an after-school/summer program in North St. Louis. The program provides tutoring, teen pregnancy prevention and gang abatement programming for youth participants between the ages of six and 18.

James is a columnist for *The St. Louis American* and *InBox Magazine*. He is a former press secretary to East St. Louis Mayor Carl E. Officer, and has served as a radio talk show host for stations KWK and WESL, and a panelist on KETC-TV's *Spectrum*.

James has worked on the mayoral campaigns of East St. Louis Mayor Carl Officer, the Illinois gubernatorial campaigns of Roland Burris, and the presidential campaign of the Reverend Jesse L. Jackson.

An alumnus of Boston University's College of Engineering, James holds a master's degree in communications management from Hamilton University. He completed post-graduate work at the Harvard University Graduate School of Education, where he completed the Bill and Melinda Gates Foundation Learning Lab and Change Leadership Program.

A proud native of East St. Louis, James is the eldest son of James and Phyllis Ingram.

James T. Ingram
Program Manager
Provident Counseling
Shreve Neighborhood Center

Francella Jackson has made significant contributions to her community through her commitment to education, public safety and the criminal justice system. She is the director of community programs for the East St. Louis Police Department.

Jackson coordinates annual vigils to commemorate homicide victims during National Crime Victims' Rights Week, and serves as coordinator of the Click It or Ticket campaign. She received recognition from the U.S. Department of Justice and the U.S. Attorney's Office for the Southern District of Illinois for her outstanding work. She also served as the volunteer coordinator for former President Bill Clinton's visit to East St. Louis.

Jackson's organizational affiliations and educational background are quite extensive. She is involved with Alpha Kappa Alpha Sorority, Inc., the United Way of Illinois auxiliary board of directors and the Community Coalition Against Violence.

A product of East St. Louis School District 189, Jackson is a graduate of Southern Illinois University Edwardsville. She is also a graduate of the University of Missouri-St. Louis Nonprofit Executive Management Program and the CORO Midwestern Center Neighborhood Leaders Program.

Francella D. Jackson
Director of Community Programs
East St. Louis Police Department

Ronald L. Jackson
Assistant Director
Neighborhood Partnership Development
St. Louis for Kids

Ronald L. Jackson is the assistant director of neighborhood partnership development for St. Louis for Kids, an organization that works to increase the number and quality of after-school programs in St. Louis and to raise public awareness and support to improve the well-being of young people. Jackson strives to improve the lives of young people. Previously, he was the executive director of InterACT St. Louis.

In addition, Jackson formerly served as the executive director of the National Conference of Christians and Jews where he developed the Dismantling Racism Institute anti-racism training program.

Jackson serves on the boards of several organizations including the St. Louis Board of Education, Catholic Community Services, the Character Plus advisory committee, the African American Churches in Dialogue, and Vision for Children at Risk. Jackson currently chairs the Black Leadership Roundtable education committee and is co-chair of the St. Louis Children's Agenda.

Jackson is the recipient of numerous awards and honors. He lives with his wife, Hattie, and their three children in the Central West End of St. Louis.

Mildred L. Jamison
Founder & Chief Executive Officer
Faith Village

Mildred Jamison is the founder and chief executive officer of Faith Village, which is comprised of Faith House Center for Child Development, Dream House and Peace Villa. She creates programs and services that assist infants, children, teenagers and seniors in the St. Louis community.

In 1991 Faith House started as a residential facility for newborns and children who have been exposed to drugs and abused. Dream House opened its doors in 2002 as the second home in the country and the first of its kind in the Midwest for homeless adolescents with HIV/AIDS. Peace Villa is a unique independent housing community for low-income seniors in the St. Louis community.

Jamison's commitment is evident in the many awards she has received including the Lifetime Achiever Award from the St. Louis American Foundation; the Spirit of Children Award from the St. Louis Pediatric Society; and the Use Your Life Award from Oprah Winfrey's Angel Network.

Jamison is the proud mother of three sons, Edgar, Daryle and Sean. She likes to spend her free time traveling and reading.

Gloria J. Johnson, Ph.D.
Founder & Executive Director
Life Source Consultants

Dr. Gloria J. Johnson is founder and executive director of Life Source Consultants, the first African-American domestic violence organization in Missouri.

Johnson received a master's degree in biblical counseling and a doctorate in marriage and family counseling from the Evangelical Theological Seminary.

In 2002 she received the Woman of Worth Award from the Older Women's League for developing specialized domestic violence programs for African-American women. She received a Certificate of Recognition for Outstanding Community Leadership in 2004 and 2005 from the St. Louis North County CARES Program.

Johnson served on the board of directors for the Missouri Coalition Against Domestic Violence and the Missouri Coalition Against Sexual Assault. She has also served on the St. Louis County Domestic Violence Council, the Missouri Coalition Against Domestic Violence Women of Color Taskforce and the St. Louis Mayor's Sexual Assault Taskforce. Johnson is a member of the American Association of Christian Counselors, Black African-American Christian Counselors and the National Council of Negro Women.

She is married to Louis and lives in Florissant, Missouri. She has three sons, Anthony, Marvin and André.

Tom Jones is the executive director of the St. Louis Agency on Training and Employment, the city agency charged with administering and coordinating workforce development services for the City of St. Louis.

Tom served as the first director of the Missouri Division of Workforce Development from 1999 to 2001; associate director of the Missouri Department of Social Services responsible for welfare reform from 1997 to 1999; and deputy director with the Missouri Division of Family Services from 1995 to 1997. From 1987 to 1995, Tom served as a principal consultant with the Maryland-based Institute for Human Services Management.

Jones is a graduate of Maryville University in St. Louis. He is also an alumnus of Harvard University's John F. Kennedy School of Government program for senior executives in state and local government.

Jones serves on numerous national and local boards, including the Workforce Development Council of the U.S. Conference of Mayors and the National Association of Workforce Boards.

Tom Jones
Executive Director
St. Louis Agency on
Training and Employment

COMMUNITY LEADERS

Wendell E. Kimbrough
Chief Executive Officer
ARCHS
State of Missouri

Wendell E. Kimbrough serves as chief executive officer of Area Resources for Community and Human Services (ARCHS), the official Greater St. Louis Community Partnership for the State of Missouri.

Kimbrough is the architect of ARCHS' Life-Long Learning partnership model, which advances education as the key to creating a successful personal life and becoming a contributing member of society. ARCHS' partnerships focus on pre-kindergarten, K-12, adult and community education.

Kimbrough is noted for 20 years of for-profit and nonprofit business experience with expertise in business administration, financial and strategic planning, marketing, relationship building, and sales and brand management. He has served as the general manager of several Atlanta and Dallas-based shopping centers and held management and marketing posts with Tropicana Products and Coca-Cola USA. He was the project manager of both the national launch of Cherry Coca-Cola and the Wendy's combo meal program.

Kimbrough serves on community boards and has received numerous leadership awards. A St. Louis native, he has a master's degree from Roosevelt University in Chicago, Illinois and a bachelor's degree from Clark Atlanta University in Atlanta, Georgia.

Ajuma Muhammad
Founder & Executive Director
Association of African American
Role Models

Ajuma Muhammad is founder and executive director of the Association of African American Role Models (AAARM). He is a community activist and a nationwide motivational speaker. A devoted husband and father of four children, he is dedicated to today's youth. His mission is to encourage every adult to "Reach One and Teach One!"

Muhammad is the author of *Understanding the Crisis of the Black Male: A Handbook of Raising Black Boys to be Responsible Black Men.* His most recent project is the AKM model for empowering black males.

Muhammad directs two residential group homes that house 12 at-risk African-American males. As residents, these young men learn the necessary life skills for future independence. A licensed psychotherapist, Muhammad engages the entire family when addressing its need to nurture black males.

Muhammad's extensive travels have taken him throughout Africa, Europe and the Caribbean, allowing him to study the impact that other cultures have made on the African-American male.

His style of motivating black males is highly effective. He is lauded for his tireless efforts in helping African-American males fulfill their dreams.

Victoria E. Nelson is the executive director of Girls Incorporated of St. Louis. Girls Incorporated operates three centers and provides programming at numerous outreach sites located throughout the metropolitan area. They provide daily, structured, educational and cultural programs to girls aged four to 18.

Victoria was selected to receive the Commerce Bankshares and William T. Kemper Foundation Community Service Award. She was recognized by *The St. Louis American* as its 2001 Salute to Excellence Stellar Performer, and by the Missouri Black Expo as an Unsung Hero. She was selected as a distinguished alumna of her alma mater, Washburn University. During her tenure, Girls Incorporated was saluted for creating quality educational opportunities. The organization received Focus St. Louis' What's Right with the Region Award and the Youth Role Model Award from the Martin Luther King Celebration Commission.

In 1975 Victoria received a bachelor of arts degree from Washburn University. In 1977 Washington University in St. Louis School of Medicine awarded her a master's degree in health administration.

A native of St. Louis, Victoria is the proud mother of two daughters, Kathryn and Isabelle.

Victoria E. Nelson
Executive Director
Girls Incorporated of St. Louis

As director of resources for Habitat for Humanity St. Louis, Courtney Pittman is responsible for planning, developing and maintaining a comprehensive, corporate, faith-based community fundraising program. Courtney also coordinates all of the marketing activities, including producing Habitat's news magazine and creating and maintaining the Web site. Additionally, she is responsible for overseeing the coordination of Habitat's hundreds of volunteers and construction site management, through the supervision of the volunteer coordinator and resource associate.

Prior to working for Habitat, Courtney spent more than 18 years in the banking industry, with a focus in community lending and neighborhood development. She gained much of her development experience while working in the St. Louis nonprofit community, serving on various boards of directors.

Courtney considers it an honor and a privilege to serve the nonprofit community and receives much personal gratification from it. She is a Coro Women in Leadership graduate and a member of the Professional Organization of Women.

A native of St. Louis, Courtney is the proud mother of two adult children, Korey and Kacie, who she considers her greatest successes.

Courtney Pittman
Director of Resources
Habitat For Humanity St. Louis

COMMUNITY LEADERS

Sponsored By Anheuser-Busch, Inc.
ONE OF THE ANHEUSER-BUSCH COMPANIES

Jo Ann Rankins-Cannon
Neighborhood Stabilization Officer
Office of the Mayor
City of St. Louis

As a neighborhood stabilization officer, Jo Ann Rankins-Cannon attends neighborhood and ward meetings. She works to build collaborative and positive relationships with the community, neighborhood organizations and police, while serving as a liaison between the mayor's office, city departments and residents.

Jo Ann was honored by the Kwame Foundation and Anheuser-Busch Companies during Women's History Month in 2006. She is vice chair of the Human Development Corporation of Metropolitan St. Louis, a board member of Gateway to Independent Transportation Company and the Horizon/Horizon North Housing Corporation, and a charter member of Friends of Fairground Park.

A native and lifelong resident of St. Louis, Jo Ann is a proud product of the St. Louis Public Schools. She received her bachelor's degree in urban education from Harris-Stowe State University, and her master's degree in human resource development from Webster University.

Jo Ann is the wife of the late Barry W. Cannon. She is a mother of three, grandmother of eight and caretaker of four. Her favorite scripture is Phillippians 4:13: "I can do all things through Christ which strengthens me."

Carolyn D. Seward
Chief Operations Officer
Better Family Life, Inc.

Carolyn has more than 21 years of corporate management and ten years of nonprofit community development experience. In St. Louis, she is recognized for her ability to develop, manage and implement major projects and initiatives in the community. She coordinates, develops and implements performance tools to qualitatively and quantitatively evaluate all programs for the organization. Under her leadership in workforce development, more than 6,000 St. Louis city and county residents receive an array of integrated services.

For 20 years, Carolyn and her family have played a major role in Better Family Life's growth and the purchase of the Cultural Center and Museum. In July of 2006, the Annie E. Casey Foundation named the MET/BFL a Center for Working Families.

Carolyn has a bachelor of arts degree in business administration and economics; a master's degree in management and human resource development from Webster University; and certification in total quality management and facilitation.

A native of Jackson, Tennessee, Carolyn is the wife of Jermal Seward and the proud mother of three children, Jermal II, Daraa' and Makida.

Brother Anthony Shahid is president of the Tauheed Youth Group, an organization dedicated to saving black youth. He has been blessed to help thousands of men and women to leave their drugs and gangs, and become positive, productive black men and women in society. He was instrumental in reducing the crime rate during Mayor Bosley's term with his gang abatement program and job fairs.

Shahid is also very passionate about helping his people to fight discrimination. He has gone up against many Fortune 500 companies with a "no compromise" position and has successfully negotiated the hiring of thousands of black people in management and non-management positions.

A native St. Louisan, Shahid graduated from Soldan High School in 1974 and is a journeyman painter/decorator by trade. He is a loving husband and father of four children.

Shahid is the embodiment of black power and strength in the community.

Anthony Shahid
President
Tauheed Youth Group

Kenneth Sowell is a senior consultant of community development in the child health advocacy and outreach department at St. Louis Children's Hospital, a position he has held since 2001. Ken serves as liaison to the City of St. Louis, St. Louis County and St. Clair County in Illinois for an initiative called Healthy Kids at Play. This initiative provides health-related programming, diagnostic screening and safe play spaces for these areas.

In 1996 Ken received the Mathews-Dickey Boys' and Girls' Club Outstanding Alumni Award and *The St. Louis Sentinel*'s Yes I Can Award. Ken has received numerous awards throughout the St. Louis area for his contribution to the community. He is a member of Kappa Alpha Psi Fraternity, Inc. and the St. Louis-Senegal Sister Cities Committee.

In 1977 Ken earned his bachelor of science degree in speech pathology from Fontbonne University. Before coming to St. Louis Children's Hospital, he was the director of special projects and facility events for the St. Louis Science Center.

A St. Louis native, Ken is married to Monita and has three children, Briana, Monique and Antwain.

Kenneth A. Sowell
Senior Consultant
St. Louis Children's Hospital

© ROSCOE CRENSHAW

Gloria L. Taylor
Founder & Chief Executive Officer
Community Women Against
Hardship, Inc.

Gloria L. Taylor is founder and chief executive officer of Community Women Against Hardship, Inc. Her responsibilities include soliciting funding and in-kind donations, attending onsite and offsite meetings, scheduling and overseeing various community education programs, and networking with organizations that share common objectives. She also solves a wide range of problems, staffs and recruits interns, schedules annual fundraisers, completes long-range strategic planning interface, and engages in hands-on involvement in manual tasks.

Gloria is a recipient of many awards including the YMCA Human Dignity Award, the Unsung Heroine Award from the Top Ladies of Distinction, the OWL Woman of Worth Award, the Dorothy Height Leadership Award, and the 2006 *Traditional Home* magazine Classic Woman Award.

A St. Louis native, Gloria is a member of St. Alphonsus "Rock" Catholic Church. She is an avid jazz lover.

Gloria has four grown children, King Jr., Jeffrey, Cynthia and Stephanie, who continue the family legacy of humanitarianism through their active support of the organization.

Reginald Williams
Director of Community Policy &
Bridges Across Racial Polarization®
FOCUS St. Louis

Reggie Williams is the director of policy and of the Bridges Across Racial Polarization® program at FOCUS St. Louis. With more than 16 years of nonprofit experience, Reggie excels as a program manager, facilitator, trainer, curriculum designer, administrator and communicator.

Most recently, Reggie served as the community programs manager at the Coro Leadership Center-St. Louis. He also served as program director for the National Conference for Community and Justice and co-facilitator in the Cultural Leadership parent program.

Reggie has received many professional honors and awards including a What's Right With The Region! award in 2004. It honored the Dismantling Racism Institute for Educators, a program Reggie directed during his tenure at NCCJ. In 2002 Reggie received the NCCJ's Excellence in Leadership Award.

Reggie holds a master's degree in management from Fontbonne University and an undergraduate degree in theater and communications from Drury University. He is an adjunct professor at Webster University.

Reggie is married to Kwamina and has three sons, Reggie II, Shaun and Brandon. His motto is "You have to dare to be great!"

Roland Williams is founder and president of the Youth Lifeline Foundation Inc., a nonprofit organization that harnesses the powerful influence of celebrity athletes, entertainers and business professionals. They teach at-risk youth valuable life skills necessary to becoming more positive and productive individuals.

Entering his ninth year as an NFL tight end, Williams has enjoyed tremendous success on the football field, which includes the 1998 Offensive Rookie of the Year honors, a 2003 American Football Conference Championship, and most notably, the St. Louis Rams' Super Bowl XXXIV Championship.

Williams has also received numerous awards including the prestigious NFL Unsung Hero Award, the Oakland Raiders Man of the Year Award, and the Press Radio Club Pro Athlete of the Year Award. He is also a multi-year finalist for the Walter Payton NFL Man of the Year Award for philanthropy and citizenship.

Regarded as one of the most engaging and energetic athletes in professional sports, Williams is also an inspiring motivational speaker, author and television sports analyst.

Williams is married to Rona, and has two children, Justice and Trustin.

Roland Williams
Founder
Youth Lifeline Foundation Inc.

Providing Solutions For Your Accounting and Tax Needs

St. Louis' Premiere Full Service Certified Public Accounting Firm

Helping Small Businesses, Individuals,
Non-Profits and Churches

Davis Associates
Certified Public Accountants

4119 N. Hwy 67
Florissant, MO 63034
314-653-0008
www.DavisAssociatesCPA.com

Call Us, We Can Help You!

- **Accounting**
- **Audit**
- **Tax**
- **Consulting**

Darlene M. Davis, CPA
Principal

MBE/WBE

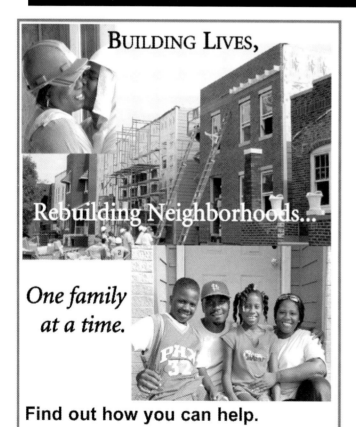

BUILDING LIVES,

Rebuilding Neighborhoods...

One family at a time.

Find out how you can help.

Call Courtney Pittman
314-371-0400

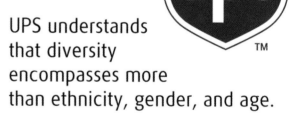

Habitat
for Humanity®
Saint Louis

At UPS, diversity is a core component of our company.

UPS understands that diversity encompasses more than ethnicity, gender, and age.

Diversity is leveraging our unique experiences and contributions which add value to our culture and contribute to our business and community success.

UPS is an equal opportunity employer. M/F/D/V.

Copyright © 2006, United Parcel Service of America, Inc. All Rights Reserved.

WHO'S *WHO*

St. Louis'
SPIRITUAL LEADERS

*"Give instruction to a wise man, and he will be yet wiser:
teach a just man, and he will increase in learning."*

PROVERBS 9:9 NKJV

SPIRITUAL LEADERS

Reverend Dr. F. James Clark
Pastor & Founder
Shalom Church (City of Peace)

The Reverend Dr. Freddy James Clark, a native of St. Louis, is the pastor and founder of the Shalom Church (City of Peace) in St. Louis, Missouri.

Clark earned a bachelor of arts degree in religion and philosophy from Bishop College in Dallas, Texas in 1981. He received a master of divinity degree in 1986 and a doctorate of ministry degree in 2001 from Eden Theological Seminary. He plans to publish his doctoral dissertation "Hospitality - An Ecclesiological Practice of Ministry" concerning the importance of embedding hospitality into every level of life or living.

Clark and his wife are the parents of three adult children, Terrence, Anthony and Michelle.

Bishop Willie J. Ellis
Pastor
New Northside Baptist Church

Bishop Willie J. Ellis is a product of St. Louis Public Schools. He attended Sumner High School and Harris-Stowe State College, and went on to receive a doctor of divinity degree from Providence Bible Theological Seminary. He also received honorary doctor of divinity degrees from the University Bible Institute in Alamo, Tennessee, and Western Bible Baptist College in Kansas City.

On June 21, 2001, he was elevated to the office of bishop by the Philadelphia Full Gospel Churches of Europe, Inc. Some of his congregation's noteworthy accomplishments include growth in the number of members from 50 to 1,500; and helping those in need through the Child Development Center, the Building Resources Education and Assistance for Tomorrow's Health (Breath) program, and the Drum and Bugle Corps.

Ellis is a chaplain for the Metropolitan St. Louis Police Department. He is also a commissioner for the State of Missouri Public Defender's Office and a commissioner of the board for the St. Louis County Housing Authority.

Ellis is the husband of Dr. Beverly Ellis and is the proud father of two daughters, six grandchildren, and one great-grandchild.

Bishop Dr. Wyatt I. Greenlee Jr.
Founder & Senior Pastor
Greater New Higher Heights
Christian Church
United Church of Christ

Bishop Dr. Wyatt I. Greenlee Jr. is the founder and senior pastor of Greater New Higher Heights Christian Church United Church of Christ located in St. Louis.

Greenlee's evangelical style of ministry places special emphasis on relevancy in ministry and targets the inner city. His unique and exhilarating teaching method enables people from all walks of life to understand and enjoy the word of God. He welcomes all to be loved through Jesus Christ, including families who can experience the free move of the Holy Spirit and have the freedom to praise and worship God in spirit and truth. His powerful outreach ministry consists of community awareness, building educational excellence, social and economic services, and support groups that affect the entire community.

Greenlee attended the St. Louis Public Schools and graduated from the University of Missouri-St. Louis, where he obtained a bachelor's degree in business administration. He also received a master of education degree and doctrine degree in education administration from St. Regis University and Covenant Theological Seminary.

Bishop James A. Johnson
Pastor
Bethesda Temple Church
of the Apostolic Faith

Bishop James A. Johnson has been pastor of the Bethesda Temple Church of the Apostolic Faith for more than 50 years.

Johnson has served as a member of the board of directors of Aenon Bible School, general secretary of the P.A.W., diocesan of the 14th and 12th Episcopal Districts, auxiliary director for the National Sunday School Association, assistant presiding bishop and presiding bishop. Considered by many to be a "gentleman of gentlemen," he is regarded highly as a loving and compassionate man.

Johnson is the author of two books, *Enduring the Night* and *Jesus Christ, With Us God*. He founded the Bible Institute of Bethesda Temple Church and as the first teacher, he utilized personal writings from *Theology of the Cross* as study material. In 1991 and 1992 Johnson was the invited morning speaker for Hampton University's Ministerial Conference.

Johnson was married to the late Sister Josephine B. Johnson for 50 years prior to her passing in 1998. She was active in Pentecostal Assemblies of the World circles. On May 16, 2004, Johnson married Sister Juana J. Johnson.

SPIRITUAL LEADERS

The Reverend Aubry Jones Sr.
Retired Pastor
United Methodist Church

Rev. Dr. Aubry Jones Sr. has been the pastor of 11 congregations throughout Missouri for 47 years. Jones served as a teacher and administrator in the St. Louis Public Schools for 34 years, and as an adjunct assistant professor for Harris-Stowe State University for six years. A Korean War veteran, he served overseas in Japan.

Jones earned his bachelor of science degree from the University of Arkansas at Pine Bluff, and a master of education degree from the University of Arkansas. He graduated from the Perkins School of Theology in Dallas, Texas, and earned a master of divinity degree and a doctor of ministry degree from Eden Theological Seminary in St. Louis.

Jones has received numerous awards including the Teacher of the Year Award, the Martin Luther King Award, the Clergy Coalition Service Award and many others.

He is married to Melva Jones and they have eight children. Jones is a member of Kappa Alpha Psi Fraternity, Inc.

The Reverend Earl E. Nance Jr.
Pastor
Greater Mt. Carmel Baptist Church

The Reverend Earl E. Nance Jr. is pastor of Greater Mt. Carmel Missionary Baptist Church. He served 15 years as co-pastor under his father, Rev. Earl E. Nance Sr., who pastored for 43 years.

Nance is a former president of the St. Louis Metropolitan Clergy Coalition. He also served as president of the Missouri Progressive Baptist Convention and as president and dean of the Progressive National Baptist Convention Midwest Region Congress of Christian Education. From 1987 to 1997, he served on the St. Louis Board of Education.

Currently, Nance serves on the boards of Faith Beyond Walls, the Mathews-Dickey Boys' & Girls' Club, the Monsanto YMCA and the St. Louis Sports Commission.

In 1980 Nance was appointed by Governor Joseph Teasdale to the 22nd Judicial Commission. He served a six-year term and was the first African-American member of the commission.

Nance holds a bachelor of arts degree in education from Harris-Stowe State College and a master of arts degree in education from Georgia State University.

He is married to Viola Harvey Nance, and has one daughter, Candice Nicole Nance.

A Monticello, Mississippi native and resident of St. Louis, the Reverend Dr. Robert Charles Scott is married to the former Pier C. Patterson. He serves as pastor of Central Baptist Church, the second oldest African-American Baptist church in St. Louis.

Additionally, Scott is co-mentor with Dr. Charles E. Booth and Dr. Jesse T. Williams at United Theological Seminary (UTS) in Dayton, Ohio.

A graduate of Jackson State University and Duke University Divinity School, Scott earned a doctoral degree from UTS. Graduating with high distinction, he was the youngest person in his doctoral group. He also graduated from the Summer Leadership Institute at Harvard University Divinity School.

One of the top 20 young preachers under 40 according to *The African American Pulpit*, Scott was inducted into the Morehouse College Board of Preachers. He was featured for the J. H. Jackson/Caesar Clark preaching forum during the National Baptist Convention. Scott is published in *Sound the Trumpet Again: Sermons for Empowering African American Men*. He is a lifetime member of Omega Psi Phi Fraternity, Inc., the NAACP, and Jackson State and Duke alumni associations.

Dr. Robert Charles Scott
Pastor
Central Baptist Church

D r. A. Michael Shaw II is founder of Perfect Love World Revival Ministries located in St. Louis, Missouri and New Orleans, Louisiana. He oversees Divine Favor Church in Italy, and multiple evangelistic ministries. He is an executive board member of Antioch Bible Colleges in Japan and Korea.

Shaw received his ministry credentials at St. Paul Church of God and Christ and Victory Assembly. On February 19, 2005, Shaw was ordained as an apostle and bishop. He attended Xavier University and Southern University at New Orleans.

In November of 1998, Shaw founded the LOVE Clubs (Lifting Our Valuable Esteem), which empower students and have had more than 27,000 participants.

Due in part to Hurricane Katrina, Shaw now resides in St. Louis. He is actively involved in the St. Louis community, serving as executive board member for First Tee St. Louis. He is also involved with the Youth & Family Center, the Downtown Optimist Club, and Skyway Gateway Investment Co. Shaw is a member of Midtown Toastmasters.

He is married to Lisa Shaw and has a son, Michael, and a daughter, Jordan.

Dr. A. Michael Shaw II
Founder
Perfect Love World Revival Ministries

SPIRITUAL LEADERS

Reverend Dr. Curtis Shelton
Pastor
Mount Pleasant Baptist Church

D r. Curtis Shelton is the founding pastor of Mount Pleasant Baptist Church. The church opened in February of 1980 and serves more than 300 members today. Under his leadership, the church is continuously expanding, resulting in the need to purchase additional land for parking. Recently, they built a new child development center. During the flood several years ago, Mount Pleasant was selected to serve as the Federal Emergency Management Agency headquarters.

Shelton is actively involved in the community. As the moderator for the Union District, he is responsible for 24 churches. A member of the Missionary Baptist State of Missouri and the National Baptist Church Convention, he co-chairs the transportation of congress 2007 committee. While working on his thesis, Shelton remained active in several community groups. Mount Pleasant is the official meeting site for community meetings of two wards in St. Louis.

Shelton graduated from St. Louis Public Schools and matriculated to college. He completed a doctorate from Glide Tidings Bible College. He is married to Annette Shelton.

Reverend Alvin L. Smith
Pastor
St. Paul African Methodist
Episcopal Church

R everend Alvin L. Smith is pastor of St. Paul African Methodist Episcopal Church in St. Louis.

An activist, Smith participated in Operation Safe Schools for children attending St. Louis Public Schools. He is a member of Clergy and Citizens United for Safety and Justice, the St. Louis Clergy Coalition and the NAACP. Smith serves as chairman of the board for St. Paul Saturdays. He was appointed to the Episcopal committee of the AME General Conference and serves on the AME Church strategic planning committee.

Smith attended public and parochial schools in Los Angeles, California. He attended Wilberforce University and the University of California, Los Angeles. He received his master of divinity degree at the Interdenominational Theological Center in Atlanta, Georgia, and was licensed to preach in the AME church in 1997. Smith completed the U.S. Naval Chaplain's Commander School and was commissioned as a lieutenant. He then served as a U.S. Naval Reserve Hospital chaplain for eight years.

A talented singer and musician, he is married to the Reverend Beatrice Phillips Smith, and they have one son, Maurice.

WHO'S *who*

The Reverend Steven G. Thompson is senior pastor and teacher of the historic Leonard Baptist Church in St. Louis. He is moderator of the Antioch District Missionary Baptist Association. In this capacity, he presides over some 40 churches in fellowship and community outreach programs.

Thompson is an award-winning gospel radio announcer for KIRL radio station in St. Charles, Missouri. He has received many awards including the Horizon Award, Gospel Announcer of the Year, and the Spoken Word Award.

Thompson is a board member of the Western Baptist College in Kansas City, Missouri. In 2001, he was elected second vice president of the Missionary Baptist State Convention of Missouri and called to preside over the southern region of Missouri Baptist churches.

In June of 1993, he received a bachelor of arts degree from Glad Tidings Bible College. In August of 2004, he was awarded a master of divinity degree from St. Regis University in Monrovia, Liberia.

A native of Luxora, Arkansas, Reverend Thompson is an accomplished author, playwright, and theater director. He is a husband, father, and grandfather.

Reverend Steven G. Thompson
Pastor
Leonard Baptist Church

Reverend Dr. Jesse T. Williams Jr. is the senior pastor of Washington Tabernacle Baptist Church of St. Louis, where he has served since 1990. Williams was licensed to preach the gospel in 1983 at Mount Carmel Missionary Baptist Church in Topeka, Kansas. He was ordained to the gospel ministry in 1990.

Williams earned a doctor of ministry degree and a master of divinity degree from the Eden Theological Seminary. He received a bachelor's degree in mechanical engineering and a degree in business administration from the University of Kansas. He recently received a certificate of participation through Harvard University's Divinity School Summer Leadership Institute.

Williams served as a delegate to the World Baptist Congress in 2000 and preached at the Fort Buchanan army base in Puerto Rico for the Martin Luther King celebrations in 1996 and 1997. On a foreign mission with the National Baptist Convention, USA, Inc., he ministered throughout Africa.

Williams is a faculty member at the United Theological Seminary in Dayton, Ohio. For the past ten years, he has blessed thousands through his radio ministry every Sunday morning.

Reverend Dr. Jesse T. Williams
Senior Pastor
Washington Tabernacle
Baptist Church

Got Billiken Tickets?
Shimmy does.

2006-07 Billiken Basketball

MEN'S HOME SCHEDULE

Fri., Nov. 3	UMSL (Exh.) ••	7:30 p.m.
Wed., Nov 8	HARRIS STOWE (Exh.)	7 p.m.
Sat., Nov. 11	QUINCY	7 p.m.
Sat., Nov. 25	HOUSTON	1 p.m.
Sat., Dec. 9	WESTERN ILLINOIS	1 p.m.
Sat., Dec. 16	UT-MARTIN	7 p.m.
Mon., Dec. 18	MISSOURI STATE	7 p.m.
Fri., Dec. 22	NORTH CAROLINA (ESPNU)	7 p.m.
Sat., Dec. 30	MISSISSIPPI	1 p.m.
Sat., Jan. 6	DUQUESNE •	7 p.m.
Wed., Jan. 10	RHODE ISLAND •	7 p.m.
Sat., Jan. 13	XAVIER •	1 p.m.
Thu., Jan. 25	CHARLOTTE • (CSTV)	7 p.m.
Sat., Feb. 3	GEORGE WASHINGTON •	1 p.m.
Sat., Feb. 17	LA SALLE •	7 p.m.
Wed., Feb. 21	DAYTON •	7 p.m.
Wed., Feb. 28	RICHMOND •	7 p.m.

WOMEN'S HOME SCHEDULE

Fri., Nov. 3	UMSL (Exh.) ••	(at Scottrade Center)	5 p.m.
Tue, Nov. 7	MARYVILLE (Exh.)		7 p.m.
Fri., Nov. 10	AKRON		7 p.m.
Mon., Nov. 13	CHICAGO STATE		7 p.m.
Wed., Nov. 15	TENNESSEE STATE		7 p.m.
Sat., Nov. 18	UT-MARTIN		7 p.m.
Wed., Nov. 29	ILLINOIS		7 p.m.
Wed., Dec. 6	UMKC		7 p.m.
Sat., Dec. 30	ARKANSAS		4 p.m.
Fri., Jan. 12	XAVIER •		TBA
Sun., Jan. 14	DAYTON •		TBA
Sun., Jan. 21	SAINT JOSEPH'S •		TBA
Sun., Feb. 4	CHARLOTTE •		TBA
Thu., Feb. 8	ST. BONAVENTURE •		TBA
Sun., Feb. 11	FORDHAM •		TBA
Sun., Feb. 18	GEORGE WASHINGTON •		TBA

• Atlantic 10 Conference games   •• Doubleheader
All men's home games played at Scottrade Center
All women's home games played at Bauman-Eberhardt Center unless othewise indicated
All dates and times are Central and subject to change

Order your Billiken Basketball season tickets today!

Shimmy Gray-Miller
Head Women's Basketball Coach

Your Home Team
SAINT LOUIS BILLIKENS

(314) 977-4SLU
sluBillikens.com

Lawrence (Larry) E. Thomas will serve as the 2006 Chair of the Charmaine Chapman Society

A vital member of the Charmaine Chapman Society from its inception, Larry Thomas, principal, Edward Jones, will take over the role of Chair, bringing renewed leadership and dedication to the position.

Thomas, a United Way of Greater St. Louis leadership donor ($1,000 and above) since 1989, joined the Alexis de Tocqueville Society ($10,000 and above) in 1998 and has been a United Way board member since 1999. His commitment to making the region stronger and healthier through United Way makes Thomas a perfect fit for his new role as chair.

Thomas sits on the boards of: Children's Hospital, Herbert Hoover Boys & Girls Club, St. Louis Zoo, Forest Park Forever, the Bond Market Association and the Bond Market Foundation. He also serves on Washington University's board of trustees, is a member of the alumni board of governors, and sits on the national advisory council of the John M. Olin School of Business at Washington University, and is a member of its executive alumni association.

"Larry has been a member of the Charmaine Chapman Society since its inception, so he has a real understanding of the impact United Way has on our region," David Steward, 2006 United Way board chair, said. "He knows how to get the job done, and I am confident he will lead the Charmaine Chapman Society to another successful year of raising funds for our local community."

"I am excited to lead this Society because I have seen firsthand the difference the United Way makes in the lives of people living right here in our St. Louis community."

— Larry Thomas
Principal, Edward Jones

United Way of Greater St. Louis

PledgeUnitedWay.org

For the best in Automotive Sales, turn to the Who's Who Team at Behlmann Buick Pontiac GMC.

From left to right:
Fred Butler,
Brett Glasby,
Will Spencer Jr., and
Craig Whitfield.

With decades of combined car sales experience for both new and pre-owned, Behlmann's Who's Who Team represent the best of their profession in St. Louis. Fred Butler, Brett Glasby, Will Spencer Jr., and Craig Whitfield are ready to help any customer find the exact vehicle they want, at a price they can afford. Whether it's a luxurious new Buick Lucerne, an exciting Pontiac Solstice convertible, or the ultimate in full-size SUV style and luxury -- a GMC Yukon Denali, Behlmann has more in stock to choose from than any other dealer in St. Louis. Behlmann is the long-time #1 selling Pontiac and GMC dealer in the area, and they're now the area's newest Buick dealer.

Behlmann Buick Pontiac GMC is located in Hazelwood just off I-270 at McDonnell Blvd. You can contact any member of the Who's Who Team by calling 314-895-1600, or go on-line at www.behlmann.com.

I-270 & McDonnell Blvd.
314-895-1600 • www.behlmann.com

St. Louis'

ENTREPRENEURS

"You can always chase a dream but it will not count if you never catch it."

MALCOLM X, 1925-1965

NATIONALIST LEADER

SPONSORED BY

Jane Abbott-Morris
President & Chief Executive Officer
Human Resources Select
Services, Inc.

Jane Abbott-Morris is the president and chief executive officer of Human Resources Select Services, Inc. HRSS provides a variety of services including employment, orientation, benefits, training, employee relations, performance management, organizational development, mediations and employment law.

Jane is a graduate of the Executive Leadership Institute sponsored by the National Forum for Black Public Administrators. She is founder of the Grand Center Toastmaster Club and Teen Leaders and Communicators. A certified EEO investigator and mediator, she is a member of Delta Sigma Theta Sorority, Inc. Jane is a founding member of the National Campaign for Tolerance for the Civil Rights Memorial Center in Montgomery, Alabama.

Jane holds a bachelor's degree in elementary education from Harris Teachers College, a master's degree in counselor education from Southern Illinois University, and a master's degree in public administration from Webster University.

Jane is an adjunct professor at Harris-Stowe State College and was included in the 2000 *Who's Who Among College Professors*.

A native of St. Louis, Jane is the proud mother of Christopher Scott Abbott-Morris, who attends Missouri Western State College.

Mark & Marlon Austin
Designers & Directors
Bespoke Group International

Mark and Marlon Austin are the designers and directors of Bespoke Group International. Having always been known as "go-getters," they started their careers as financial planners. With the sales experience they gained as financial planners coupled with their love for art and fashion, they turned a part-time hobby into a full-time passion for fashion. These days, the self-taught twin brothers are designing many of the latest styles and haute couture designs for some of the top players in the fashion industry.

After many years of playing an integral part in the success of many fashion houses, the brothers have recently launched MarkMarlon Bespoke Couture, their own clothing label, and Gemello Fratello, their bridge collection. Although they reside in St. Louis, they spend much of their time at their Chicago office and flying from New York to Italy to the United Kingdom and back, setting up wholesale trade accounts with small boutiques and department stores.

They are natives of St. Louis, Missouri. Mark is married and has a daughter; Marlon is also married.

Reggie Blackwell is the managing partner of MAC Sports & Entertainment, a full-service agency representing professional athletes, speakers, entertainers and media personalities. He is fully certified by the NFL and NBA Players Associations.

Blind in his right eye from birth, Reggie was raised in the troubled Fairgrounds Park neighborhood. He credits his list of achievements to ambition and his family, who kept him on track.

Blackwell attended Ritenour High School, where he shined in football, basketball and track. He was voted All-State, All-Conference, All-Metro, senior class president, and graduated with a 3.2 GPA. He received a football scholarship to Kansas State University where he was a three-year starter and team captain. He was president of Omega Psi Phi Fraternity, and earned a degree in public relations/marketing with a minor in education.

Following graduation, Blackwell attained high-profile positions as a sales and marketing manager for both Anheuser-Busch and Nike. He co-founded MAC Sports & Entertainment in 2005.

In his free time, Blackwell volunteers as a football coach at Mathews-Dickey Boys' & Girls' Club, where he helps others overcome the obstacles he faced.

Reggie Blackwell
Managing Partner
MAC Sports & Entertainment

Pearlina Boyd is the president and chief executive officer of Accession Consulting, LLC. Accession provides consulting services in the areas of public policy, nonprofit management and strategic planning. Boyd has worked with several prominent dignitaries and professionals in the U.S. and Japan.

Boyd is a proud member of Sigma Gamma Rho Sorority, Inc., the National Association of Female Executives and the American Society for Public Administration. She serves as a community leader and concerned advocate for minorities, women and youth in the nonprofit sector. Boyd serves on the advisory board of Lincoln University's Cooperative Extension Program. She also serves as a policy advisor on the statewide public policy committee for Citizens for Missouri's Children, and the FOCUS St. Louis community policy committee.

Boyd is a candidate for a master's degree in public policy administration and holds a graduate certificate in nonprofit management, both from the University of Missouri-St. Louis. She also holds a bachelor's degree in socio-political communications from Missouri State University. She is single with no children.

Pearlina Boyd
President & Chief Executive Officer
Accession Consulting, LLC

Floyd Boykin Jr.
Editor
SpokenVizions Magazine

Floyd Boykin Jr., a.k.a. IMPAKT, is an internationally published poet, a spoken word performer, musician, songwriter, music producer and lupus activist. He is the founder and editor of *SpokenVizions Magazine*, the only publication in the country that is geared toward the accomplishments and lifestyles of spoken word poets.

Boykin has opened for legendary group, The Last Poets, Gil Scott-Heron, Malik Yusef, Goapele and Murphy Lee. In 2001 he was featured at the National Black Poetry Festival in St. Louis. The festival also featured national poets such as Amiri Baraka, Jessica Care Moore, Reggie Gibson and Dahveed Nelson, one of the founders of The Last Poets.

Boykin was featured in the 2005-2006 edition of *Who's Who in Black St. Louis®*. Recently, he was presented with The Keith Rodgers Founder of the Year Award in Tallahassee, Florida, in recognition of his visionary leadership and community service. Boykin appeared on Floetry's live DVD release, *Floacism*, and was featured on DefPoetryJam.com. He is also a celebrity judge on the American Idol Underground Web site.

Ernest Bradley
Founder & President
Biddle Group, LLC

Ernest Bradley is founder and president of Biddle Group, LLC, a community development company specializing in youth and property development since 1994. The Biddle Group has two historic real estate development properties, refurbished to their original grandeur in St. Louis and metropolitan Illinois. Currently, Ernest works for the Lincoln University Cooperative Extension - Urban Impact Center of St. Louis, helping four schools to develop 4-H clubs.

The Biddle Group has mentored youth in metropolitan St. Louis, building leadership and life skills through tennis and golf. Ernest has more than ten years of involvement collaborating with various organizations including Carr Square Public Housing, the Human Development Corporation, Alternative Unlimited High School, the Herbert Hoover Boys and Girls Club and Missouri Black Expo.

Ernest is a proud member of Lone Star #2, Masonic Order. He is also a member of 100 Black Men of Metropolitan St. Louis. As a member, Ernest served as chairman of the Black Tie Gala, worked on national staff and served as mentoring chairman. Community rebuilding is Ernest's passion.

Linda Calmese is founder and executive director of Bits and Bytes Training Institute. She was a pioneer in personal computer-based vocational training when she opened her business in 1985. She holds bachelor's and master's degrees in business education and a specialist degree in counseling from Southern Illinois University Edwardsville. She has traveled abroad and was employed by the Department of Defense Overseas School, where she taught at Torrejon Air Force Base High School in Madrid, Spain for 11 years. Linda's passion for her community brought her home with a vision to reach out through training.

Her vision was revolutionary in the business environment. She introduced potential office staff with a new level of computer skills. Many were either unskilled or under-skilled in computer software and technology in the mid 80s. Training was also provided to businesses to upgrade workers' skills and knowledge to meet the demands of the growing high tech environment.

In August of 2005, the local Workforce Investment Board recognized Linda for her innovative Youth Entrepreneurial Program. The Honorable Congressman Jerry Costello presented her with a recognition award.

Linda Calmese
Founder & Executive Director
Bits and Bytes Training Institute

Deanna Carroll owns and operates a State Farm Insurance agency in West St. Louis. Her agency markets and sells all lines of State Farm insurance and financial products. Deanna has owned her agency for seven years and has been a part of the State Farm family for 14 years.

Deanna is committed to giving back to the St. Louis community through her participation in the Urban League Young Professionals (ULYP). She has held several offices as a member of this organization and is currently serving her second term as president. During her term as president, ULYP has been dedicated to generating proceeds in support of the Urban League of Metropolitan St. Louis' programs and completing community service programs throughout the community.

Deanna received her bachelor's and master's degrees from Drake University. She has earned the designations of CLU (Chartered Life Underwriter), CASL (Chartered Advisor for Senior Living) and FLMI (Fellow of Life Management Institute).

In addition, Deanna is a member of the Kirkwood Chamber of Commerce, Alpha Kappa Alpha Sorority, Inc., and First Baptist Church of Chesterfield.

Deanna Carroll
Owner
Carroll State Farm Agency

Charles E. Crump
President
Charles Crump
Insurance Agency, LLC

Charles Crump is the president of Charles Crump Insurance Agency, LLC, an Allstate Insurance agency located in St. Louis. He has been with Allstate for 35 years. During that time, he has won numerous company sales awards including Agent of the Year in 1984 for the Kansas City region. He has also been appointed to many national agent advisory groups.

A product of St. Louis Public Schools, Charles attended Hadley Technical High School where he was a starting end on the football team and vice president of his graduating class of 1963.

Charles attended Truman University, formerly Northeast Missouri State, in Kirksville, Missouri. During his years in Kirksville, he became the first African-American president of a class and was selected to *Who's Who in Colleges and Universities in America* in 1965. He graduated in 1967 with a bachelor of science degree in education.

Charles has been a member of Kappa Alpha Psi Fraternity for 40 years and remains an active member of the St. Louis alumni chapter. He was a founding member of Tee Masters Golf Club, a 501(c) 3 nonprofit corporation that established the St. Louis Metropolitan Minority Golf Program.

Some of Charles' hobbies include golf and travel. He has traveled to the African continent on several occasions.

Eddie G. Davis
Co-Founder & President
Integrity Recyclers, LLC

In 2004, Eddie Davis formed Integrity Recyclers, LLC with Mr. Robert L. Coleman; they operate as consultants and merchants of scrap metals and other recyclable materials. Davis also formed DaLite & Associates, LLC in order to serve as a business consultant for small and mid-sized businesses.

In his more than 25 years of business experience, Davis has served as president of the St. Louis Minority Business Council, as president of the St. Louis Board of Education, and as a member of the board of directors and the executive committee of the National Minority Supplier Development Council.

Davis currently serves as chairman of the economic development committee for the St. Louis Black Leadership Roundtable, as a trustee of the St. Louis Science Center, and as treasurer of the St. Louis Chapter of the National Association of Securities Professionals.

Davis holds a bachelor of science degree in business studies from Saint Louis University, and he has completed Missouri Continuing Legal Education Advanced Business Acquisition Studies presented by the Missouri University Law School.

Davis is married and is the father of an adult daughter and two adult sons.

Clifton W. Gates is president and chief executive officer of Gates Realty Investment Company and the National Assurance Agency. He is also the founder and board chairman emeritus for Gateway Bank of St. Louis, the only minority-owned and operated bank in St. Louis.

Gates served as the city's first African-American police board commissioner from 1967 to 1974. In 1975 he founded Lismark Distributing Company.

Gates has served on numerous professional organizations including as president of the St. Louis Urban League, director of the Missouri State Chamber of Commerce, and director of the Better Business Bureau. He sits on the board of directors for the Municipal Opera and Forest Park Forever. He is vice president of Boy Scouts of America.

Gates has received numerous awards and honors including Distributor of the Year and Regional Distributor of the Year from the U. S. Department of Commerce; the Management Award from the Labor and Management Committee; the Public Service Award from the *St. Louis Argus*; and an honorary doctorate of philosophy in business administration from Hamilton State University.

Clifton W. Gates
President & Chief Executive Officer
Gates Realty Investment Company
National Assurance Agency

Kerri Gwinn Harris is chief executive officer of KGHarris & Associates, LLC, a premiere training and development consulting firm. She is also developer of the firm's flagship Keys To Global Diversity Training.

Gwinn Harris authored *Keys To the Executive Suite: The Quintessential Guide to Getting Empowered and Getting Employed*, hosts *Keys To The Executive Suite© The Radio Show*, and is a highly sought columnist and orator.

The 2005 Entrepreneur Extraordinaire for the national sorority of Phi Delta Kappa, Alpha Nu Chapter, Gwinn Harris is also a women's ministry speaker. She lends her talents to the United Way of Greater St. Louis' allocations committee, Charmaine Chapman Society cabinet, Forest Park Forever women's committee, and the Monsanto Family YMCA Tennis & Tuxedo committee.

Gwinn Harris holds a bachelor of arts and a master of science from Fontbonne University, and is currently pursuing a Ph.D. in organizational development with an emphasis in leadership. She holds memberships in several organizations including the National Council of Negro Women, the National Association of Female Executives, the American Business Women's Association, and Alpha Kappa Alpha Sorority Inc.

Kerri Gwinn Harris
Chief Executive Officer
KGHarris & Associates, LLC

Jeanetta Hill
Chief Executive Officer
Personal Touches by Jeanetta, Inc.

Jeanetta Hill, a Detroit native, is president and chief executive officer of Personal Touches by Jeanetta, Inc. She has owned and managed the company for more than 18 years. Personal Touches is a multifaceted special events production company that provides décor for themes, corporate and social events, grand openings, new product launches, press conferences and marketing promotions.

After being in sales for ten years and in the education field for more than six, Jeanetta began designing. Upon discovering that she had a natural knack for design and a long list of clients, she used her sales experience and business savvy to turn her desire into a successful production company.

Jeanetta currently operates her business from an office and warehouse in St. Louis and just recently opened an office in Detroit. She produced a half-million dollar event at the America's Center in St. Louis, dropped 6,000 balloons for President George W. Bush in Arkansas, and provided event décor for Anheuser-Busch, Enterprise Rent-A-Car, DIA-Bal Africain, and The Jackie Joyner-Kersee Foundation.

Jeanetta strongly believes that it is our responsibility to give back.

Crystal Howard
President & Chief Executive Officer
C3 Real Estate Investors

After 12 years as a public relations professional, Crystal Howard launched her own company in a completely different field – real estate investing. She acquires residential and commercial properties for resale and rental.

Crystal is a board member of Citizens for Modern Transit. The organization advocates efforts to expand light rail as the critical component of an integrated, affordable and convenient public transportation system, enabling economic growth to improve the quality of life in the St. Louis region. She also serves on the community advisory board of Ameristar Casinos, offering valuable feedback on community strategies and charitable giving opportunities, and assisting them with their mission to help people improve the quality of life in the communities where their properties are located.

Crystal earned her bachelor's degree in communications and public relations from Saint Louis University. She received accreditation in public relations from the Public Relations Society of America.

A native of St. Louis, Crystal is the proud mother of two sons, Clayton and Carlin.

L .D. Ingrum Gallery & Studio was conceived and formally organized in 1991. The L.D. Ingrum Gallery & Studio is an innovative photography company that has earned a respected reputation in the local industry. It quickly developed an impressive client base, including Reebok International LTD, the St. Louis Cardinals, Monsanto Company, and BET Publication Group.

L.D. Ingrum Gallery & Studio is expanding its line of services by introducing Ingrum Signage Project Management. As a signage project management team, they are able to incorporate this form of visual art while maintaining focus on photo documentations.

Lois' dedication to photojournalism and her community shows through her numerous organizational memberships, including the St. Louis Minority Business Council, the National Press Photographer Association, the Freelance Photographer Association, Iota Phi Lambda Sorority, Inc., and the NAACP. For the past nine years, Lois has also been instructing students, from the ages of ten through 21, in the art of photography.

A St. Louis native, Lois has been married to Eric Ingrum for 18 years, and she is the mother of 15-year-old Alexander Ingrum.

Lois Ingrum
Owner
L.D. Ingrum Gallery & Studio

R ose Jackson-Beavers is the publisher and owner of Prioritybooks Publications. She has published several novels including *Summin T' Say, Quilt Designs and Poetry Rhymes*, co-written with Edna Patterson-Petty, *Backroom Confessions* and *A Hole in My Heart*, a novel she co-authored with 16-year-old Edward Booker. The East St. Louis native also works as a freelance journalist. She currently lives in Florissant with her husband of 22 years, Cedric, and her daughter, Adeesha.

Jackson-Beavers received her bachelor's and master's degrees from Illinois State University and Southern Illinois University. She has a vast amount of experience working with people of all ages. In addition to pursuing her interests in poetry and short stories, she also spends time working in church and volunteering with local organizations in her community.

Jackson-Beavers has freelance work and columns published in numerous publications including *A-Magazine, Spanish Lake Word Newspaper* and the *North County Journal*. In addition, she has published the works of ten local authors.

Rose Jackson-Beavers
Publisher & Owner
Prioritybooks Publications

Leah Jewel
Model, Actress,
Comedienne & MC

Leah Jewel has a lucrative acting career in commercials, voice-overs and modeling. She has appeared in two movies, *Divas of Comedy* and *A Ghost Image*, with celebrities from hit television shows *CSI*, *Nip/Tuck* and *The Sopranos*.

Leah is a successful comedienne, having performed at venues throughout the nation. She covered arts and entertainment, hosting the talk show, *Spotlight St. Louis*, and writing the column, My Spirit's Keeper. Leah has also written theatre, film and music reviews for *Intermission Magazine*, *Take Five* magazine and *The St. Louis American* Newspaper.

Leah earned a bachelor's degree in education and master's degrees in communications, education and business/human resources. She is a playwright and the author of *My Soliloquy* and *Mojo Woman: A Conjuring of Poems*. She has published poems and short stories in anthologies. Previously, Leah worked as an on-air personality at KFUO-FM 99.1.

Leah is available as an MC for events, comedienne and motivational speaker. Her most cherished job is that of wife and mother to her husband, Adrian, and daughter, Lauren. "The job just keeps on giving!" she says.

K. Kalimba Kindell
President & CEO
Legacy Management Institute, Inc.

K. Kalimba Kindell is the president and CEO of Legacy Management Institute, Inc., a full-service consulting firm. She develops and implements adolescent, family, business, religious, and community service delivery systems to build teams, wealth, health, and goals. She is world renowned for her instruction and facilitation skills in the public and private sectors.

Kindell is a certified trainer, lecturer, consultant, life coach, and public speaker. Under her direct leadership, a cadre of expert consultants provides services and programs to local and national communities.

She is affiliated with and appointed or elected to many organizations that "empower greatness and build legacies" in the community such as Beyond Housing/Neighborhood Housing Services, the United Way of Greater St. Louis' Allocation Panel, the CORO Foundation of St. Louis-Women in Leadership, and FOCUS St. Louis. She is also the executive vice president of the National Black MBA Association.

Kalimba earned her bachelor of arts degree in business administration from Webster University, and in 2000, she was awarded a master of business administration degree from Lindenwood University.

A Philadelphia, Pennsylvania native, she is the proud mother of four, Hameed, Mustafa, Saidah, and Yusef.

Jacque Land is co-founder and co-owner of the Platinum Group, Inc. (along wife/partner Leata Price-Land). Platinum Group specializes in a variety of promotional functions, including event planning, marketing, public relations, concert promotions, product and street promotions. With years of experience, Platinum Group has established a reputation for developing successful ventures and producing some of the largest events in the region.

Jacque is president-elect of 100 Black Men of Metropolitan St. Louis. Additionally, he is an on-air radio personality with KATZ-Gospel 1600, a board member of St. Louis Public Library, member of Alpha Phi Alpha Fraternity, Inc., and a dedicated member of New Sunny Mount Missionary Baptist Church.

In 1996 Jacque received his bachelor's degree in biology with a minor in chemistry from the University of Missouri-St. Louis.

A St. Louis native, Jacque is married to Leata Price-Land and is the proud stepfather of Chip Price and Jaime Price. His mission in life is to be a positive role model in the community and break the shackles of sheer materialism that confront our youth on a daily basis.

Jacque M. Land
Co-Owner
Platinum Group, Inc.

Maurice Meredith is an accomplished freelance photographer. For more than 28 years, his keen eye has led him to photograph 500-plus celebrities and national figures. For the last 22 years, Maurice has documented many recurring events in St. Louis and the country, including the Million Man March and the 25th anniversary of the March on Washington.

Maurice pursued and developed his career by working as a freelance photographer with Fleishman-Hilliard Public Relations Company, which led to substantial contacts with Anheuser-Busch Companies, Southwestern Bell, and Bank of America. He has also worked with *The St. Louis American*, *The St. Louis Sentinel* and the *St. Louis Post-Dispatch*.

Additionally, Maurice has spent 20 years as the photographer for the St. Louis Black Repertory Company. During those years, he also documented the Annie Malone Parade and has been the Missouri Black Expo's and Gateway Classic's photographer since inception.

Maurice holds degrees in commercial photography and a degree in electronic engineering technology. In 1998 he received an award from the United Way, and in 2001 he received a community service award from the city.

Maurice Meredith
Photographer

Arvin Mitchell
President
Full Plate Entertainment

Arvin Mitchell is a comedian, actor, and host. He is familiar to television viewers for his appearances on BET's *Club Comicview*, *Spring Bling 21 Questions*, and *Coming to the Stage*. He has also headlined on college campuses and worked the comedy club circuit. Tapping into his ancestral roots of entrepreneurship, Mitchell started his own publication company, Full Plate Entertainment, which provides opportunities for other artists to showcase their talents.

Arvin performed in the 2003 Las Vegas Comedy Festival and was a finalist for the 2004 Just For Laughs Montreal Comedy Festival. His reviews highlight his technical comedic skills, his engaging and authentic connection with the audience, and his dazzling smile.

Mitchell provides community service to Better Family Life, The Black College Expo, 4 Sho Fo Kids Foundation, and other community organizations in the St. Louis area.

Arvin was born in the heart of St. Louis and is the proud father of one beautiful and charismatic daughter.

Kem G. Mosley
President & CEO
Mosley Construction, Inc.

Kem G. Mosley founded Mosley Construction, Inc. in November of 1979. Mosley Construction, with the motto of "The Courage to Do It Right," has grown into one of the largest minority-owned construction companies in Missouri and has completed projects in Missouri, Illinois, Kansas, Nebraska, and Iowa.

Mr. Mosley has received several awards and has been recognized by many groups including the Small Business Administration (SBA), St. Louis American's Top 25, Minority Youth in Construction, Ft. Leonard Wood Corp of Engineers, and Kirkwood/Webster Boys Club. In addition, he has been featured in *Construction Digest*, *Small Business Monthly*, *The St. Louis American*, *St. Louis Business Journal*, and the *St. Louis Post-Dispatch*.

Kem sits on the boards of the Kirkwood Church of God, Crisis Nursery, the Construction Industry Diversity Council, the St. Louis Minority Business Council, and SPROG, Inc.

Mr. Mosley holds a bachelor of science degree from Kansas State University and a master of education degree from Washington University. Kem credits his business training to SPROG, Inc.—a youth organization that he directed in the 1970s.

Diane Page is the owner of ChildFirst Education Consultants. She believes that children must be put first in order to assure that they will have healthy, productive and successful futures. ChildFirst was created for parents and educators to help them navigate their children to success. They offer professional development workshops that promote academic success for all children. Recently, she wrote a children's book entitled *Come Sit Next To Me,* which encourages families to make literacy important in their lives. She has also created numerous inspirational posters to help us find those "teachable and learnable moments."

Page earned her bachelor's degree from the University of Michigan. She has more than 15 years of experience working with children and families, and more than ten years of management experience.

Page is the mother of twins, Brianna and Errynne, who are high school sophomores. She is also a foster mother of three girls. Her hobbies include reading, cooking and spending time with her girls. She is also very active on numerous committees in her community.

Diane Page
Owner
ChildFirst Education Consultants

Leata Price-Land is the founder of the Platinum Group, Inc., a full-service public relations and marketing firm in metropolitan St. Louis equipped to service national and international clientele. Her expertise consists of event marketing, advertising, street marketing, concert promotions, media relations, and placement. Traveling around the country to service upscale consumers, Land's reputation has evolved as a remarkable and credible public relations practitioner.

This consummate marketing guru has been involved in business endeavors namely, the Missouri Black Expo, the United Negro College Fund (UNCF), and *The St. Louis American*'s Salute to Excellence series. Moreover, Land is an avid writer for *The St. Louis American* newspaper. Her commitment to the community is evident in her victorious record in political campaigns and public activism.

Truly cultivated in the word "service," Land is a participant with Women in Transition, and is a member of the Forest Park advisory board. A commissioner on the Planned Industrial Expansion Board, Land also served as a board member of the George Washington Carver House, and Allegiant Bank.

Leata Price-Land
Founder & Co-Owner
Platinum Group, Inc.

Lanear Rhodes, ABR, ABRM
Broker/Owner
Rhodes Realty Service, LLC

Lanear Rhodes is passionate about real estate and community involvement. She promotes fair housing, consumer education and seminars that enhance awareness of predatory lending practices. Of the two million real estate licensees in the nation, Rhodes is among the top four percent who have earned the certified residential specialist (CRS) designation, setting herself apart from the average agent. Her advanced training helps clients turn transactions into prudent deals, which many call the "Rhodes Difference."

Rhodes has received awards and recognition throughout the region. Her enthusiasm to serve allowed her to carry out the responsibilities of 2003 president of the St. Charles County Women's Council of Realtors, and currently includes being a board member for the Father's Support Center, St. Louis and the Missouri Association of Realtors. She is a member of the National, Missouri, St. Charles and St. Louis Associations of Realtors®.

Despite a busy real estate career, she never forgets the importance of acknowledging God, family, friends and past clients. She and her husband, Rudolph, often host appreciation parties that allow her sphere of influence to mix and mingle.

Richard Smith
Owner
Richard Smith Tax Service

Richard Smith is an expert in crisis tax matters and owner of Richard Smith Tax Service in Hazelwood. He serves more than 2,500 clients yearly in tax preparation, financial counseling and accounting. With 25 years of experience in tax preparation, Smith offers the best service for financial security and dedicates his resources, knowledge and expertise by assisting clients in achieving their financial goals.

He is a recipient of the prestigious Financial Services Advocate Award from the Small Business Administration and was featured in the *St. Louis Small Business Monthly*. A member of the National Association of Tax Professionals, Smith represents the Missouri National Association of Tax Professionals, Eastern District. He is well connected in the community as a sponsor of football teams, summer camps and religious organizations.

Smith is a graduate of Florida International University with a bachelor of science degree in industrial technology.

I t was 1990 when the world of broadcasting beckoned Ruth "Starr." After six months in radio, she decided to chase a lifelong dream, which led to the birth of the Gospel television show *City Lights*. Today, *City Lights* has been extended to a full-service video production company and advertising agency.

Although Ms. Starr possesses a theatrical flair, she has a natural gift of communicating with people, which is demonstrated by her tenure in the field of broadcasting and psychology. Her designation as a certified specialist in prevention and crisis intervention reveals her love for people and her heart for the community.

Also an accomplished motivational speaker, Starr is the recipient of numerous awards including The Judge Billy Jones Contribution to the Community Award.

Inspired and mentored by longtime friend, "The Motivator" Mr. Les Brown, Ruth "Starr" is a trendsetter with a vision and a message for God's people.

Ruth "Starr"
Chief Executive Officer
City Lights Gospel Video & Advertising

S t. Louis native Demetrius L. Stewart called American Family Insurance home for ten years. After beginning his career as a casualty claim adjuster, he has successfully owned and operated his own American Family Insurance agency for the past seven years.

Most recently, Demetrius earned his second consecutive J.D. Power and Associates Distinguished Agency Award for excellence in customer service. He has also received multiple honors from American Family for outstanding sales achievement of its multi-line insurance products and financial services. His next project is the future construction of the Trinity Wash Center.

Demetrius serves as associate minister and Sunday school teacher at West Side Missionary Baptist Church. He also serves other organizations including Habitat for Humanity, Beyond Housing/NHS, the St. Louis Gateway Classic Sports Foundation, Alpha Phi Alpha Fraternity, Inc. and the Epsilon Lambda Charitable Foundation.

A proud graduate of University City High School in St. Louis, Demetrius earned a bachelor's degree in business management from Columbia College in Missouri.

Demetrius is married to Shantana, and is father to Samuel and Sydney.

Demetrius L. Stewart
Multi-Line Insurance Agent
American Family Insurance

Kwame Thompson
Executive Vice President &
General Counsel
Kwame Companies

Kwame Thompson practices law in Atlanta, Georgia and Missouri. He was previously employed as executive vice president and general counsel of the Kwame Companies. He is also a co-owner and member of The Nia Investment Group, LLC and K&I Investment, LLC.

Previously, Thompson served as an associate in the corporate transactions group of the prestigious law firm of Bryan Cave, LLP, where he represented owners and contractors on various construction-related claims and drafted construction contracts on behalf of the owners.

In addition to his professional career, Thompson is an active member of the St. Louis Nonviolence Coalition and Kappa Alpha Psi Fraternity, Inc. He is the regional director for the National Bar Association and is affiliated with the Missouri Bar Association committee on minority affairs.

Thompson obtained his bachelor of arts degree in biological sciences from the University of Missouri-Columbia, and his juris doctorate from the Washington University in St. Louis School of Law.

A member of the Kwame Companies' management committee, Thompson studies the U.S. Constitution, statutes, court decisions, ordinances and rules of quasi-judicial bodies.

Tyrone Thompson
President
Kwame Constructors

Tyrone Thompson is president of Kwame Constructors. He is responsible for coordinating projects, developing contacts, creating opportunities, and building Kwame Constructors as an emerging force in the construction business. Thompson also forms strategic alliances with key players in order to gain access to emerging projects.

Previously, Thompson was the chief of police for the City of Pagedale, Missouri. He grew up in University City, Missouri and graduated from University City High School in 1982. He went on to pursue a bachelor's degree at Lincoln University.

A proud father of three children, Tyrell, Kayla, and Tyler, Thompson is a dedicated father. He serves as a parent booster club member for the Royal Knights Track Team in North County, where he is often seen taking the entire team to lunch or dinner after a track meet.

Thompson is president of the Dr. Martin Luther King St. Louis Support Group where he encourages and teaches youth to be positive leaders in the community. He is also managing Club Formula, formerly Club Isis, as well as working for the Kwame Building Group.

Tommy Tucker is the president of Tucker's Investment, LLC, parent company of Inner City Sports, which was formerly known as Tucker's. He has also founded two nonprofit corporations—ICCDA, for the purpose of developing elderly housing, and Tommy E. Tucker Ministries, which honors inner city C-average students.

Tommy has been a successful retail business owner for over 26 years in the inner city. This entrepreneur has created jobs for many people in the community. After being honorably discharged from the United States Army, Tucker attended Forest Park Community College. He later bought the historic building at 2800 North Grand and St. Louis Avenue, where he founded Tucker's Department Store, the first black-owned department store in St. Louis.

A life member of the NAACP and 100 Black Men of Metropolitan St. Louis, Tommy has received awards from the St. Louis Minority Business Council and Northside Preservation. He is the former president of the North Grand Business Association.

Tucker is a native of Starkville, Mississippi; the husband of Denise Tucker; the father of seven; and a grandfather of ten.

Tommy Tucker, Sr.
President
Tucker's Investment, LLC

Artis "Keith" Turner founded TurnGroup Technologies, LLC. in 2002. Keith leads a small staff at TurnGroup, an information technology consulting firm that focuses on providing cost-effective technology solutions to small corporations and municipalities. TurnGroup was awarded the Emerging Business of the Year Award by the *St. Louis American*, the St. Louis Regional Commerce and Growth Association, and the Urban League of St. Louis.

Keith was raised in St. Louis, and returned after he graduated cum laude from Morehouse College in 1995. Since his return, Keith has received various awards for community service and activism. Recently, he was honored by the Annie Malone Children and Family Service Center.

Keith is president of the Morehouse College Alumni Association, St. Louis chapter. He is a board member for the Bakari Institute and the Accra Foundation for Intercultural Communication and Awareness (AFRICA). Keith volunteers for St. Paul Saturdays, a manhood, leadership and development organization focused on improving the quality of life for African-American males in the St. Louis metropolitan area. He is a member of the finance committee at Friendship Missionary Baptist Church.

Artis "Keith" Turner
President & Chief Information Officer
TurnGroup Technologies, LLC.

Linda M. Wash
Broker Associate
Linda M. Wash Real Estate, LLC

Linda M. Wash founded Linda M. Wash Real Estate, now a limited liability company, in 1994. The company provides assistance to sellers and purchasers of commercial and residential real estate. A Realtor, Linda is an active member of the National Association of Realtors.

While she has received recognition for her real estate production throughout her real estate career, which began in 1988, she maintains the philosophy that her clients are always number one. Linda uses her expert negotiation skills and unparalleled customer service to continually exceed her client's expectations. She was recently named a Five Star Agent, Best in Client Satisfaction, by *St. Louis Magazine* (April 2006).

Linda's volunteer efforts advance causes related to leukemia, kidney disease, and health care. She is a foundation board member for St. Mary's Health Center in Richmond Heights, Missouri.

She received a bachelor of science degree in business administration with a minor in accounting from the University of Missouri-St. Louis.

A native of St. Louis, Linda enjoys being a mother, grandmother, sister, aunt, daughter and friend.

Todd Weaver
President
Legacy Building Group, LLC

Todd Weaver started his construction career at 12 years old by completing odd jobs. He later joined the union and worked on large construction sites for Clayco Construction Company.

Excited by the opportunities for minority contractors, Todd started his own firm, Legacy Building Group, LLC, in 2002. Specializing in design-build, Legacy's projects range from distribution centers and institutional facilities to retail buildings. In 2003, the *St. Louis Business Journal* featured Todd as a Top 40 Professional Under 40.

Todd has taken his passion for building into the community, building ball fields for Cardinals Care. Todd is active with the Matthews-Dickey Boys' and Girls' Club where he has been a guest speaker. He is also involved with Big Brothers/Big Sisters.

Todd serves on the board of directors for the Associated General Contractors, Giant Steps, and the Central Institute for the Deaf. He is a member of the St. Louis Regional Chamber and Growth Association. He holds a bachelor's degree in marketing from the University of Missouri-St. Louis.

Todd and his wife Sara welcomed their first child, Dominic, in August of 2004.

United Way of Greater St. Louis unites people of diverse backgrounds and interests who work together to strengthen health and human services in Missouri and Illinois.

Cheryl Polk (left), Executive Vice President, Chief Operating Officer and lead staff person for the Charmaine Chapman Society, says: "The United Way is fortunate to have such a distinguished and diverse cadre of volunteer leaders and staff who are committed to helping people in our community."

Other members of our management team include (*top row*) John Glenn, Earline Huddlestone, and Diane Peal; (*bottom row*) Vanessa Wayne, Wray Clay, Lonnie Williamson, and Cassandra Griffin.

PledgeUnitedWay.org

United Way of Greater St. Louis

OUR STAND

LIFE CHANGES.
YOUR INSURANCE SHOULD
KEEP UP.

Loyce Alexander
(314) 739-4444
3430 McKelvey Rd #N
Bridgeton
LAlexander@allstate.com

Pam Bonds
(314) 652-7387
4242 Lindell Blvd
St. Louis
a032660@allstate.com

Charles Crump
(314) 423-1823
10434 Page Blvd
St. Louis
a029087@allstate.com

Rithel Dent
(314) 382-5300
7605 Nat Bridge 103
Normandy
a029351@allstate.com

Karen Gilkey
(314) 355-8760
4435 N Hwy 67
Florissant
a045324@allstate.com

Deborah M. Johnson LUTCF
(314) 434-8122
106 Four Seasons Ctr, Ste 105C
Chesterfield
djohnson2@allstate.com

Randy Littlejohn
(314) 355-5370
11897 Benham Rd, #101
St. Louis
a034521@allstate.com

Yolanda Lockhart-Gibbs
(314) 521-2020
9191 W Florisant, #205
Ferguson
a097192@allstate.com

Willie Morris
(314) 423-7600
3629 St Gregory Ln
St. Ann
a043908@allstate.com

We can help you with your changing
insurance or financial needs.

Allstate.
You're in good hands.

St. Louis'

PROFESSIONALS

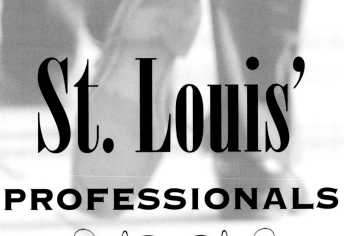

"Don't think you are going to go on forever because you are not and begin to plan something that will compensate as you reduce your capacities to leap or turn on this or that or the other, begin thinking of something else."

KATHERINE DUNHAM, 1909-2006

DANCER, CHOREOGRAPHER, HUMANITARIAN

SPONSORED BY

Gregory L. Anderson
Counselor
Operation Excel YouthBuild
Housing Authority of St. Louis County

Gregory Anderson is a counselor for the Housing Authority of St. Louis County's YouthBuild program in North St. Louis County. There, he works with at-risk youth, changing their perceptions, choices and behaviors through the use of effective therapy and communication techniques. He is responsible for planning, program implementation and supervision.

Gregory completed counselor fellowships in Reno, Nevada, Snowbird, Utah and Clearwater, Florida. Through effective personal and group counseling, 83.3 percent of his counselees earn admission to college or vocational training programs of their choice. His program was featured on *The Today Show*.

Gregory received a bachelor of science degree from Eastern Illinois University, and a master's degree in counselor education from Missouri Baptist University.

Gregory is a member of Shalom Church (City of Peace). He also belongs to Kappa Alpha Psi Fraternity, Inc. A native of Milwaukee, Wisconsin, Gregory has one son, Gregory, 14.

David Barnes
Youth Coordinator
Community Action Agency
of St. Louis County

David Barnes is the coordinator for youth services at the Community Action Agency of St. Louis County. He manages case managers assigned to several St. Louis County school districts, coordinates special events centering on youth and provides counseling services and training workshops. David is also a consultant with Advanced Learning Potential, whose clients include Chrysler and Mercedes-Benz.

David is the former president of the St. Louis County Juvenile Justice Association. He is a member of the Juvenile Minority Overrepresentation Project of St. Louis County, the St. Louis County Juvenile Justice Association and the Clayton Optimist Club. In addition to those activities, David collaborates with the St. Louis County victim impact panel for those affected by juvenile crime. He is a proud member of Grace Church.

David holds a bachelor of arts degree in sociology from Iowa Wesleyan College, certification in child abuse and neglect, and certification in community action management.

David is married to Faith Barnes, and they are the proud parents of Micah Barnes. David is the father of Phyllisa, Parris and Danielle Barnes.

Y vonne Berry is coordinator of volunteer resources for the American Red Cross - St. Louis Area Chapter. There, she works closely with the chief executive officer to coordinate the agency's community outreach to faith-based organizations, community leaders, professional organizations and the African-American Outreach Initiative.

A veteran staff on the American Red Cross disaster response team, Yvonne has had assignments in San Juan, Puerto Rico, St. Thomas, Virgin Islands and areas throughout the U.S. She is the recipient of the 2001 Tiffany Award, the national organization's highest recognition for excellence in professional service.

Yvonne is president and founder of the Midwestern District Council deaf ministry and the New Christ Temple Church media ministry. Her training in sign language and deaf culture involved travel to Paris, France.

Yvonne received a bachelor of arts degree from Albany State University and a master of social work degree from Washington University in St. Louis.

A native of Georgia, Yvonne resides in St. Louis and is grateful for her supportive family. She has a nephew, Alex, and a brother-in-law and sister, Pastor James and Bettie Coats.

Yvonne Berry
Coordinator of Volunteer Resources
American Red Cross
St. Louis Area Chapter

P amela Bonds, a personal financial representative with Allstate Financial Services, LLC, has more than 20 years of experience in the financial services industry. She works closely with Allstate exclusive agents in St. Louis, Kansas City, and the metro east area. She is committed to serving the needs of the agents and their clients. Bonds also has her own online travel agency, Star Travel.

Bonds holds degrees in business administration, finance and marketing from Beacon College in Washington, D.C. She is fully licensed in Series 7 and 63 for investment services, and is licensed to assist clients with their life and health insurance needs.

A native of Alton, Illinois, Bonds is president of the Black Chamber of Commerce of Greater Metropolitan St. Louis. She is a member of the Professional Organization of Women, and co-chairs the professional development committee.

Bonds has organized several fundraisers, health fairs and career fairs. She has fulfilled numerous pro bono speaking engagements for educational, corporate, community and charitable organizations.

Bonds is a member of Transformation Christian Church and World Outreach Center.

Pamela Bonds
Personal Financial Representative
Allstate Financial Services, LLC

The Bosman Twins
Artists & Entertainers

St. Louis' most popular jazz artists, the Bosman Twins, are described by audiences as mesmerizing, dazzling, and exhilarating. Masters of several woodwind instruments, the Emmy Award-winning duo are true ambassadors of music. Whether performing as a duo or accompanying many jazz greats, their rendition of jazz, rhythm and blues, funk, and gospel has gained them notoriety both nationally and internationally.

The twins' passion for jazz started at an early age after listening to greats like Louis Armstrong, Charlie Parker, John Coltrane, Oliver Sain, Cannonball Adderly, and their stepfather, the late Lloyd Smith, once sideman for Count Basie and Duke Ellington. Over the years, the Florida A&M music scholars, classically trained and jazz-inspired identical twins, have come into their own, energizing audiences from St. Louis to London.

Recipients of the Harmon How To Listen and the Missouri Folk Arts grants, the Bosman Twins have traveled across the country as music directors and champions for youth music education. They also assisted in implementing the St. Louis Symphony Community Music School-Herbert Hoover Boys and Girls branch. Currently, they are faculty members at the Community Music School of Webster University.

Lloyd Bruce
Sales Specialist, Linux Solutions
IBM Corporation

Lloyd Bruce, a sales specialist responsible for a 14-state territory, is focused on helping customers meet their business and technology goals. He specializes in creating strategic solutions based on the Linux operating system and involving IBM computer equipment, software, and services. During his 16 years in the information systems industry, Lloyd has held positions in sales management, systems analysis, and technical architecture.

An active supporter of St. Louis community organizations, Lloyd is a board member of Annie Malone Children and Family Services. He is also a member of the United Way Charmaine Chapman Society, and has served as a mentor at Dunbar Elementary School with the Mentor St. Louis program. Lloyd has received numerous awards and honors. His most unique honor involved his designing an experiment that was flown aboard the space shuttles Challenger and Discovery.

Lloyd received a bachelor of general studies degree from the University of Missouri-Columbia, and a master's degree in computer resources and information management from Webster University.

A St. Louis native, Lloyd is the husband of Estelle and is the proud father of two sons, Preston and Clayton.

Isaac L. Butler
Clinical Program Manager
Express Scripts, Inc.

Isaac Butler is a clinical program manager for Express Scripts Inc., a pharmacy benefits manager located in Earth City, Missouri. He serves as the primary client contact for all clinical issues and initiatives. In this consultative role, Isaac helps his clients achieve their goals by performing thorough clinical and economic evaluations. The results are improved quality of care for patients and cost containment for plan sponsors.

Isaac received his doctor of pharmacy degree from the University of Missouri-Kansas City. He earned a bachelor of science degree in chemistry from the University of Missouri-Columbia.

Isaac is an active member of the Academy of Managed Care Pharmacy. Within the academy, his primary focus is promoting the pharmacy profession and student development. In his spare time, Isaac enjoys exercising, playing golf and spending time with his family and fiancée.

Guided by his faith, the foundation for Isaac's life is summarized by Proverbs 3:5-6: "Trust in the Lord with all your heart, and lean not on your own understanding. In all your ways acknowledge him and he shall direct your paths."

David Carroll
Fixed Income Trade Specialist
Edward Jones Investments

David Carroll is a fixed income trade specialist at Edward Jones. In his current role, he executes fixed income trades and provides fixed income support to the firm's 9,500 brokers.

A native of Lake Charles, Louisiana, David graduated with honors from McNeese State University in May of 2005. He was selected for the Beta Gamma Sigma international business honor society and the Phi Kappa Phi honor society.

David has a firm commitment to the community. He has been involved with Junior Achievement, Big Brothers Big Sisters and Americorps. He currently volunteers at the Mathews-Dickey Boys' & Girls' Club, where he recently received the Volunteer Tutor of the Year award.

David is an active member of the Urban League Young Professionals of Metropolitan St. Louis and the Beta Gamma Sigma St. Louis Alumni Chapter. His hobbies include investing, trading and empowering others to achieve their financial goals. David is working on a book entitled "Financial Fitness for Teens and Young Professionals." He is also pursuing his chartered financial analyst designation. Upon completion of that program, he will begin law school.

André L. Edwards
Manager of Gateway Center
UPS

André Edwards is currently the business manager for the Gateway Center, an intricate part of United Parcel Service's Missouri operations. André oversees daily operations and is responsible for maintaining financial stability. This operation generates $3 million per month in gross revenue.

André has been employed at UPS for 29 years. He was the first black male promoted to the newly formed air division in Missouri, as well as the package division in Earth City, and he was the first male in his family to hold a managerial position in a Fortune 500 company.

The owner of Poems Express, a greeting card business, André was last year's recipient of the Legacy Award, presented from the National Council of Negro Women.

A noted public speaker, André published his first book in 1978, and his latest book is *Too Black: When Your Color Gets in the Way!*

A native of St. Louis Missouri, André holds a bachelor of arts degree from Lindenwood University. He is the husband of Ellen Edwards and the proud father of five children, André, Eric, Adrian, Alexis, and Blake, and a granddaughter named Kaley.

Reginald Farrar
Manager
Human Resources & Safety
BJC Behavioral Health

Reginald Farrar, manager of human resources and safety for BJC Behavioral Health, has been in human resources for 20 years. In addition to BJC, he has spent time at US Bank, AG Edwards, and Edison Brothers Stores.

Reggie is a member of the Society of Human Resources Management, the National Association of African-Americans in Human Resources, and the Urban League of Greater St. Louis' employment committee. He is a past mentor in the St. Louis Business Diversity Initiative's mentoring program and a former member of the Beaumont High School Academy of Finance advisory board. He has also been involved in his community by volunteering his time to the Mathews-Dickey and the Herbert Hoover Boys' & Girls' Clubs. Reggie is a member of Kappa Alpha Psi Fraternity, Inc.

Reggie believes that human resources is a critical component to every organization and should be a strategic partner in helping an organization meets its goals and objectives. In addition, human resources should be a driving force behind continuing to move an organization and its most important resource, people, to the next level.

Reggie Garrett is entering his second year as director of ticket sales and promotions for the Saint Louis University athletics department. In this capacity, he is responsible for implementing and managing all marketing efforts for the athletics department. He also assists in game-day operations, community outreach programs, game-day promotions and the negotiation of corporate and media partner contracts.

Through Reggie's marketing efforts, the men's and women's basketball teams surpassed and set record revenue marks for the 2005-2006 season. In addition, the men's team finished in the top 50 in the country for average attendance per game.

Reggie received a bachelor of science degree in political science from Seton Hall University. While at Seton Hall, he was a four-year letterman and captain of the men's basketball team as a senior. He earned his juris doctorate from the University of Houston Law Center and is a member of the Sports Lawyers Association.

A recipient of the Frieda D. Warner Citizenship Award from his hometown in New Jersey, Reggie volunteers with Big Brothers Big Sisters of Eastern Missouri.

Reggie Garrett
Director of Ticket Sales & Promotions
Saint Louis University

Kunita Gear is a senior manager in the process and technology department of Express Scripts, Inc. She identifies, prioritizes and supports operations process improvement activities through the analysis of process data, standardization of processes and implementation of best practices.

Kunita is a senior member of the American Society for Quality and a recipient of the RR Donnelley President's Award. She is an ASQ-certified quality engineer and a certified Six Sigma Master Black Belt.

Kunita holds a bachelor of science degree in industrial engineering and a master of science degree in manufacturing management from the GMI Engineering & Management Institute.

Kunita serves her community through her involvement in church activities. As a result of her interest in missions, she co-led a musical missions team on a two-week concert tour to the Czech Republic, during which they raised more than 300,000 Czech korunas (nearly 12,000 American dollars) to help in their flood relief effort. An avid reader, volunteer usher at the Fox Theatre and vocalist, Kunita currently resides in St. Louis.

Kunita R. Gear
Senior Manager
Express Scripts, Inc.

Marcus Hawkins
Senior Manager,
IT Systems Monitoring
Express Scripts, Inc.

Marcus Hawkins is the senior manager of information technology at Express Scripts, Inc. He is responsible for end-to-end systems monitoring and outage coordination.

Marcus studied mechanical engineering at the Illinois Institute of Technology where he was selected by NASA to research the dynamics of dirigibles, and sponsored to assist in developing a stethoscope for the hearing impaired.

Marcus continued his research for NASA in conjunction with the Center for Computational Mechanics at Washington University in St. Louis. He went on to hold lead engineering roles at Monsanto's world headquarters and Anheuser-Busch Companies.

A native of Dumas, Arkansas, Marcus is the husband of Vanessa K. Hawkins, and the proud father of three daughters, Kayla, Sydney and Chelsey. He is a member of West Side Missionary Baptist Church.

Eric Henderson
Workforce Planning Manager
UPS

Eric Henderson is the workforce planning manager for UPS in the state of Missouri. In this position, he is responsible for overseeing all employment responsibilities in the state. UPS currently employs more than 4,800 employees in Missouri.

Eric is in his 19th year at UPS. He started as a part-time preloader working on the sunrise sort in Earth City while attending college. Within two years, he was promoted to part-time supervisor and five years later, was promoted to full-time supervisor in the finance department. Eric was recently promoted to the workforce planning manager position in March of 2006.

He is involved with St. Charles Community College, the Hispanic Chamber of Greater St. Louis, and participates in many UPS volunteer events. Eric is the husband of Jennifer Henderson and is the proud father of one daughter, Amanda.

Rory Hennings is branch manager for 1st Metropolitan Mortgage in St. Louis. 1st Metropolitan Mortgage specializes in FHA, VA and conventional home loans, as well as sub-prime mortgages.

Hennings has been in the mortgage business for 17 years. A native of St. Louis, he is married to Nedra Hennings. He is the proud father of Rory and Tiffany Hennings.

A former professional football player for the Kansas City Chiefs, Hennings enjoys running, tennis and participating in track and field competitions.

Rory Hennings
Branch Manager
1st Metropolitan Mortgage

Dawn Higgins is the human resources generalist of the local GLOBE organization for Nestlé Purina PetCare. In this position, she provides human resources support for the company's 200-person team responsible for delivering common business process architecture, and standardizing an information systems infrastructure across Nestlé markets around the world. Prior to Nestlé, she was a manager of executive recruitment with the May Merchandising Company.

Dawn is an active alumna of INROADS Midwest, Inc., St. Louis Chapter, an organization geared toward developing and placing minority youth in industry and business to prepare them for leadership in the business community. She is a member of the first St. Louis Initiative Fellows Program, a structured leadership development program for minority individuals. She serves on Nestlé Purina's Diversity Council and is also a member of Delta Sigma Theta Sorority, Inc.

Dawn is a graduate of Central Missouri State University where she earned a bachelor's degree in business management.

A native of Bethesda, Maryland, Dawn lives in St. Louis with her husband, Sherman, and two children. She enjoys event planning and creating crafts.

Dawn Higgins
Human Resources Generalist
Nestlé Purina PetCare Company

St. Louis' PROFESSIONALS

Sponsored By

Rita Holmes-Bobo
Senior Manager, Public Affairs
Express Scripts Inc.

Rita Holmes-Bobo serves as senior manager of public affairs for Express Scripts Inc., where she is responsible for media relations and other projects relating to external audiences.

Rita has 22 years of experience in communications, fund-raising and marketing research, and has received various awards and recognition for her work. She has also achieved her APR (Accredited in Public Relations) national certification.

Rita will serve as president of the local chapter of the Public Relations Society of America in 2007 and currently chairs the programming committee. She also serves on the Kansas University Black Alumni Organization chapter leadership team and the North County Inc. inclusion taskforce. Rita is a member of First Baptist Church of Chesterfield and Delta Sigma Theta Sorority, Inc. She is a graduate of Coro Women in Leadership.

A Wichita, Kansas native, Rita graduated from the University of Kansas with a master of business administration degree in marketing research and a bachelor of science degree in business administration.

Rita and her husband of 23 years, Reverend Luke Bobo, are the proud parents of Briana and Caleb.

P. Michele Holton
Manager of Inclusion
Edward Jones

P. Michele Holton is the manager of inclusion at Edward Jones. In this role, she partners with business areas across the firm to create and execute strategies to build a diverse and inclusive organization for customers and associates.

Michele, who became a limited partner in 2000, holds Series 7 and 63 licenses and is a Senior Professional in Human Resources (SPHR). She has completed Edward Jones executive education courses at Harvard Business School and The Drucker Institute at Claremont College.

Prior to Edward Jones, Michele worked for Washington University in St. Louis and was responsible for undergraduate multicultural recruitment.

Michele graduated, cum laude, from Washington University with a bachelor's degree in history. She serves on the Professional Organization of Women (POW) board and is board secretary for INROADS/St. Louis. She chaired the St. Louis Diversity Officers' Network and now chairs the Securities Industry Association (SIA) diversity committee. Michele was recognized in 2004 among the *St Louis Business Journal's* 40 Under 40.

Michele is the wife of Matt Holton and is the mother of two wonderful sons, Michael, 5, and Maxwell, 3.

Angelina Jackson
Master of Real Estate
Rhodes Realty Service, LLC

Angelina Jackson is a master of real estate with Rhodes Realty Service, LLC. Although she spends most days writing contracts and demonstrating negotiating strategies, she also answers technology questions, serves on local and state real estate committees and exercises her wit. She maintains a positive attitude by thinking of something funny and not allowing herself to worry about things beyond her control.

Jackson received the Women's Council of Realtors' Excel Award for Missouri and St. Charles County. A fair housing advocate, she is director for the Missouri Association of Realtors, and member of the National, Missouri and St. Louis Associations of REALTORS®.

Numerous St. Louis communities require specialists who are aware of municipal ordinances, occupancy restrictions and other expertise that differentiates between competent and unqualified. Jackson provides access to specialized technical information that generates customized strategic plans, enabling her clients to make confident, informed decisions and ultimately reach their goals.

When she is not showing property (her favorite part of the real estate business), Jackson relaxes with her husband, Nathaniel, three sons and two dogs, a Rottweiler and Shih Tzu.

Karl Jones
Missouri District Operations Manager
UPS

Karl holds the position of Missouri district operations manager for United Parcel Service (UPS). In this position, Karl is responsible for all transportation operations throughout the state. He began his career with UPS in 1984 as a part-time employee in the Georgia district, and a year later he was promoted to a full-time supervisor. He also held positions in human resources before being promoted to a manager in 1992. In 2002 Karl was promoted to a staff manager in the Alabama district. He was recently relocated to St. Louis and is excited about getting involved in the St. Louis community.

Karl has been involved in the communities in which he has worked by volunteering with the Urban League, the Boy Scouts, and the Fellowship of Christian Athletes. He is also an avid golfer and loves to spend time with his family.

Karl is married to Minerva Jones and they have three children, Anthony (18), Alexis (15), and Austin (4).

Ron Jones
Business Manager
UPS

Ron Jones is currently the business manager for the UPS St. Charles Center. The St. Charles Center provides service on approximately 10,000 packages per day with an average of 4,600 customers. The area spans more than 3,100 miles and it includes St. Charles, St. Peters and O'Fallon. There are 39 delivery drivers assigned to this area out of the 50 assigned to the operation. Ron also manages 50 inside part-time and full-time employees, who process packages and are responsible for unloading and staging the Earth City fleet of more than 287 delivery vehicles. Ron has a staff of 17 management people that report to him. This year, he celebrated 30 years of exemplary service with UPS.

A native of East St. Louis, Ron served in the U.S. Army and attended the University of Maryland. He and his wife, Terry, are the proud parents of two daughters, Nila and Gloria. He also has three wonderful granddaughters, Alyssa, Krystal and Courtney, and one grandson, Justin.

Vernon Jones
Technical Sales Specialist &
Business Partner Advocate
IBM Systems Storage Group

Vernon Jones is a technical sales specialist within the IBM System Storage Group. His work includes providing complex storage solutions, educating business partners on IBM storage products and configuring storage hardware configurations.

Vernon is co-founder of the Black Family Technology Awareness Association of St. Louis. He holds the vice president position within the IBM Black Network Group of St. Louis and is a member of the Unity PAC.

A native of East St. Louis, Illinois, Vernon entered the United States Marine Corps in 1988 and served a four-year tour of duty in which he participated in Desert Shield/Storm. Upon finishing his tour, he graduated from Southern Illinois University Edwardsville with a bachelor of science degree in management information systems.

Vernon enjoys participating in hobbies such as snorkeling, bowling, fishing and traveling with good friends. He was married to Priscilla in 2003, and they both attend Mt. Nebo Missionary Baptist Church in Madison, Illinois.

WHO'S *WHO*

Kelli Jordan is an information technology (I/T) architect with IBM Global Services. Her duties include design, installation, maintenance and integration of complex client information systems worldwide. She is responsible for determining hardware requirement definitions and configurations, developing solutions and resolving technical implementation issues to optimize performance within the Linux, UNIX and Windows environments. She also provides technical facilitation, currency reviews and recommendations for multi-vendor server, SAN, disk and tape storage products.

A member of the IBM Diversity Council and an officer with the St. Louis IBM Black Network Group, Kelli is also co-founder of the Black Family Technology Awareness Association of St. Louis. She serves on the board of the Gifted Resource Council, is a volunteer for Mentor St. Louis, and is a member of the Ladies Auxiliary Post 397, Unity PAC and Delta Sigma Theta Sorority, Inc.

Kelli is a graduate of Ranken Technical College, and she sits on Ranken's computer networking technology advisory board.

Born in Chesapeake, Virginia, she considers herself a lifelong St. Louis resident. She is the proud mother of two sons, Kyle and Kendall.

Kelli M. Jordan
I/T Architect
IBM Global Services

Katherine Kendrick is employed by IBM Global Services Strategic Outsourcing Systems Support as a senior technical service professional. Focusing on the AT&T account, she is responsible for system support billing for the North and Midwest regions. As a team, Kendrick and her coworkers received an award for creating the standard guidelines for new and existing accounts.

Kendrick has participated in a variety of projects on other IBM cites. She spent three months in New York, California, and Chicago implementing some of the standards and guidelines she helped create. She was also selected to attend the prestigious Woman of Color Conference in Atlanta, Georgia.

Sharing her leadership skills, Kendrick actively participates as a mentor in St. Louis Public Schools; is an active member of the St. Louis-IBM Black Network Group; and is a member of Shalom City of Peace Church, where she serves as a greeter.

She is the proud mother of three wonderful children, Ricky, Amber, and James Kendrick. Ricky and Amber have completed college and James is pursuing a career as an electrical engineer.

Katherine Kendrick
Senior Technical
Services Professional
IBM Corporation

Hubert L. Kerr Jr.
Sr. Manager of Quality Assurance
Express Scripts, Inc.

Hubert Kerr is the senior manager of quality assurance in the manual claims department of Express Scripts, Inc. His role is to oversee all quality and training initiatives for the St. Louis and Bloomington operations. Hubert's main focus is to maintain a consistent approach to quality assurance tracking and reporting, new-hire training and curriculum development, and to solidify a "best practice" process approach while developing new quality metrics and reporting tools.

Hubert is a dedicated community service volunteer who gives his times to several organizations. When he is not spending time with his family, he volunteers for the March of Dimes, the United Way and the Edwardsville YMCA as a youth soccer coach.

Hubert received a bachelor of business administration degree from the University of Houston, and Fontbonne University awarded him a master's of business administration degree in 2005.

A native of Houston, Texas, Hubert is the husband of Tammy Foster-Kerr and the proud father of a son, Gabriel, and a daughter, Autumn. He enjoys Cajun cooking, playing baseball, bike riding and fishing.

Lee Lewis Jr.
Community Relations Manager
Enterprise Rent-A-Car

Lee Lewis Jr., community relations manager for Enterprise Rent-A-Car, is responsible for community, diversity and government relations initiatives in the St. Louis and southwestern Illinois region. Lewis oversees programs in inclusion management and employee recruitment. A 15-year employee of Enterprise, Lewis has held a number of revenue-producing management and marketing positions during his tenure in San Antonio, Texas.

A native of Houston, Lewis earned a business administration degree from Texas Southern University. He has won numerous awards for outstanding accomplishments in community involvement. He currently serves the St. Louis region as board president of the Professional Organization of Women, and member of the corporate advisory boards of the St. Charles Workforce Investment Board and the Hispanic Chamber of Commerce. Lewis also sits on a number of committees for the St. Louis Urban League and is a mentor and board member with Mentor St. Louis.

His philosophy is, "To be truly successful, one must play a role in the success of others." Lewis, an ordained minister of O'Fallon Church of Christ, enjoys spending time with his wife and eight children. They live in St. Charles.

WHO'S *Who*

Victor Little is a psych tech for Peter and Paul Community Services' program, Positive Directions, a transitional housing program for people living with HIV and AIDS. Victor is also a local actor that performs for schools, churches and other events in the area. He has performed with Unity Theatre Ensemble as Walter Lee in *A Raisin in the Sun* and Sgt. Waters in *A Soldier's Play*.

Victor holds a bachelor of science degree from Central State University in Ohio, and is currently pursuing a master of public policy administration degree in not-for-profit management at the University of Missouri-St. Louis.

Victor Little
Psych Tech
Positive Directions
Peter & Paul Community Services

Ozzie L. Lomax is a plant manager for AmerenUE's Meramec Generation. He is responsible for the operation of a 1,000 megawatt power plant. Prior to joining Ameren, he worked with Kansas City Power & Light Co. for 23 years in various leadership positions.

Ozzie chairs the project management advisory team for Ameren Generation. He also sits on the advisory boards of Southern Illinois University at Carbondale's (SIU-C) college of engineering, and SIU at Edwardsville's school of business. He is on the board of directors of the YMCA and an advisor for the Boy Scouts of America, Explorer Post 2994.

Ozzie received a bachelor's degree in electrical engineering technology from SIU-C. He is a pulpit pastor at West Central Church of Christ and received certification as a marriage enrichment facilitator from the Family Dynamics Institute.

Ozzie is a recipient of SIU-C's Alumni Achievement Award, the United Way's Loaned Executive of the Year Award, and the Southern Christian Leadership Council's Achievers Award. He has been married to Joe Lomax for 27 years. They have two daughters, Amanda Lomax-Owens and Brittany Lomax.

Ozzie L. Lomax, PMP
Plant Manager
Meramec Generation Station
AmerenUE

St. Louis' PROFESSIONALS

Karla R. McClendon
Learning & Development Manager
UPS

Karla McClendon is the learning and development manager for the Missouri district of United Parcel Service (UPS). In this position, she facilitates training; coordinates the delivery of driver training; communicates information concerning training rollouts from corporate to the region and district; and sets up panels for the management promotion call, the opt-in promotion process.

Karla is a member of Southern Missionary Baptist Church located in Kinloch, Missouri, where she is involved in a multitude of activities including choir, finance, and teaching new membership orientation classes.

Prior to the consolidation of the Ferguson-Florissant Districts, Karla attended school in the Kinloch School District. She received a bachelor of science degree in criminal justice from the University of Missouri-St. Louis in January of 1980.

In her free time, Karla enjoys exercising, traveling, and spending time with her family and friends. Her favorite scriptures are Matthew 6:33 and II Timothy 2:15.

Anisha Morrell-Charles
Coordinator of Diversity Recruitment
St. Louis Community College

Anisha Morrell-Charles is coordinator of diversity recruitment at St. Louis Community College. She manages minority recruitment and community and immigrant outreach. She is also an adjunct instructor of communications and business at the Forest Park campus.

Anisha serves as vice president of administration for the National Black MBA Association, St. Louis Chapter; treasurer of the Hispanic Leaders Group of St. Louis; and national judge for the Black MBA Fortune 1000 scholarship competition. She is on the board of directors for the Hispanic Chamber of Commerce. Additionally, she is a member of Focus St. Louis' New Americans implementation team, and United Way's Charmaine Chapman Society and Women's Leadership Giving Initiative.

Anisha received a bachelor of arts degree from the University of Missouri-Columbia. She earned a master of arts degree in communications and a master of business administration degree in marketing from Lindenwood University.

A native of New Orleans, Anisha is a true southern griot who lives for family, cooking, entertaining and "tellin' tales." She resides in St. Louis with her husband, Mario Pascal Boyard Charles, a high school educator and musician.

WHO'S WHO

Sponsored By

St. Louis'

PROFESSIONALS

Celeste Player is a clinical program manager in the workers' compensation division of Express Scripts, Inc. She is dedicated to achieving and maintaining a quality, cost-effective pharmacy benefit and meeting the unique needs of workers' compensation clients.

As the pharmacist on her team, Celeste's responsibilities include developing and implementing clinical programs, monitoring clients' drug trends and examining unique opportunities for intervention. She serves as a liaison between clients and Express Scripts, responding to client inquiries regarding drug expenditures, program designs and injured worker communications.

Celeste received a doctorate of pharmacy from Xavier University College of Pharmacy in New Orleans, Louisiana. She is an active member of Delta Sigma Theta Sorority, Inc. and the Academy of Managed Care Pharmacy. In her spare time, she is an avid St. Louis Rams football fan and enjoys event planning and traveling.

A native of St. Louis, Celeste is the wife of Dr. Steven Player and is the proud mother of Mason, 4, and Kourtney, 1.

Celeste Player
Clinical Program Manager
Express Scripts, Inc.

Robert Pullen is the manager responsible for sales support and sales operations in Missouri for United Parcel Service (UPS). His responsibilities include working in partnership with all UPS functions and managing day-to-day sales operations in Missouri. His staff of 37 employees provides specialized support and service needed to achieve worldwide leadership in package distribution.

For more than 15 years, Robert demonstrated drive and ambition in ten different positions, including management positions in operations, middle market sales, and national account sales. He has more than 13 years of sales management, sales marketing, account management, and program management experience. Robert has been recognized three times for the UPS Chairman's Award, recognizing the top sales people at UPS worldwide.

Robert remains committed to community outreach, and as such, he has been involved in Junior Achievement, the Urban League, and Habitat for Humanity. He is also an active supporter of the United Way as a leadership contributor.

A native of St. Louis, Robert holds a degree in business management from Friends University. He is the husband of Jacqueline Martinez Pullen and the proud father of one daughter, Maya Rose.

Robert Pullen
Manager, Sales Operations
UPS

Toryn Rhone
Missouri District
Employee Relations Manager
UPS

Toryn Rhone is the employee relations manager for United Parcel Service (UPS) in the state of Missouri. In this position, he is responsible for developing strategies to address any concerns the district employees might have, as well as coordinating community involvement programs that provide volunteer opportunities for the district's employees.

Toryn is in his 28th year with UPS. He started as a part time loader working the night shift while he was attending college. Within a year, Toryn was promoted to part time supervisor and then, five years later, was promoted to full time supervisor. He has held full time management positions in hub operations, human resources, security, and package operations. He has performed special assignments in Nashville, Tennessee, and New York, New York.

A native of St. Louis, Toryn has volunteered with the Boy Scouts, Junior Achievement, and 100 Black Men. He is the husband of Marcelle Perry-Rhone and is the proud father of two children, Jeremy and Taylor.

Jeanne Roberts
Co-owner
Roberts Twins & Associates, LLC

Jeanne Roberts is a transactional attorney specializing in real estate, corporate, and entertainment law with the firm of Gallop, Johnson & Neuman, L.C. She is the first African-American attorney out of 90 attorneys at Gallop.

Jeanne also assists in real estate developments for her father's companies, The Roberts Companies. Additionally, she formed three entertainment companies with her twin brother, Michael Roberts, Jr. First, they formed Sho-town Entertainment, LLC, a music production and sports management company. Their second company, Gateway Live, LLC, consists of event planning and production, lifestyle marketing, endorsement opportunities, promotions, and artist relations. Third, they formed Roberts Twins & Associates, LLC, a television production company. Roberts Twins will co-produce its first television show along with Eric Rhone and Cedric the Entertainer. Both Jeanne and her twin will host the UPN 46 television talk show, entitled *The Mike and Jeanne Show*.

Jeanne attended Spelman College in Atlanta, where she graduated cum laude with a bachelor of science degree in mathematics. Subsequently, Jeanne attended and graduated from Pepperdine University School of Law in Malibu, California, where her main focus was entertainment law.

Alicia R. Smith is the Charles Drew Program Coordinator for the American Red Cross. In this position, she manages and implements the African-American Initiative for the Missouri/Illinois region to meet blood collection goals. She is also responsible for a special donor recruitment program which benefits children with sickle cell disease.

Smith has been involved in the government and nonprofit sectors for more than 20 years. Throughout her long career in community affairs she served as executive assistant to Mayor Clarence Harmon, and as St. Louis director for the Missouri State Treasurer.

Smith received a master of arts degree in public policy administration from Saint Louis University and a bachelor of arts degree in business administration from Colorado College. She was honored as an Urban League Scholar, a National Merit Scholar and was featured in *Who's Who in American Colleges*.

Active in the community, Smith is a member of The Links, Inc., Jack & Jill of America, Alpha Kappa Alpha Sorority, Inc., and the Central West End Association. She has also served on the boards of numerous organizations.

Alicia R. Smith
Charles Drew Program Coordinator
American Red Cross

Robin N. Smith is employed as a manager of slot operations for President Casino. Her job responsibilities include developing and maintaining training systems for electronic gaming device personnel and application of federal cash reporting. She also administers the electronic gaming device department in accordance with management's directives and the policies and procedures as described in the systems of accounting and internal controls.

Robin is a lifelong resident of St. Louis, Missouri. She attended school in the University City School District. After graduating from University City High School in 1987, she attended Southeast Missouri State University were she studied early childhood education and business management.

An aspiring author, Robin loves to read in her spare time. In addition, she often finds herself lost in her very own writings.

Robin is a member of Shalom Church (City of Peace) in Florissant. She currently resides in Florissant with her three children, Charon, Kristin and Cameron.

Robin N. Smith
Manager of Slot Operation
President Casino

John Sumlin
Sales Manager
Lou Fusz Automotive Network

John Sumlin is the sales manager for the pre-owned department of Lou Fusz Automotive Network, one of the top privately-owned automobile groups in the country. There, he manages sales staff, purchases the vehicle inventory and handles print and Internet advertising.

John has worked in several capacities of the automotive industry for more than ten years. His positions have included new and pre-owned sales and leasing, finance manager and sales manager.

John was chosen as an Outstanding Young Man of America in 1998. He is a 1997 graduate of Leadership Clarksdale, a program that brings together future leaders of the community to achieve goals for the city. He earned a bachelor of science degree in business administration from Alcorn State University in 1993.

A highly involved member of Progressive Baptist Church, John volunteers with the YMCA and Habitat for Humanity. A life member of Kappa Alpha Psi Fraternity, Inc., John is a past potentate with the Shriners of Hira Temple #31.

A proud native of Clarksdale, Mississippi, John is married to Angela Shaw-Sumlin, and they have two adorable daughters, Johnalynn and Anna-Marie.

Tony Taylor
Missouri District Hub Manager
UPS

In the 20 years that Tony Taylor has been with United Parcel Service (UPS), he has held various management positions. Currently, he is the Missouri district hub division manager. Tony directs a workforce of more than 1,000 employees in the progression of millions of packages within the UPS system.

Two of Tony's most memorable career experiences were assisting with logistical support for the 2004 G8 Summit, and spending a month performing community service work as part of a UPS internship program.

Tony has volunteered his experience to Family House, Inc. and has served on the board of directors for Junior Achievement of Rock River Valley. In addition, he was appointed to the executive committee of the Rockford Chamber of Commerce.

The Taylor family has enjoyed residing in Wisconsin, Illinois, and Georgia in addition to their current home in Missouri. Tony and his wife, Kim, have three children, Kelly, Quinn and Ashley.

Sponsored By

St. Louis'
PROFESSIONALS

Ellen Thompson is a senior manager with Express Scripts, Inc., supporting the eligibility services department. In her role, she is responsible for leading projects and project teams that are engaged in the planning and execution of Express Scripts' corporate initiatives.

Elected in 2005, Ellen currently holds the active board position of vice president of professional development for the Project Management Institutes' St. Louis Chapter. Her role supports and encourages the development and training of project management professionals (PMPs) within the St. Louis metropolitan area.

Ellen completed her master's studies at Webster University, where she earned a master of arts degree in computer resources information management in 2003 and a master of business administration degree in 2004. She completed her undergraduate studies at Saint Louis University in 2000, where she earned a bachelor of science degree in computer science with honors.

A native of St. Louis, Missouri, Ellen is the proud wife of Marcus Thompson, Esq., a practicing attorney in the St. Louis area.

Ellen Thompson MBA, PMP
Senior Manager, Eligibility Services
Express Scripts, Inc.

Rodney White is currently on assignment as a learning and training coordinator for the local GLOBE organization within Nestlé Purina PetCare Company. As a member of this team, his primary responsibility is the coordination and planning of training for more than 6,500 associates in the Nestlé Purina PetCare Company.

Rodney is a member of the Society for Human Resource Management and is a certified senior professional in human resources. He has served as a volunteer counselor for the Ethnic College Counseling Center, a private nonprofit organization with the purpose of serving young people in the Denver community. The mission of the Center is to recruit, encourage, train and prepare students to pursue education beyond high school. He continues to participate in the bi-annual college tour of historically black colleges and universities with the Center. Rodney is also a member of Alpha Phi Alpha Fraternity, Inc.

Rodney received a bachelor of science degree in 1985 from the University of Florida. In 1990 he was awarded a master of business administration degree from Florida Agricultural and Mechanical University.

Rodney A. White
GLOBE Learning &
Training Coordinator
Nestlé Purina PetCare Company

 WHO'S WHO

Tony White
Agent
State Farm Insurance

Tony White is an agent for State Farm Insurance, in his hometown of East St. Louis, Illinois. He has worked in the insurance industry for more than 16 years. During his early years as a fire claims representative, he logged more than 350 days of storm duty as a catastrophe volunteer.

Tony received a bachelor of science degree in education from Northwest Missouri State University, where he also was a full ride scholarship member of the nationally-ranked Division II men's basketball team.

Tony hosts a fire prevention festival and a child safety seat event at his office annually. He also chairs a scholarship program at his church, Emmanuel Temple COGIC, and coaches a youth AAU basketball team.

A member of the business workforce/development committee for the Greater St. Louis Regional Empowerment Zone, Tony is an executive committee member of the Mid-America Workforce Investment Board. Likewise, he is a member of the NAACP, and a member of the executive board of directors for the Okaw Valley Council of the Boy Scouts of America.

Tony and his wife, Lisa, are the proud parents of three children, Joshua, Lauren, and Justin.

Eric Williams
Manager
UPS

Eric Williams is a manager for UPS, assigned to the package division. Eric's current assignment is in the Southeast Center, where he oversees the daily delivery and pick-up operations, in addition to managing the center's workforce of approximately 61 employees.

Eric distinguished himself early in life as an exceptional athlete. He excelled in football at the University of Southern California. He capped off his collegiate career by being named both team captain and Defensive Most Valuable Player in 1976.

In 1977 Eric entered the National Football League as a 8th round draft choice for the St. Louis Cardinals. He was rewarded for his leadership by being named Rookie of the Year in 1977. Eric played eight successful years in the NFL and one year in the USFL.

Eric has been married to his wife, Debra, for 18 years. He is the proud father of two sons, J.V. and Nicholas, and a grandson, Eric. In his spare time, Eric enjoys hunting, fishing and children's charities, including the NFL alumni-sponsored Big Brothers/Big Sisters organizations.

Jim Williams is responsible for the service delivery for several technical platforms for IBM in St. Louis. He has responsibility for the service teams that support check processing in the banking group, large printing systems, and the large mainframe platforms.

Jim's career started in 1978 as a customer engineer in Pittsburgh, Pennsylvania. He relocated to Charlotte, North Carolina, where he became a service planning representative from 1985 to 1989. He was promoted to management in 1989 and has since held several service management positions in the St. Louis area.

As a service manager, Jim has won numerous awards including several directors awards and the IBM Means Service Award. A military veteran, he served in the United States Air Force from 1965 to 1970. After his discharge, he attended the University of Pittsburgh.

Jim has been active in the Boy Scouts of America, serving as a Cub master and other positions in his Scout troop. He also coached Midget League football in the Pittsburgh area.

Jim is married and has two sons, Marvin and Parren Williams. Parren is a graduate of Webster University.

James E. Williams
Service Delivery Manager,
Integrated Technology Solutions
IBM Corporation

Loretta Wilson is diversity marketing manager for GMAC's St. Louis Business Center, where she coordinates diversity events and programs in seven states. Her responsibilities are to create opportunities for increased GM dealer sales in all diversity segments via cultural awareness, product knowledge, and credit education. Loretta is GMAC's regional spokesperson for the SmartEdge Educational Program, and she is a past recipient of General Motors's Business Woman's Leadership Award.

A St. Louis native, Wilson received her bachelor's degree in business administration and marketing at Lindenwood University. She has continued her education by taking business and sales related courses.

Loretta is a member of the Association of Finance and Insurance Professionals and a committee member for the Annual National Kidney Foundation Golf Tournament. A past member of the United Way's advisory board, she is also a member of the National Association of Female Executives.

Loretta is the wife of Harry Wilson, a proud mother of two children and an active member of Greater Grace Church in St. Louis. One of her favorite quotes is, "To whom much is given, much is required."

Loretta Wilson
Diversity Marketing Manager
GMAC

Barbara Malone Youmans
Human Resources Manager
St. Louis Blues/Scottrade Center

Barbara Malone Youmans is human resources (HR) manager for St. Louis Blues/Scottrade Center. St. Louis Blues/Scottrade Center is a premier sports and entertainment arena located in beautiful downtown St. Louis, Missouri.

As HR manager, Barbara is responsible for recruitment of part-time event staff as well as full-time administrative staff. She created and maintains Scottrade Center's Hepatitis A program, creates recruitment advertisements, facilitates new hire orientations, and conducts investigations. She has been with St. Louis Blues/Scottrade Center for more than six years.

Barbara is a dynamic public speaker and trainer. She delivers superb, high-energy training for various social service agencies with job readiness programs. She is currently a board member for True Vine Christian Center, a former board member for Vincent Gray Alternative High School, and a former advisory board member for The Fathers' Center. Barbara also served as chairperson for AAIM's Metro East executive roundtable in addition to serving on the AAIM recruitment advisory board.

DaVonna D. Young
Senior Marketing Specialist
President Casino

DaVonna D. Young has been employed by President Casino for 11 years. She has managed the fields of slot operations and marketing. DaVonna is currently the senior marketing specialist who focuses on public relations. It is her responsibility to uphold the civic duty of the company as well as ensure its role as a corporate citizen of St. Louis. She also creates, implements, and executes marketing promotions and advertising as well as provides training and development to President Casino's workforce.

A native of East St. Louis, Illinois, DaVonna is a graduate of East St. Louis Senior High School. She furthered her education at the University of Illinois Champaign, majoring in business administration with an emphasis in marketing.

Although DaVonna enjoys her work life, she also likes the challenges of golf and motherhood. She is the proud mother of five-year-old Christian Kai. She is a strong believer in God and family.

One of DaVonna's favorite quotes is, "Life may not be the party we hoped for, but while we're here we might as well dance!"

WHO'S WHO

ADVERTISERS' INDEX